THE NOVELS OF HENRY GREEN

The Novels of
HENRY GREEN

———❖———

Edward Stokes

1959
THE MACMILLAN COMPANY
NEW YORK

© EDWARD STOKES 1959
PRINTED IN GREAT BRITAIN BY
BUTLER AND TANNER LTD

Contents

I

Preliminaries

I write books, but I am not proud of this any more than anyone is
of their nails growing.

(Pack My Bag, p. 238)

I

IT is strange that no full-length critical study of Henry Green
has yet been written, since in the last ten years he has come
to be regarded, at least by critics and fellow-writers, as one of
the most individual and important novelists now writing.
Elizabeth Bowen has described him as "one of the novelists
most to be reckoned with", W. H. Auden considers him "the
best English novelist alive"[1] and Robert Phelps has proclaimed
him "easily the best English novelist of his generation".[2] But
perhaps the comparative scarcity of criticism of Green's work
is not surprising, because he is one of the most elusive, tantaliz-
ing and enigmatic of novelists, whose work is extremely difficult
to define or categorize. His work appears puzzling and difficult
partly because he has always resolutely insisted on being an
artist, never an essayist, propagandist or journalist. Moreover,
as an artist, Green is more akin to the poets than to most
novelists. V. S. Pritchett has described him as a "dispossessed
poet";[3] and Jean Howard has remarked that "the continuous
close-co-operation he exacts is of a kind associated with poetry
rather than prose".[4] Since so much of the meaning of Green's
novels is conveyed through poetic methods, criticism of his
work necessarily involves study not only, or mainly, of characters,
plots, themes and narrative techniques, but also and chiefly of
vision, imagery, symbolism and language. This study attempts
to treat all these aspects of Green's work more thoroughly and
systematically than they have yet been treated, but I gratefully
acknowledge my indebtedness to many previous critics, whose
work has suggested various lines of enquiry. For if there has
been no extended criticism of Henry Green, there have been a
number of valuable shorter commentaries on aspects and
sections of his work, in chapters of books, essays and reviews,

by such critics as Walter Allen, Nigel Dennis, James Hall, Jean Howard, Arnold Kettle, John Lehmann, Rosamond Lehmann, Giorgio Melchiori, Robert Phelps, V. S. Pritchett, Henry Reed, Mark Schorer, W. Y. Tindall and Philip Toynbee.

All these critics have admired Green's novels, but there have been some adverse critics of his work. One of his most hostile critics has been his fellow-novelist, C. P. Snow, who in a *Spectator* article ("Books and Writers", September 22, 1950), claimed that he saw in Green's work "all the signs that we have come to associate with artistic diffidence and decay". It is interesting to note that these two writers, Green and Snow, lead two of the strangest double lives in the history of the English novel. Dr. Snow, when not writing novels, until 1945 was an eminent physicist, and since that date has been Civil Service Commissioner. By day Henry Green is not Henry Green; he is Henry Vincent Yorke, managing director of H. Pontifex and Sons, manufacturers of equipment for the food and drink trade, and has been chairman of the British Chemical Plant Manufacturers' Association.

It is paradoxical that Green, the conservative business man, should describe his own work, perfectly accurately, as "an advanced attempt to break up the old-fashioned type of novel";[5] it is doubly paradoxical that Snow, the experimental scientist, should be content, in the main, to work within the limits of "the old-fashioned type of novel", and that, partly for this reason, he should view Green's work with disfavour. In the article already quoted, Snow compared Green, unfavourably, with William Gerhardi. "In the last few years Mr. Henry Green has occupied a position similar to that of Mr. William Gerhardi in the twenties. In both cases the name was in the literary air, though the books were not much read; both were admired by brother-writers; both had a vision of life which was poetic and oblique, and both gained a kind of esoteric topical interest insomuch as they spoke for a tiny sector of the cultivated world, part-raffish, part-cultivated, part-prosperous, which was enjoying its last butterfly-day when Mr. Gerhardi began and by Mr. Green's time was already far gone into decay." Some of the comment is just, but the charge that Green is a spokesman, champion or apologist of "a tiny sector" is absurd; his presentation of this sector is, in fact, remarkably objective and detached. The insinuation that all of Green's work is concerned with this tiny sector is even more misleading, for only three of Green's nine novels (*Party Going, Doting* and *Nothing*) present, as principal figures, people even remotely corresponding to Dr. Snow's description. One suspects that Dr. Snow has somehow overlooked all of the novels written by Green in the forties.

Snow's is a surprising charge, because one feature of Green's work that makes him almost unique among contemporary novelists is the variety of social strata that he explores. Indeed Joyce Cary is the only British novelist who rivals him in diversity and versatility. Cary seems to be equally at home with Nigerian natives, juvenile delinquents, well-to-do Anglo-Irish, professional men, eccentric artists, politicians and domestic servants. Similarly, Green has portrayed, with equal fidelity, artisans and office-workers, public school boys and professional firemen, business men and butlers, the gilded youth (and middle-aged) of Mayfair and an eminent scientist in his lonely old age. He is one of the few English novelists who can portray the well-born and the rich without being vulgar or snobbish, supercilious or deferential; he is also one of the few English novelists who can present working-class people without condescension, or fake vaudeville humour. As a *Time* reviewer put it: "Green's novels bubble like a social melting-pot that can boil down everything from cutaways to galluses."[6] He is extremely fortunate that his way of life has enabled him to mix freely with all classes, and freed him from what (according to Nigel Dennis) he considers "the English novelist's worst restriction—ignorance of life in all social classes but his own".[7]

The variety of subject-matter in Green's novels does, to some extent, reflect the circumstances of his own life, but Green has never been content with fictionalized autobiography—not even in his first novel, *Blindness*. He has never been content either with reportage or documentary realism—not even in the two novels (*Living* and *Caught*) in which the temptation to rely on the appeal of the unfamiliar or the topical was strongest. Indeed Henry Green was probably one novelist whom Louis MacNeice had in mind when he contended: "The single-track mind and the single-plane novel or play are almost bound to falsify the world in which we live. The fact that there is method in madness and the fact that there is fact in fantasy (and equally fantasy in 'fact') have been brought home to us not only by Freud and other psychologists but by events themselves. This being so, reportage can no longer masquerade as art. So the novelist, abandoning the 'straight' method of photography, is likely to resort once more not only to the twist of plot, but to all kinds of other twists which may help him to do justice to the world's complexity. Some element of parable, therefore, far from making a work thinner and more abstract, ought to make it more concrete. Man does, after all, live by symbols."[8] The ensuing chronological discussion of Green's work will have three objects —to outline his artistic development, to indicate the variety and objectivity of his work and to point out some of the ways in which Green transcends "the 'straight' method of photography".

2

Henry Green, like several other British writers of his generation (including Christopher Isherwood, Evelyn Waugh, William Plomer and Graham Greene) made a precocious start as a novelist. Green was actually first in the field with *Blindness* (1926), written while he was an Eton Schoolboy and Oxford undergraduate, and published when he was only twenty-two.

Blindness attracted less attention from the critics and reviewers than Waugh's *Decline and Fall* and Greene's *The Man Within*. When noticed it was usually lightly dismissed. Green himself, fourteen years later, in his autobiography, *Pack My Bag* (1940), was to laugh at its passages of conventionally poetic prose. (E.g. "He would never again be able to go out in the morning and recognize the sweep of lawn and garden again, and to wonder that all should be the same. He would never again be able to appreciate the miracle that anything could be so beautiful, never to see a bird again, or a cloud, or a tree, or a horse dragging a cart, or a baby blowing bubbles at his mother", p. 56.) Yet the novel wears remarkably well; it is an extraordinary book to have been written by a youth in his teens. In its elegance, intelligence and prevailing unsentimentality, one clearly sees Green's original and striking talent.

The book has an unusually ambitious theme—the attempts of an impressionable, sensitive and cultivated youth to reconcile himself to accidentally caused blindness, and to start life afresh. It is unique among Green's books in being divided into three separately named sections—"Caterpillar", "Chrysalis" and "Butterfly". Part I is a transcript of John Haye's journal during his last year at school; Part II an account of his first months of blindness; Part III an account of the later period when he is beginning to overcome his handicap, and discover the compensating development of his other senses. The only part of the book which seems at all autobiographical is the first; John Haye's journal is probably largely a record of Green's own experiences and mental attitudes. It is a desultory and informal diary of school happenings, holiday incidents, with interspersed comments about books and school. (E.g. "What is bad is that this school tends to turn the really clever into people who pretend for all they are worth to be the mediocrities which are the personification of the splendid manhood phase", p. 9.)

But although there may be a close temperamental similarity between the youthful Henry Green and John Haye, the potentially tragic situation in which Green's character finds himself and his reactions to this predicament were wholly imagined. Unlike many writers of first novels, Green was not merely shuffling and rearranging what he had known and experienced, but venturing, with an alert intuitive sympathy, into the unknown. And already, in his unforgettable portrayal of an almost Faulknerian household, in which a defrocked, gin-soaked clergyman and his primitive, uneducated daughter live in squalor on tinned herrings, he showed his interest in the abnormal, his capacity to understand and convincingly depict people outside the orbit of the usual middle-class novelist.

Henry Green spent two hectic years at Oxford, but no one would guess it from his novels. None of his characters seems to have been near a university; if any of them has (presumably Mr. Rock, the old scientist in *Concluding*, at least, must have), Green does not consider it important enough to mention. Oxford certainly was not (or has not yet been) important to Green as a novelist; apparently it made no appeal to his creative imagination.

Far more important to him was the period immediately after Oxford, which he spent at his father's foundry in Birmingham. There, he records in *Pack My Bag*, he "lived in lodgings, worked a forty-eight-hour week first in the stores, then as a pattern maker, then in the iron foundry, in the brass foundry and finally as a coppersmith and wrote at night" (p. 236). What he wrote was his second novel, *Living* (1929).

The contrast between *Blindness* and *Living* is as startling as the contrast between Eton and Birmingham. *Living* was one of the first novels about factory workers and factory life. Such books appeared in shoals during the thirties, but *Living* is still probably the best, and one of the few that gives an apparently accurate, and certainly convincing, portrayal of the attitudes, the ways of thought and feeling of factory workers. Walter Allen has remarked that "the title of the book is itself defiant, as though Green had discovered life for the first time. No working-class writer, I think, could have written the book; the author's delighted sense of novelty is carried over to the reader."[9] This is true, but it does not mean, as it might seem to imply, that the novel is a *record* of Green's discovery of life. The delighted sense of novelty suffuses the book, but it is not shared by any of the characters. There is no thinly-disguised self-portrait of the author in *Living*, no Stephen Dedalus or Paul Morel, no Philip Quarles or William Bradshaw. It is true that the chief character who is not a member of the working class is a young man of the same class, and about the same age, as Green himself. But if young Dupret, the boss's son, is, in any sense, a self-portrait, the disguise is perfect. Far from working in the foundry, Dupret junior is content to remain in London, except for occasional ill-advised and disastrous visits to Birmingham. He has none of his creator's interest in the workers as human beings; to him they remain alien and incomprehensible, dirty and rather frightening. In fact if young Dupret is a self-portrait, it is a self-portrait completely in the Chaucerian tradition of ironical self-belittlement.

The subject-matter of *Living* is important, but the book is not primarily, as it was originally considered, a realistic novel. Although the main settings for the book are the foundry and the drab streets, pubs and workers' homes, Green constantly transforms dinginess into beauty, not by romanticizing, but simply by seeing things with fresh eyes and registering them with an unconventional accuracy. Green also constantly breaks through the boundaries of simple realism through his masterfully unorthodox arrangement of words, through poetic and symbolic incident, and through recurrent patterns of imagery (especially the image of homing pigeons).

It was ten years before Green published another novel. These, it is worth recalling, were the ten years from the beginning of the depression to the war, the decade dominated in literature by the "Pylon school" and social realism, the movement to which, as Walter Allen remarked, "the subject-matter of *Living* gave [Green] honorary membership . . . [but] to which he never truly belonged".[10] For most of this stormy time of economic breakdown and unemployment at home, and the terrifying growth of Fascism abroad, Green was apparently working on *Party Going*, which was eventually published in the year the war began. When one turns to Green's novel from some of the typical documentary, political and propagandist works of this period, whether in poetry or prose (e.g. Auden's *Spain*, Ralph Bates' *The Olive Field*, Calder-Marshall's *Pie in the Sky*, Day Lewis' *Magnetic Mountain*, Orwell's *Road to Wigan Pier*, Upward's *Journey to the Border*, Warner's *The Wild Goose Chase*), one is reminded a little of Sir Thomas Browne meditating on ancient funeral rites and the significance of the number five, while Milton thundered, harangued and exhorted. But the parallel, though enticing, is inexact, for, despite its appearance of triviality, *Party Going* shows a keen awareness of the social realities of the time. And paradoxically, it is less personal and introspective than most of these "political" works.

Party Going is not a long novel (255 pages) but it has, on its last page, the note "London 1931–1938". Nigel Dennis, apparently with Green's concurrence, explains this protracted gestation by saying that Green was "faced for the first time with the problem of 'creating an abstract situation out of new conditions'" and that in this novel Green "crossed the hazardous divide which separates 'real' fiction from autobiographical".[11] This, as already suggested, does Green less than justice. A novel, surely, should be described as autobiographical only if it introduces a character who is basically similar in temperament and outlook to the author, and whose crucial experience of life parallels the author's own. *Living* is exempt from the autobiographical charge on the first count, *Blindness* on the second. It is true, however, that from *Party Going* on there is in Green's novels scarcely a single character with whom there is the slightest temptation to identify the author. Certainly in *Party Going* there is none, among the group of blasé and irresponsible young society people waiting at a London railway terminus for the fog to lift so they can proceed on their continental jaunt. The author is present only in solution, not by proxy, except perhaps for a momentary precipitation in an

B

important passage of reflection of Alex Alexander's, which is the nearest approach to a direct statement of the book's theme.

Party Going is a relatively slight book, but it is a complex work of art which fuses into a unity the diverse elements of allegory, symbolism, poetry and the realistic and comic exposure of futility. Like all of Green's books it is *sui generis*, stubbornly itself and irreducible to any neat formula. Indeed this book has provoked Arnold Kettle to remark: "The truth is that about a successful work of art there is in an important sense nothing whatever to say. Any discussion of what goes to make it up remains simply a discussion of what goes to make it up."[12]

Walter Allen, writing about Green in 1941, expressed the opinion that *Living* and *Party Going* were as important as anything published in the preceding decade. But most of Green's critics would agree that the novels on which his place chiefly depends are those published during and just after the war— *Caught* (1943), *Loving* (1945) and *Back* (1946). All three are (to borrow Elizabeth Bowen's phrase describing her collection of stories, *The Demon Lover*) "studies of war-climate and the strange growths it raised", but none of them, not even *Caught*, with its extraordinary descriptions of the fires of the blitz, depends mainly for its interest on the transitory and abnormal circumstances of the war-years.

For some years, during the war, Henry Green was a member of the Auxiliary Fire Service. He served throughout the tense expectancy and dreary boredom of the "phoney war", and through the fury of the blitz. According to Nigel Dennis, he was struck by the fact that "proletarian inspiration was essential to his artistic development".[13] Fortunately there was plenty of it among the butlers, valets, waiters and porters who were his fellow amateur-firemen. *Caught* was based partly on this experience and this inspiration, for it describes the life of a wealthy Auxiliary Fireman, Richard Roe, in a London sub-station, from the beginning of his pre-war training down to a period of sick leave spent in the country in late 1940, after he had been knocked out by a bomb that came too close. But the similarity between Richard Roe and his creator does not seem to extend beyond membership of the same social class.

Just as Green's period of training in his father's factory had provided him with a wealth of new factual material and showed him how business-life looked from below, so the war with its enforced contacts between inhabitants of separate worlds gave him an increased insight into the ways of life, the attitudes and behaviour-patterns of a class very different from his own, and revealed even more clearly what his own class looked like to its servants. But in *Caught* as in *Living* Green refused to be circumscribed by the limits of documentary realism; again he showed complete control of his material and refused to be hypnotized by the merely topical and adventitious. The war is certainly more than an incidental circumstance; it places the characters in unfamiliar situations which accelerate their development (or disintegration), but we are made to feel that this same process would have gone on, more slowly perhaps, but no less surely, if there had been no such disruption of their normal lives.

Even in its documentary, factual aspect the novel is one of the best that the war produced. It compares favourably with books like C. S. Forester's *The Ship*, Anthony Thorne's *I'm a Stranger Here Myself*, Roger Grinstead's *Some Talk of Alexander* and Gerald Kersh's *They Die with Their Boots Clean*, which were among the best of those that dealt with life in the various Services. The descriptions of station life are authentic and vivid, the dialogue carries immediate conviction. But intimately grafted to the account of the boredom and petty intrigues of the sub-station, interwoven with it, giving it depth and tension, is a sinister and macabre sub-plot of almost Jacobean horror. And interspersed amongst the prosaic, circumstantial detail are several passages of highly elaborate poetic prose, used mainly for the monologues of Richard Roe. Green's treatment in this novel of the facts of the war-situation illustrates the truth of Henry James' comment on the artist's imagination: "We can surely account for nothing in the novelist's work that hasn't passed through the crucible of his imagination, hasn't in that perpetually simmering cauldron his intellectual *pot-au-feu*, been reduced to savoury fusion."[14]

This book undoubtedly marked an important stage in Henry Green's development, because it not only united all the qualities he had previously displayed, but also revealed a greater depth of psychological insight, and an ability to make the abnormal and the bizarre as authentic as the mundane.

The second, and very different, fruit of Green's war-time association with valets, footmen and porters was *Loving*, which many critics consider to be Green's finest achievement to date.

Loving is a slighter, less tragic novel than *Caught*, but its various elements are more perfectly fused. The whole action of *Loving* is confined, even more strictly than that of *Party Going*, to a single scene—a huge Irish castle in war-time where the owner, a rich widow, and her daughter-in-law struggle along with a dozen servants, most of them English. The book is a masterpiece of life below stairs; the two ladies are completely dependent on their servants and are important in the novel only as they affect the kingdom below. Actually it is not a single kingdom but a loose confederation of independent states ruled over by butler, housekeeper, cook and nurse. No one has the hardihood to enter the kitchen unless expressly invited by the cook. Charley Raunce is regarded as a vile usurper by some of the old guard when he assumes the prerogatives belonging to his rank as acting-butler.

Like all of Green's novels *Loving* exists on more than one plane. Most obviously it is a convincing portrayal of several typical but individual characters; of these Raunce is one of Green's best characters. On a second level it is both a subtle study of the complex status relationships within the servant hierarchy and, by implication, a study of the decay of the class system. But beyond these levels the book owes much of its delightful individuality to the fact that it is a deliberately inverted fairy-tale. Green suggests the connection with legend and fairy-tale by beginning the novel with the words "Once upon a day" and ending it with "Over in England they were married and lived happily ever after". The castle, with its vast, opulent, disused rooms, its trappings of onyx and alabaster, its flocks of strutting, screaming peacocks and hordes of doves incessantly fighting and making love, is a place of enchantment and its inhabitants under a spell, which Raunce (extraordinary Prince Charming!) and Edith eventually break when they escape to the reality of England at war. Mrs. Tennant's lost ring and Edith's "love potion" of preserved peahen's eggs are only two of the most obvious mythological elements. The novel, moreover, is studded with symbolic scenes and episodes—moments which occur quite naturally in the flow of narrative, but which carry overtones of meaning, beyond their immediate context. Some of the finest of these epiphanies are, as in several of Green's other novels, concerned with the omnipresent birds.

One American reviewer summed up trans-Atlantic opinion

of the book when he described it as "the richest and most entrancing novel that has come out of England since Virginia Woolf's *Between the Acts*".[15]

Back is perhaps not quite so impressive as its two predecessors, but it is, nevertheless, probably the finest English novel about the return to civilian life of a war-veteran, and in some ways it is Green's most remarkable *tour de force*. Here there is no single focal setting; the novel ranges through a series of London middle-class milieux—suburban homes, flats, lodgings, restaurants and business offices, in which normal activity is hag-ridden and almost ham-strung by the controls and directives of war-time committees, bureaux and departments, all known by mystifying initials. Through the maze of S.E.C.O., S.E.V.B., S.E.P.Q., S.O.M.F., A.B.P., etc., the book's hero, Charley Summers, an executive in an engineering firm which lost its factory in the blitz, recently returned home after years in a German prisoner-of-war camp, with one leg missing and the balance of his mind disturbed, despairingly gropes his way.

The book is valuable for the veracity of its depiction of war-time business life, a subject with which Green was thoroughly familiar. But, as always, Green was less interested in a specific, contemporary set of conditions than in the individual human being, whose perplexities are not only typical of those of all bewildered servicemen trying to readjust themselves, but symbolical of universal human problems. To present this deeper level effectively Green uses many unrealistic or anti-realistic devices. Important again are the legendary overtones; the book, indeed, is a modern *Romance of the Rose*. Its action arises from Charley's obsession that his mistress, Rose, who died during his captivity, is actually alive and deceiving him, and from his efforts to make her reveal and confess herself. The woman, Rose, and the flower, rose, are the dominant symbols of the book. In *Back* Green also introduces coincidence (of which he has always been fond) more freely than ever. Mistaken identity and what Jean Howard calls "the appalling knock and echo of coincidence"[16] are not used carelessly or capriciously, but deliberately and responsibly to emphasize the madness of the world in which Charley finds himself, the split in his own mind, and his eventual reintegration.

The unusual quality of *Back* then (like that of *Caught*) derives from the subtle interplay of two different levels—the outer level of realistic and semi-satirized suburban and business life and conversation, and the inner level of mental disturbance, hallucination and neurotic fantasy.

Indeed all of Green's work up to this point derives its distinction from a fusion (not always perfect) of two levels of interest, which may be defined as, first, the prosaic, circumstantial and contemporary level, and, secondly, the poetic, symbolic and universal level. The factual, specific truth of his novels arises largely from his gift for dialogue; few novelists have possessed his uncannily accurate ear for ordinary conversation—for its desultoriness, haphazardness and repetitiveness, and for its concealments and evasiveness. But in all his books, while preserving verisimilitude of surface, Green connects his contemporary characters and situations with universal and timeless emotions, and with man's perennial predicaments and perplexities, the most important of which, for Green, is the problem of human happiness and how it is to be attained. He does this not overtly and explicitly, but allusively and obliquely, by methods which are often thought of as belonging essentially to poetry (though they have also been used by, for example, Forster, Lawrence, Joyce and Virginia Woolf); chiefly through symbolical and mythological overtones and through the use of colour and imagery. These are not, as they have been called, "random beauties"; they have an appropriateness arising from, and in turn reinforcing, a central theme and a dominant emotion.

In Green's three post-war novels these two levels appear to have been separated, so that first one and then the second has been dominant, almost to the complete exclusion of the other. The first of these novels, *Concluding* (1948), is the strangest and most controversial of all Green's books. A few of his admirers (Jean Howard, Nigel Dennis, Robert Phelps) consider this novel Green's masterpiece, but some reviewers regarded it as an obscure anti-climax to his best work. Whatever its eventual place may be, the book represents yet another, and apparently Green's most revolutionary, departure in subject-matter. All his previous novels had comparatively ordinary settings (though viewed always from an unusual angle, and invested always with novelty and wonderment). But in *Concluding* Green moved on from the public school, the foundry, the railway station, the

fire station, the servants' hall and the business office to a training school for girl civil servants, established in a former Great
House in the English countryside, in a state-dominated brave
new world of the future. Mark Schorer has aptly described the
novel as "a non-political *1984*".[17]

Concluding seems, at first, the most ironical of all Green's
intriguing titles, for this is one of the most inconclusive of novels.
At the end of this single summer's day (for here Green observes
the unities both of place and time) in the lives of the girls and
teachers of the school, and in the life of Mr. Rock, the once
famous scientist, who, for having in the distant past evolved a
now-forgotten Great Theory, is allowed to occupy a cottage in
the grounds, nothing has been resolved or concluded. The
mystery of the missing girl is still unsolved; Mr. Rock's tenure
of his cottage, in face of the determination of the school
principals to evict him as a menace to their bureaucratic
heaven, is even more precarious. Yet the title is perfectly fitting,
for if nothing specific has been settled, the total effect of this
beautiful but frightening nightmare is of a whole civilization
coming to an end.

Concluding is a quite logical culmination of one side of Green's
work. By projecting the action into an indeterminate future,
he avoids any danger of the book's being judged as a report on
a contemporary situation and tacitly emphasizes the timelessness
of the conflicts (between the sexes, between different generations, between the state and the individual) which it presents.
Despite the dream-like quality of the book it is far from being
a work of unbridled fantasy; if the time is indicated only as
"Sometime in the future" and the location only as "Somewhere
in England" that "somewhere" is described (or evoked) in full
sensuous detail. It *is* a particular place, but it is also much
more. Green's settings have always tended to be symbolic and
in *Concluding* this tendency is carried a stage further, for the
setting here stands for Western Civilization itself endeavouring
to repress and regiment itself into non-humanity. The school
is clearly a symbol for a sterile, mechanized, denatured civilization. But the setting also includes the forest surrounding the
school, and this mysterious forest, bird-haunted, heady with the
scent of flowers, drowsy with summer heat and again shrouded
in dense fog, is equally clearly a symbol for the elemental,
instinctive life which humanity attempts to deny, but which

will not be denied. But again, however indeterminate time and however symbolic place may be, the characters are clearly and sharply drawn. In fact few novels fit more literally Marianne Moore's description of poetry as presenting "for inspection imaginary gardens with real toads in them".

It is not only in this regard that *Concluding* is "poetic"; its whole organization, even more than that of earlier books, is akin to that of music or of poetry rather than that of conventional narrative or drama. In all the earlier books there had been scenes and episodes, often apparently trivial or even irrelevant, which reverberated with mysterious feeling. *Concluding* consists almost entirely of such scenes, and the way in which they are ordered and combined depends more on their emotional relationship to one another than on simple narrative logic.

There are few such scenes in Green's two most recent books, *Nothing* (1950) and *Doting* (1952), which are generally considered to be inferior to, at least, the four novels which preceded them. These books are disappointing for several reasons. One reason is that in them, for the first time, Green begins to repeat himself, for both deal with the same small segment of upper-class, well-to-do society in post-war London. One of the chief interests in these novels is that the people they introduce— John Pomfret and Mrs. Weatherby in *Nothing*, the Middletons and Charles Addinsell in *Doting*—are essentially the same people as the Max Adeys, Angela Crevys, Amabels and Alex Alexanders of *Party Going*, now some twenty years older, and the parents of children reaching adulthood, and now, as a result of the war and high taxation, not quite so privileged and affluent. Indeed they can now scarcely afford their regular luncheons at the Ritz, and they can do little to assist their children who have already been devoured by the bureaucracy.

Green described *Nothing* as "a frivolous comedy of manners", and the description fits *Doting* equally as well. Far more than any of his other novels they tend to coalesce in the reader's mind shortly after they are read, for although they have quite distinct plots, their whole tone and treatment are the same. *Nothing* concerns the devious machinations of the beautiful, middle-aged and unscrupulous Mrs. Weatherby to prevent the marriage of her son to the daughter of her ex-lover, John Pomfret; *Doting* concerns a middle-aged husband, Arthur

Middleton, who loves his wife but is infatuated by a young girl, and his wife's retaliatory intrigue with a handsome, raffish widower. These plots are worked out with a consciously artificial geometrical precision, through a series of conversations in smart restaurants, night clubs and apartments. Both plots and manner inevitably remind one of Etherege and Congreve.

There is, in these novels, a good deal more than is immedidately obvious. Beneath their shimmering, elegant, trivial surface they are acute and perceptive studies of the disintegrating society of the wealthy. But even so, if in Henry Green's work *Concluding* represents one extreme, they represent the other. In *Concluding* the poetic, symbolic and universal level of meaning is almost all-important; in *Nothing* and *Doting* there are comparatively few glimpses of this level, for they are confined almost exclusively to a specific time, place and social condition. They will certainly date (as *Loving* and *Back*, for example, will not) when the situation to which they refer has altered. This Green apparently recognizes, for he is quoted (by Nigel Dennis) as remarking that in "fifteen years' time [*Doting*] will be thought quite soppy".[18]

The difference between *Concluding* and the later novels is partly a difference of technique. Between the writing of *Concluding* and the writing of *Nothing* Green became convinced that "communication between the novelist and the reader will tend to be more and more by dialogue",[19] and so he deliberately set out to write a novel consisting almost entirely of what the characters say aloud, keeping descriptive passages and even "stage directions" to the barest minimum. The dialogue is certainly thoroughly real, as always in Green's novels. But here, where it is almost unrelieved, it is too painfully real, since most of it is trivial, well-bred, inane chatter which carefully conceals what the characters really think and feel. The concealment is so perfect that one suspects at first that these people are actually incapable of thought and feeling, that there is no more to them than their impeccable exteriors. One does eventually penetrate a little beneath the surface, but whether one finds enough to make the effort worth while is debatable.

It is impossible to say whether Green, having decided that all commentary, description and character analysis should be eliminated from the novel as impurities, found that only such people and situations as those presented in *Nothing* and *Doting* lent themselves to this kind of treatment; or whether, feeling himself no longer capable of work of the complexity and richness of *Caught*, *Back* and *Concluding*, he devised this restrictive theory of the novel to fit his new limitations of sympathy and insight. Perhaps neither explanation is correct, though the fact that he has twice employed the same method to present the same kind of subject-matter suggests that one of them must be. One hopes, however, that Green will not continue to deny himself most of the varied technical resources of the novel, and that he will not continue to restrict his scrutiny to this tiny social area. He has, up to *Concluding* (and indeed up to *Nothing*, for it is only the failure of *Doting* to break new ground which is disappointing) been so versatile and adventurous a novelist that one will not be surprised if his next novel renounces the dialogue theory, and has its setting in a coal-mine, a television studio or a dressing-room at Lords.

3

In this chronological survey of Green's work, I have attempted to bring out certain general features. First there is the variety of subject-matter. There are in Britain, it seems, an almost infinite number of distinct social classes and sub-classes. Most British novelists, however observant and perceptive they may be, seem to be unable to portray convincingly life in more than one or two of these strata. Henry Green is one striking exception. Secondly there is the variety of tone, method and manner. His novels are never pure comedy or pure tragedy, but they cover most of the spectrum between these two extremes. They may be arranged in ascending order from frivolity to poignancy as follows—*Doting*, *Nothing*, *Party Going*, *Loving*, *Living*, *Blindness*, *Back*, *Concluding*, *Caught*. Style and method are always subtly adjusted both to subject-matter and to emotional atmosphere.

A third feature, however, is that, although no two novels (except *Nothing* and *Doting*) are much alike, although in each novel Green has investigated a different condition of life, all of them are unmistakably Henry Green's. Green has made many different linguistic experiments but certain stylistic idiosyncrasies have remained constant. More important, however, is the thematic continuity. All the books are, at least tangentially and by implication, studies of disintegration and dissolution, but Green's view is more hopeful than this suggests. As Jean Howard remarks, Green has "a belief in the possibility of happy endings which is unshared by most modern novelists. He ends when he has straightened things out for his characters and given them somewhere to go."[20] No less important is the continuity in his view of human beings, his feeling for the strange complexity of the most ordinary mortals, his perception of the contrast between the commonplace, inarticulate social self and the fears and fantasies beneath. The strength of his characterization rests on his ability simultaneously to see his characters as others see them, as they see themselves, and as they really are. Beyond this also he is able to see his characters both as definite, specific individuals and as symbols of humanity and human problems generally. From this arises the most important element of continuity in his work, already sufficiently emphasized—its fusion of accurate realism with symbolism and poetry.

Despite their variety of subject and tone Green's novels, then, do carry the unmistakable imprint of his individuality. Like every novelist he is inevitably present in his work. His sympathy, judgment, irony—all the qualities that make up his special vision—are implicit in the selection and ordering of characters and incidents, and in style. But, even more than most contemporary novelists, Green is present in his novels only in solution, and not by proxy. From the beginning he has aimed at (and now insists on) a strict objectivity and self-suppression. He has stated Stephen Dedalus' theory of the artist's withdrawal and the impersonality of art simply and categorically: "The writer has no business with the story he is writing."[21] So none of his work is autobiographical in substance: even in *Living* and *Caught* no character is a *persona* or mask for Green himself. Even these novels are based far more on acute observation and imaginative sympathy than on private experience. The use of penetrating observation rather than personal experience as a main source of subject-matter is in line with certain other dicta of Green's, reported by Nigel Dennis, e.g. "The writer's duty is to meet as many pedestrian people as possible and listen to the most pedestrian conversation." "Unlike literary men factory workers are interested, passionately interested in one subject above all—the lives and habits of other *people*. Get into conversation with any group of workmen—and *other people* is what they talk about."[22] If this is true Green is far more like a factory worker than a normal literary man. He is very different from most of the writers of his generation who, however much they tried to immerse themselves in the "destructive element" of contemporary realities, remained interested, above all, in themselves. As C. Day Lewis has said of them:

> We who 'flowered' in the Thirties
> Were an odd lot; sceptical yet susceptible,
> Dour though enthusiastic, horizon-addicts
> And future-fans, terribly apt to ask what
> Our all-very-fine sensations were in aid of.[23]

Moreover Green, in his quest for objectivity, has always avoided the kinds of viewpoint which tempt the reader (though often erroneously) into assuming some sort of identification between a character and his creator. He has never used any kind of internal point of view: that is, none of his novels has, as narrator, a character within the novel, either major or minor, who tells his own or someone else's story, either accurately or evasively (such view points as are used, for example, in *A Farewell to Arms*, *The Great Gatsby*, *Lord Jim*, *The Good Soldier*, *The Immoralist*). He has never used either the point of view adopted by Joyce in *A Portrait of the Artist as a Young Man*, where, although Joyce speaks of Stephen always in the third person, he is virtually always inside Stephen's mind (as Lawrence is inside Paul's mind in *Sons and Lovers*, and Wolfe is inside Eugene's mind in *Look Homeward Angel*), nor that used by James, for example in *The Ambassadors*, where Strether's is the presiding consciousness through which all is seen. Green's nearest approach to this latter point of view is in *Back*, but whereas Strether is chosen as the point of observation because of his proximity to his creator in moral perceptiveness and values, Charley Summers is clearly an "obtuse observer", whose obsession is such that he sees little and understands less. He is much more like such characters as Jane Austen's Emma Woodhouse (*Emma*) or Melville's Amasa Delano ("Benito Cereno").

But if Green generally refuses to adopt the various points of view which limit the author's knowledge to the content of one mind and consciousness, he does not adopt either the traditional mode of omniscient author narration. More and more he has eschewed commentary, explanation, interpretation and character analysis. "For", he argues, "if you want to create life the one way not to set about it is by explanation." And, he asks, "Do we know, in life, what other people are really like? I very much doubt it. We certainly do not know what other people are thinking and feeling. How then can the novelist be so sure?"[24] The result is that there is seldom a passage in Henry Green's novels which one can isolate from its context and assert that in it the author is identifiably present. Nigel Dennis is right when he remarks that a Green novel is "subtly designed in such a way that Green himself . . . seems to be the one personality who has had nothing to do with it".[25]

It is interesting to note that much the same thing has frequently been said about another important contemporary British novelist, Joyce Cary. Mark Schorer, for example, has said of Cary's novels that they are "objective and widely various, and they never quite seem to have been written by Cary".[26] Nevertheless the resemblances between the two novelists are slight; their approach and emphasis are different, and the variety of their work is achieved in entirely different ways. In Cary's case the effect of diversity and objectivity results mainly from his preoccupation with characterization. He has an extraordinary ability to slough his own individuality and submerge himself in his characters. In several of his most important books, particularly *Herself Surprised*, *To Be a Pilgrim* and *The Horse's Mouth*, he creates a central character who dominates the book and whose personality determines its form, method and general tone. Even in novels where this central character is not the narrator, like *Mr. Johnson* and *Charley is My Darling*, it is the characters rather than the novelist who (as Schorer puts it) "set up the imaginative focus and the moral reference".[27] Green, in contrast, almost always remains detached from his characters: we seldom get the impression that one of his characters has taken charge, and is imposing on us his special vision of the world. The exception, again, is *Back*, which is unique among Green's novels in keeping through-out close to the nerves and consciousness of a single character. But generally Green achieves his startling authenticity, as well as his illusion of objectivity and withdrawal, and the variety of his work as a whole, not by putting himself behind the eyes and inside the mind of single characters, but by, in each novel, immersing himself in a different condition of life, a different pattern and texture of experience, and making that condition of life and that texture of experience concrete and alive through his unfailingly accurate dialogue and his extraordinarily flexible and resourceful narrative and descriptive prose.

II

Proletarians and Plutocrats

> People, in their relations with one another, are continually doing
> similar things, but never for similar reasons.
>
> *(Party Going*, p. 114)

I

WHATEVER else the novel can do without, it cannot do without characters. From whatever angle they may be viewed, however they may be presented (whether through detailed description and analysis, through the objective recording of their behaviour and speech, or through the ever-changing flow of their consciousness), and for whatever symbolic purposes they may be employed, characters, in whose existence, at least within the reference of the novelist's created world, the reader can believe, are the indispensable primary requirement of the novel. Although Henry Green has sometimes been criticized by those who maintain that the novelist's chief business is the creation of large, definite, memorable characters, one of his greatest and most easily appreciable virtues is the range and livingness of his characterization.

The variety of social areas from which Green's characters are drawn has already been mentioned, but certain limitations in his range of characterization must be noticed. Virginia Woolf's remark : "Since he [the artist] is a single person with one sensibility, the aspects of life in which he can believe with conviction are strictly limited"[1] is clearly relevant to Green. Though his range of characterization is unusually wide, it omits large groups and classes of people, and several important aspects and areas of experience.

One major omission, which puts Green at the opposite pole from a writer like Aldous Huxley, reflects both Green's determination that his work shall not be autobiographical, and the unusualness of his double life as business man and novelist. According to Nigel Dennis, Green, "in private life, practises a nervous temperamental detachment from art"; "he declines to hold any literary opinions whatever or to pass judgement on

27

any other author, dead or alive"; "he believes that the artist can survive only by becoming a business man and that he can learn about art only from non-artists", and that "conversation is the principal way of learning anything about life, and it is absurd to waste good talk on topics such as art, that come after life, not before it."[2] Hence it is not surprising that among the characters of Green's novels there are no writers (except the briefly-glimpsed young poet, Campbell Anthony, whose projected anthology gives *Doting* its name), no creative artists of any kind, and, after *Blindness* at least, not even any aspiring artists or people of artistic temperament or with artistic interests. None of Green's characters even seems to read—except Mr. Craigan, the old iron-moulder in *Living*, who reads and re-reads Dickens.

Nor are there any scholars or intellectuals among Green's characters. It might be objected that Mr. Rock, the old scientist of *Concluding*, upsets this generalization; but it is difficult seriously to regard Mr. Rock as a scientist. Like everyone else Mr. Rock seems to have forgotten the great theory which won him fame; his bedroom is packed with books, but he has not opened one in years; even the daily paper is destined for use, unread, in the lavatory; his voluminous mail from scientific societies, never opened, serves as fire-lighters. Whatever Mr. Rock may have been (and whether he was astronomer or zoologist, botanist or physicist, chemist or geologist is impossible to guess) he is now simply an old man; whatever this sage's horizons may once have been, they are now narrowed to include only his cottage and his mentally-sick grand-daughter, and his whole life is now centred in his determination to cling to the one as a refuge for the other.

Presumably Mr. Rock, more than half a century before we meet him, must have attended a university; there is even less evidence that any of Green's other characters has done so. Most of his well-to-do characters—the Richard Duprets, Max Adeys, Richard Roes, John Pomfrets, Charles Addinsells—are obviously products of exclusive public schools; but one feels that if any of them went on to Oxford or Cambridge (nowhere else is thinkable), it was only in conformity with the traditions of their class, for it has obviously been of even less importance in their lives than Green's two years at Oxford were in his. Moreover, there are very few professional men and women among

Green's characters; the few doctors (e.g. the hotel doctor in *Party Going* who attends Miss Fellowes, the doctor in *Caught* who questions Pye about his sister), lawyers, and teachers (in *Concluding*) have little more than walk-on parts. Even Miss Baker and Miss Edge, the school principals in *Concluding*, are administrators and state executives rather than teachers.

None of Green's characters is a thinker; none of them is concerned with abstract ideas of any kind, or with any of the insoluble problems of man's destiny and place in the world, which hang over such diverse characters as Virginia Woolf's Lily Briscoe, E. M. Forster's Mrs. Moore, Henry Handel Richardson's Richard Mahony. In complete contrast to Graham Greene's characters none of Henry Green's characters is religious; but for that matter none of them is anti-religious. They are not Catholics or Protestants, agnostics or atheists: they are simply unaware of any spiritual dimension; none is tormented by fears of damnation, none has hopes of salvation. Such things simply never enter their heads. Similarly hardly any of them is interested in, or even seems aware of, wider social or political questions. One might guess how most of them would vote in an election, but it would be purely a matter of habit, not of conviction. (Pye seems to be the only one with political views of a sort.) This too is to be expected; in *Pack My Bag* Green briefly summarized some of the main events and conditions of the 1920s—the aftermath of the war, unemployment, discontent and disillusionment—and added "All this is common ground and none of my business" (p. 174). The remark applies as much to Green the novelist as to Green the autobiographer.

Green's range seems to exclude a great deal; but, since artists, intellectuals, philosophers and university trained professional men (virtually the cast of *To the Lighthouse*, one notices) are, after all, a small minority, it actually includes far more than it excludes. Green's characters are mainly workers of various kinds (factory workers, office workers, domestic servants), business men (directors, managers, accountants, etc.) and the wealthy. Nearly all are people who are preoccupied with their own personal problems (their jobs, their family and other relationships), and who have neither time nor training nor inclination for larger, more abstract or more abstruse interests. Most of them are commonplace, average, ordinary—not at all promising material for a novelist, one would think. Yet Green

c

manages to make these people and their unspectacular lives absorbingly interesting. Several things contribute to the success of his characterization; one important factor is Green's pleasure in the human spectacle, his keen awareness of people, his eye and ear for oddities of class-speech and behaviour. But this awareness of externals is only half of the "double vision" which enables him to penetrate beneath the mask of class and type to the individual human soul beneath, to the compulsive anxieties and strange imaginings. V. S. Pritchett has truly said that Green's "special gift has been the awareness of shut doors in people's lives [and] the ability to open them, to show the haze of fantasy in which they exist".[3] So the strength of Green's characterization rests mainly on his ability simultaneously to show his characters clearly and vividly as a keen-sighted ob- server would see them, as they imagine themselves to be, and, by implication at least, as they really are—though what Green's major characters "really are" is usually too complex for easy definition. For Green's main characters, at least, are never static or predictable; they often seem peculiar and incompre- hensible, but this is because they are more like actual human beings than like most fictional characters. Their behaviour, like that of people in real life, is often contradictory, impulsive and irrational; they are always quite likely to perform some unexpected act either of charity, magnanimity or heroism or else of treachery, cruelty or greed. Though Green has not been obviously affected by current theories of psychology, his is an unusually close-up view of human personality and behaviour, which records, usually without explanation, every blush and stammer, every quiver of the nerves, and generally leaves interpretation to the reader.

2

Green has created perhaps only half a dozen really major characters, but his gallery of subsidiary characters is large and varied. A comprehensive discussion would require the sorting of these characters into a score or so of different groups (based on sex, age and social status), but I shall consider only a few representatives of four groups—the young, workers, the middle class and the wealthy.

Pack My Bag makes it clear that Green's memories of his own childhood are vague and fragmentary. So, unlike several prominent contemporary novelists (including Elizabeth Bowen, Joyce Cary, L. P. Hartley and Rumer Godden), he has never taken children as central characters in a novel, nor used a child's mind and consciousness as the perceptional focus. There are comparatively few children in his novels—Richard Roe's five-year-old son, Christopher, in *Caught*; the two little Tennant girls and the cook's nine-year-old Cockney nephew, Albert, in *Loving*; young Ridley Philips, who Charley Summers is convinced is his son, in *Back*; and the six-year-old Penelope Weatherby, in *Nothing*, who is (at least according to her deviously plotting mother) so upset by the mock-marriage with John Pomfret. It is probably unnecessary to remark that his treatment of them is completely unsentimental.

Christopher Roe, Green tells us, "was like any other child of his age, not very interested or interesting, strident with health. He enjoyed teasing and was careful no-one should know what he felt" (p. 5). Christopher is seen almost exclusively through the eyes of his widowed father, who finds him unapproachably young and is shy with him. Richard wants to be close to his son, but the years between make this impossible; he cannot help seeing the boy with adult eyes and registering every slight imperfection in his behaviour, as when he shows off or "laughs too much" when Richard slips over in the damp park. But though his appearances are few, Christopher is important in the novel because Roe's inability to share in the life of this "cold, unquestioning, yet perfectly happy" little boy makes him all the more aware of the loss of his wife; this contributes heavily to the melancholy, elegiac tone of the opening chapters. He is also important because his brief abduction by Pye's mad sister, some months before the novel opens (retrospectively described in one of the most brilliant sections of *Caught*), greatly complicates the relationship between Pye and Roe.

The trio of children in *Loving*—the two little rich girls, Moira and Evelyn, separated from their mother, who bothers little about them, by a screen of servants, and their new companion, "the little 'Itler", Albert, who, soon after his arrival, strangles one of the peacocks, and later causes more trouble by finding and hiding Mrs. Tennant's sapphire ring—are older and more distinctly drawn. Green does not attempt to make a *What Maisie Knew* out of the girls' situation; but though they are not aware of their mother's adultery, they are hostile and resentful towards her lover, Captain Davenport, for usurping time that should be theirs. They are fascinated by the strange behaviour and speech of young Albert, and enter into his schemes delightedly. Albert, in some ways a younger version of Cary's Charley Brown, is an engaging little monster—a strange blend of childish ingenuousness and self-protective slyness, deceit and cunning.

Adolescents are rather more important in Green's novels than children. Green has remarked, in *Pack My Bag*: "Any account of adolescence is necessarily a study of the fatuous and yet it would be wrong to treat it on the lines of comedy, as could easily be done" (p. 166). Green's characterization always shows an unusual ability to perceive and reveal both the comic and the pathetic aspects of his characters; as his comment suggests, adolescents are especially susceptible to this treatment. One of Green's finest adolescents is the other Albert in *Loving*, Raunce's yellow pantry boy—sheepish, miserable, obstinate, in a hopeless, inarticulate agony of love for Edith, who regards him as a child, though she is only a few months older than he. Albert is alternately bullied and treated with big-brotherly comradeship by Raunce; he is teased and tormented by Edith and Kate who flaunt their untouchable bodies before him, until, in a stupidly heroic attempt to protect Edith, he blurts out his "confession", "I've got it", to the insurance investigator questioning the servants about the missing ring. He refuses to give any explanation to Mrs. Tennant, and leaves for England under a cloud, mulishly determined to be an air-gunner and die a hero's death.

Almost the same age, but near the other end of the social scale, is the seventeen-year-old public schoolboy, Peter Middleton, in *Doting*. He is old enough to be taken to night-clubs, where he smokes cigarettes and drinks his pints of shandy (and surreptitious glasses of champagne) with man-of-the-world aplomb; but he is still at the stage of "doting" on food and fishing more than anything else, and of being incredulous that a mere girl, like Annabel Paynton, should know anyone as exalted as one of the school prefects. Returned home from hospital after his slight injury in a car-accident, he is self-consciously heroic about his excruciating suffering. Though a minor figure, Peter is deftly presented, like all the characters in this novel, entirely through his own speech.

In his portrayal of girls and young women Green's strong streak of romanticism is most clearly evident. Not for him any plain Jane Eyres; his young women, whatever their social class, are bewitching, enchanting and desirable. Mark Schorer has asked: "What other contemporary writer can bring before us with such force and shock the physical beauty of women, the shocking splendour of girls' drapery, hair, mouths, skin . . .?"[4] Who else indeed could make such a poetic fancy out of a schoolgirl's knee? "A knee which, brilliantly polished over bone beneath, shone in this sort of pool she had made for herself in the fallen world of birds, burned there like a piece of tusk burnished by shifting sands, or else a wheel revolving at such speed that it had no edges and was white, thus communicating life to ivory, a heart to the still, and the sensation of a crash to this girl who lay quiet, reposed" (*Concluding*, p. 56). Or of the hands and arms of an untidy typist? "He began to take in her forearms, which were smooth and oval, tapering to thin wrists, with a sort of beautiful subdued fat, also her hands light nimble bones with fingers terribly white, pointed into painted nails like the sheaths of flowers which might at any moment, he once found himself feeling late at night, mushroom into tulips . . ." (*Back*, p. 43).

The heaviest concentration of young girls is in *Concluding*; in this novel there are no less than three hundred trainee civil servants of the bureaucratic state. Apparently their names have even been prescribed by the state, for they all begin with M— Maisy, Margot, Marion, Mary, Melissa, Merode, Mirabel, Moira, Muriel. For the most part they are a picturesque part of the physical setting, and of the novel's atmosphere. None of them is distinctly individualized, though we do on a few occasions overhear their shrewd, slangy, highly speculative gossip about the principals, matron and staff, about Mr. Rock, his unbalanced grand-daughter Liz, and her lover, the economics tutor, Sebastian Birt. One remembers them most vividly, however, as an undifferentiated mass of femininity, in the scene of the ball which climaxes the novel, as white-clad, rapt, surrendered utterly to the music, they circle in one hundred and fifty pairs to the strains of waltz-music from an ancient gramophone, beneath azalea and rhododendron.

This scene inevitably recalls another, in Green's earlier novel, *Loving*, when those two other young temptresses, the housemaids Edith and Kate, waltz together, among the white-sheeted furniture, in the vast, empty ballroom of the Irish castle, their purple-clad bodies reflected a thousand times in the crystal chandeliers. But these two are much more fully delineated. Edith is a partner in one of the most ordinary yet most unusual, most trite yet most wildly romantic, love-affairs in modern fiction; Kate with her doll's face and tow-hair, herself, it seems, also in love with Raunce, is driven into an "affair" with Paddy, the Irish lamp-man, uncouth, unkempt and incomprehensible as he is. The changing relationship between these two girls—the intimate confidences, the coolnesses, the hostilities, the enviousness and the magnanimity—is traced by Green with a remarkable subtlety and perceptiveness.

There are several other finely portrayed adolescents in Green's two most recent novels, *Nothing* and *Doting*, but they will be discussed, with their elders, in their social context.

Of the many workers in Green's novels three groups are most important—the foundry workers in *Living*, the firemen in *Caught* and the servants in *Loving*. Apart from Mr. Craigan, one of Green's major characters, *Living* presents a number of memorable smaller figures, all of whom are startlingly authentic, mainly because they are observed and presented with such complete detachment and such complete freedom from sentimentality and patronage. There is Jim Dale, Mr. Craigan's young workmate, whom Mr. Craigan approves as a suitor for Lily Gates—steady and reliable, but inarticulate, ineffectual and unromantic. Jim is made more and more miserable and frustrated by Lily's obvious preference for Bert Jones, but his campaign to win her back consists of throwing a pebble at them in a fit of childish petulance, and hoping that Bert will lose his job and leave Birmingham. Lily compares these two rivals in images—"Mr. Dale was to her like being on verge of sleep in safe bed . . . . When she was with Bert it was like she had just stretched then waked then was full of purposes" (p. 76). Bert Jones, a fitter, is much flashier, much more articulate (though even he is not exactly eloquent) than Dale; but he is unreliable and lacking in stamina. He is vaguely discontented and rebellious ("Us working people we got to work for our living till we're too old. It's no manner of use thinking about it, it's like that, right on till we're too old for them to use us", p. 75) but he soon gives up the technical school course that Lily badgers him into attending and plans vaguely to take Lily to Canada where he hopes his talents will be more appreciated. They do eventually "elope", but when they cannot find his parents in Liverpool he deserts her in ludicrously painful circumstances. Bert is no villain or vile seducer, however; he is just a weak and spineless drifter, incapable of planning or accepting responsibility.

The older generation includes Lily Gates' father and Tupe. Joe Gates is a shiftless, loud-mouthed, boastful buffoon; he is afraid of and servile towards Craigan, in whose house he lives; but, resentful of the old man's dominance, he makes occasional foolish and feeble efforts to reassert his parental authority over Lily. At the beginning of the novel he is loud in his condemnation of Tupe, the manager's spy, but soon he is pally with Tupe, treacherously laughing at and criticizing Craigan over the beer Tupe buys him, and equally treacherously denying the association. Tupe, always creeping round looking for a chance to curry favour with the manager, Bridges, by reporting some breach of the rules, envious and vindictively hostile towards Craigan, receives poetic justice when Bridges' favour does not save him from being pensioned off with the other over-age workers. These two are thoroughly contemptible, but they are presented by Green without a hint of indignation or moral condemnation.

Most of the amateur and professional firemen in *Caught* are seen only in groups and they are not clearly differentiated (their function in the novel does not require that they should be) but they impress one as real people—for the most part mean, selfish, sensual, coarse, absorbed in gossip, intrigue and petty grievances, but capable of feats of casual bravery. A few, however, do stand out—notably Shiner Wright, the huge ex-seaman with his expressive epithet "conga", who is killed in one of the first of the raids, after performing almost superhuman feats; and Arther Piper, the toadying, trouble-making, tale-bearing old ex-soldier, on his "fifth campaign", with his maddening habit of repeating the speaker's last words or confirming them with a "so there you are then". The accuracy of Green's characterization is indirectly attested by Stephen Spender, who was also in the A.F.S., and whose account of station life in his autobiography, *World Within World*, tallies closely with Green's. Indeed some of the firemen briefly depicted by Spender seem like the originals of those in *Caught*. "Grannie", who was "always grousing in a tone of voice which the others imitated" and "who had the reputation of getting lost on fires", and Bill, the great, ungainly Cockney with enormous limbs, roaring at everyone he met: "You worry too much, that's what's wrong with you",[5] are like first sketches of Piper and Shiner.

The first servants to walk into Green's novels are the "two nannies dressed in granite with black straw hats and white hair" in *Party Going*, who come upon Miss Fellowes washing her dead pigeon in the Ladies, and whose reaction is so exactly right. "They did not care to retire as that might seem as if they were embarrassed by what they were seeing, speak they could not as they had not been spoken to, nor could they pass remarks with this attendant out of loyalty to homes they were pensioners of and of which Miss Fellowes was a part" (p. 10). Later Green comments: "Those nannies, like the chorus in Greek plays, knew Miss Fellowes was very ill. . . . They had . . . an unfailing instinct for disaster. By exaggeration, and Fate they found rightly was most often exaggerated, they could foretell from one chilblain on a little toe the gangrene that would mean first that toe coming off, then that leg below the knee, next the upper leg and finally an end so dreadful that it had to be whispered behind hands" (p. 73). (Incidentally, this is just what does happen to Arthur Morris, in *Nothing*, from whom bits are ripped as from a human calendar.) This is virtually all that Green tells us about the nannies, and throughout the book they are never heard to speak intelligibly, but these ancient, mute prophets of doom are memorable figures.

The type is more fully developed in the elderly retainers, Nannie Swift and Agatha Burch, the head housemaid, in *Loving*. Nannie Swift, deaf, ill and growing simple, can still boast of *her* instinct for disaster. "After all there's not a woman after a life spent with her charges but doesn't get an eye for illness. It may start as no more than a snivel when you put 'em to bed and then before you've time to adjust yourself you're right in the middle of it, day and night nurses under your feet with oxygen bottles and all that flummery" (p. 120). The be-wigged Miss Burch bitterly resents Charley Raunce's usurpation of the butler's place with his predecessor (and, apparently, her paramour) "not yet in the ground", and the fact that, in all this great mansion, she has no "more than a door opening into the sink" to call her own, while the Nannie has her nursery

and Mrs. Welch her kitchen to rule. There are many lonely
people in Green's novels, but these two solitary old women,
with nothing in their lives except memories of the children
they have tended or the floors they have polished, are among
the most pathetic.

Green's first menservants also appear in *Party Going*.
Thompson and Edwards, who sit around gossiping and taking
full advantage of the opportunities for casual amorous dalliance,
while they keep watch over their employers' fitted pigskin
dressing-cases, are first sketches for the fully developed individuality of Charley Raunce.

A trio of nicely differentiated cooks complete Green's gallery
of servant-class minor characters—Mary Howells, the char
turned cook's off-sider in *Caught*, gossiping, inquisitive, lachry-
mose, harassed by the matrimonial troubles and unbalanced
mental condition of her daughter, who, by going adrift, drives
yet another nail into Pye's coffin; Mrs. Welch, in *Loving*, gin-
soaked, spying, truculent, hiding her fierce love for young Albert
(who is suspected to be a nearer relation than her nephew)
under a mask of bullying rage; and Mrs. Blain, the cook in
Concluding, less fully delineated, but obviously a woman to be
reckoned with, massive, dictatorial and "a terror for her rights".

The middle-class denizens of Henry Green's world are mainly
office workers and executives; they are concentrated chiefly in
Living and *Back*. Probably no novel has ever given a more convincing representation than *Living* of the constant intrigue which
goes on in any large organization—the attempts to curry favour
with the bosses, the incessant jockeying for position and
treachery among the higher ranks. The executives are presented
with the same sharp fidelity as the workers. There are such
figures as the ambitious chief draughtsman, Mr. Tarver,
bumptious, self-opinionated, aggrieved, writing letters of complaint to the London head office of the firm, vicariously
annihilating the works manager, Mr. Bridges, in the shape of a
tennis ball; and his confederate in the London office, the
cunningly plotting accountant, Mr. Archer. But the two finest
portraits are those of Mr. Bridges, the manager, and Richard
Dupret, the owners' son (who actually belongs to the wealthy
class, but will be considered here, since he is generally seen
"at work"). Bridges, a Brummagem man, who has himself
risen from the working class, illiterate, irascible, is perpetually

in a frenzy of anxiety about the intrigue above and below. ("And all through today them others, like crows after sheep's eyes, trying to get 'old of 'im and tell lies", p. 11). Like so many of Green's characters, Bridges lives simultaneously in the outer world and in a world of private fantasy, where he dramatizes himself into a figure of powerful and noble personality, grievously afflicted and under-valued. One passage, in particular, shows Green's skill in delineating character through vivid images.

"Mr. Bridges in his thinking and in most of his living was all theatre. Words were exciting to him, they made more words in him and wilder thinking.

Sometimes liquid metal foundrymen are pouring into moulding box will find hole in this, at the joint perhaps, and pour out. Sometimes stream of metal pouring out will fall on patch of wet sand or on cold iron, then it will shower out off in flying drops of liquid metal. To see this once or twice perhaps is exciting. But after twice, or once even, you just go to stop hole up where metal from box is pouring.

So with Mr. Bridges.

You were to him speaking, and he began quietly answering, then, suddenly, he was acting, sincere in feeling, but acting, and words were out pouring, fine sentiments fine. At first you said 'Fine old man' in your mind, at last you were thinking only how to plug him. And with him this was not only with his talking, it was also in his silent thinking" (pp. 112–13).

The callow young Dupret, allowed to play around with the business, as with a toy, while his tycoon father is ill, succeeds on his death to the managing directorship. He is an empty, conceited, foolish young man, all the more determined to assert his authority because he is so acutely self-conscious, and so aware that the older men, like Bridges and Walters, who have worked for his father for years, measure him against his father and find him wanting. He, too, is much given to declaiming to himself about the iniquities of the loathsome, horrible, stupid old men and their intrigues. It is, however, his complete failure with Hannah Glossop, the frivolous, empty-headed girl with whom he is infatuated, that drives him to dull the anguish he imagines he feels in "work"; his conception of work is to do something, anything, however rash and ill-considered. But all that he (egged on by Tarver and Archer) can think of to do is to sack all the elderly men, even though some of them are the most skilled and dependable workers in the factory. Without the faintest trace of didacticism or propaganda, Green, through the portrayal of Dupret, indicates some of the capriciousness of private enterprise.

A very different specimen of managing director is Charley Summers' boss, Corker Mead, in *Back*. He has not inherited wealth, like Dupret, but has risen to his present position from an apprentice, like Bridges and Walters, whom he resembles somewhat. Outwardly hard ("Corker is mustard") and efficient in running his engineering firm (which, having lost its factory in the blitz, depends on various government departments' making other companies turn out its product), he is sympathetic, though uncomprehending, in his attitude towards Charley in his difficult period of adjustment; he is eager, indeed, to give him fatherly advice that he should marry, while he is himself embroiled in a violent telephone wrangle with his wife. Like Dodge, the Fire Brigade superintendent in *Caught*, he is really an old woman at heart, loving a cosy chat about illnesses and symptoms and treatments.

Another executive (of some kind) in *Back* is Green's example of the exuberant libertine, the sensual man about town, Arthur Middlewitch, who, undaunted by his chromium-plated artificial arm, is determined to make up for all the time he has lost in a prisoner-of-war camp. Completely self-centred beneath his effusions of bonhomie, he scarcely pretends to listen to what anyone else is saying in his eagerness to recount his amorous exploits. But his mask of self-confident importance fails altogether to hide his vacuity, and it is no surprise when we learn that he has been sacked. Middlewitch has some affinities with Sebastion Birt, Liz Rock's lover (in *Concluding*); Birt is a creature of Protean mimicries and no real identity. It is surely significant that this weak, worried, treacherous poseur, sensually enslaved by Liz, is the nearest approach in Green's work to a portrait of an intellectual. He is, at least, the only one of Green's characters who ever attempts to speak (though always in mockery) in abstractions.

Skilful as is Green's portrayal of those contained within the large, amorphous tract of society usually loosely classified as the middle class, his characterization of the wealthy is even more distinguished and unusual. The wealthy make their first appearance, in force, in *Party Going*, but there are foretastes in *Living*. Interspersed throughout the earlier book are occasional glimpses of the factory-owner's family, and of the social circle, with its round of dinner-parties, balls, night-clubs and house-parties, in which young Dupret moves. Richard is infatuated with a foolish, spoilt, vaguely yearning young woman named Hannah Glossop ("You look into crystal globe and its round emptiness makes a core in it you can't see through, there is nothing there only the transparency is confused. That was like Hannah Glossop . . .", p. 134) who is a forerunner of the females of *Party Going*.

Party Going is almost entirely composed of the gossip, the intrigues, jealousies, rivalries and complicated amours of a group of young society people who are on the point of departure for the continent for three weeks as the guests of a fantastically rich young man, when they are delayed at the station by fog. David Garnett, reviewing the novel when it first appeared, tried to define the book's individual flavour in this way: "Suppose Groucho Marx fell completely under the spell of Mrs. Woolf and sat down to write a novel about the rich . . . and then suppose that it turned out to be almost photo-graphically realistic, screamingly funny, but quite lacking in Mrs. Woolf's love of the long catalogue of life which for her, and for us, is poetry. . . . It turns out not to be a work of love . . . but shrewd and cold."[6] This is a graphic description, but it over-simplifies and, to some extent, mis-states the effect of the book. It is true that the book is highly effective as a piece of "photographic realism"—or better, of "radiographic realism" —for Green shows an almost indecent insight into the (to be charitable) minds, feelings and motives of his gilded butterflies, and he presents his malicious portraits with devastating skill. Prominent among them is the perfectly named "Angela" Crevy, who makes such cruel scenes with her young man (who is not one of the party, and is opposed to Angela's going to France at Max Adey's expense) that she efficiently reduces him to an abject "crawling frenzy of love". She taunts, torments, derides and humiliates him until he wishes he were more worthy of one so marvellously adorable. Partly because she is a comparative newcomer to this exclusive clique, has not yet mastered its private idiom, and is still scheming desperately to consolidate her position, Angela is the nastiest of them all: she is also the one most shrewdly and coldly observed. One encounters few young women in fiction at once so convincing and so frightening—she is almost in the Rosamond Vincy class. Compared with Angela, Julia Wray is almost tolerable, for she has the faint, evanescent charm of semi-idiocy. Her thoughts are dominated by her "charms" ("her egg with elephants in it, her wooden pistol and little painted top") in which she places her trust. Occasionally she wonders what Max will do with her during the trip, but when he begins to make love to her, she refuses to be "mussed up" and is annoyed because he interrupts her account of the acquisition and importance of her top. At least that is part of the reason for her rebuff; but also (for she has a streak of cold calculation in her feather head) she realizes that with three weeks ahead of them "it would never do to start too fast and furious".

It is not until half-way through the book that the female star of this ballet-like comedy, Amabel, makes her dazzling appearance, overshadowing all her rivals by her poised arrogance, complete self-possession and wary distaste for her own sex. Her competitors enviously acknowledge her pre-eminence. "Amabel had her own position in London, shop girls in northern England knew her name and what she looked like from photographs in illustrated weekly papers, in Hyderabad the colony knew the colour of her walls" (p. 140).

The male lead is Max Adey, the enormously rich young man at whose expense the whole party is travelling. Seldom has the effect of great wealth on the character of a young man been more economically suggested. Green, in *Pack My Bag*, has remarked: "Without exception the rich of that generation were the most unpunctual people I ever met. They behaved like stage favourites and when you were invited to a meal it was usual to be kept waiting three-quarters of an hour before the host, languid with money, deigned to come in" (p. 205). Such a one is Max Adey. Although this is his party, he has not even decided whether he will accompany it, or stay in London with his mistress, Amabel, when the boat-train is almost due to depart. But when his valet announces that his bags are packed he decides that he may as well go, and leave Amabel lamenting.

Amabel, however, is as rich and mobile as he. She sees no

reason why these girls who are after Max's money should be
given a clear field, so she refuses to be deserted and, uninvited
and unexpected, she joins the party at the station hotel. With
complete aplomb she makes herself at home (even to taking a
bath), sets the whole group by the ears with her intrigues, and
much more subtly, but equally effectively, reduces Max to the
same abject state to which Angela had brought Robin Adams.
Garnett, in the comment already quoted, was a little astray in
describing the book as "shrewd and cold"; despite the clear-
sighted accuracy of the portraiture the total effect of the book
is not "cold". Green's attitude towards his characters is not one
of unmingled distaste and reproof. His attitude towards Amabel
(who is favourably compared with the others by Alex Alexander,
the most intelligent member of the party—"It was not Amabel's
fault, she was all right even is she did use him [Max], it was
these desperate inexperienced bitches, he thought, who never
banded together but fought everyone and themselves . . .",
p. 196) is much more complex. Green's awareness of the triviality of her existence is strangely blended with an enchanted
appreciation of her physical beauty and sophisticated poise, a
delight in her as the culmination of her species. There may be
little of Mirabell in Max, but there is much of Millamant in
Amabel, and Green's portrayal of her, like Congreve's portrayal
of Millamant, is poetic rather than satirical.

The same is true of his portrayal of Mrs. Weatherby, who is by
far the most memorable of the characters in either of Green's
two recent comedies of manners, *Nothing* and *Doting*. Most of
the characters in these books are deliberately kept flat, and
even Mrs. Weatherby herself scarcely escapes the bounds of
the type. But she, like Amabel, represents the very crown and
flower of her type. It is, indeed, essentially the same type—the
beautiful, selfish, unscrupulous, spoiled, intriguing (in both
senses) woman—aged some twenty years; in the fluttery speech
which masks Mrs. Weatherby's craft there is also a suggestion
of Julia Wray.

Much of the interest of *Nothing* arises from the basic similarity
of its characters to those of *Party Going*. But now these fashion-
able Mayfair people, instead of being in their irresponsible,
sophisticated, self-indulgent twenties, are in their irresponsible,
sophisticated, self-indulgent forties; they can still afford their
lunches at the Ritz, and their intimate dinners in their flats

(caviare, sturgeon's eggs, lobster mayonnaise—a "scratch meal"), but they are beginning to feel the financial pinch, and the family lawyer, who handles their affairs, is becoming something of an ogre. But their children, who are now almost as old as they (or their friends) were in *Party Going,* feel the pinch much more. The children—the widower John Pomfret's daughter, Mary, and the widow Mrs. Weatherby's son, Philip—are completely different from their parents, and their lives are completely different. Whereas their parents' lives, during the long weekend between the wars, were a ceaseless round of house-parties, hunt-balls, dinner-parties, and trips abroad, the children have to drudge for a living in the government departments of post-war London. Not that the children yearn for the lost privileges of their parents' youth; for while the older generation retains in middle age all the careless, frivolous hedonism of its youth, the younger generation is serious-minded, public-spirited, puritanical and painfully aware of its responsibilities. The children have a touching filial devotion and family loyalty, but they cannot help being disquieted and disgusted by their parents' selfishness and immorality. In one of the tête-à-têtes between Philip and Mary (the novel is composed almost entirely of such dialogues) the following conversation takes place (p. 69).

" 'They all ought to be liquidated,' he said, obviously in disgust.
'Who Philip?'
'Every one of our parents' generation.'
'But I love Daddy.'
'You can't.'
'I do, so now you know.'
'They're wicked, darling,' he exclaimed. 'They've had two frightful wars they've done nothing about except fight in and they're rotten to the core.'
'Barring your relations, I suppose?'
'Well, Mamma's a woman. She's not really to blame. Nevertheless I do include her. Of course she couldn't manage much about the slaughter. And she can be marvellous at times. Oh, I don't know though, I think I hate them every one.'
'But why on earth?'
'I feel they're against us.'

'You and me, do you mean?'

'Well, yes if you like. They're so beastly selfish they think of no one and nothing but themselves.'

'Are you upset about your twenty-firster then?'

'Not really,' he answered. 'I wouldn't 've had one in any case.'

'Then what is actually the matter?'

There was a long pause.

'It's because they're like rabbits about sex,' he said at last."

But if the parents are, in their children's eyes, wanting in stability, morality and responsibility, the children are, in their parents' eyes, wanting in elegance and elan, sparkle and vivacity. It is Mrs. Weatherby who eventually wins; by a series of subtle insinuations and evasions she wrecks the projected marriage between her son and Mary Pomfret, and instead herself marries her lover of years before, Mary's father. But the strength of this comedy arises mainly from its impartiality, from Green's refusal to take sides. For if Green recognizes the earnestness of Philip, he recognizes also his dull passivity, his lack of drive and imagination and adventurousness; and if he recognizes Jane Weatherby's utter selfishness, he also recognizes and conveys (as with Amabel) her charm.

The other characters in this novel are perfectly common-place—John Pomfret, the well-bred, diabetic snob, perfectly groomed, suavely sensual, not very intelligent and plasticine in the hands of Mrs. Weatherby; Liz Jennings, his mistress, who seems perfectly happy to be passed around from man to man; Dick Abbott, the typical curtly spoken, pompously dignified stooge, who chokes at inauspicious moments, and when he loses Jane, solaces himself with Liz. They are completely lacking in depth; nothing seems to stir them, though they may pretend it does; but in their rather infuriating way they are alive.

The same may be said of the characters of *Doting*. The time and the background are virtually the same; the characters, though different, are from the same segment of society. Again there are representatives of two generations, but the aspect of the relationship between the generations which this novel explores is different. The centre of the action is the infatuation of a member of the older generation, Arthur Middleton, with a girl young enough to be his daughter, Annabel Paynton.

Three others are eventually involved in an intricate pattern of amorous intrigue and counter-intrigue—Arthur's wife Diana; the Middleton's widower-friend and Diana's prospective lover, Charles Addinsell; and Annabel's friend Claire Belaine. No more than *Nothing* is *Doting* a tract or a moralized fable, but again the characters are typical rather than highly individualized. Arthur Middleton is any middle-aged, well-to-do married man who wants both to have his cake and eat it—to keep his wife, with whom he is perfectly happy, and also to go to bed with someone else; Diana is any attractive wife who loves her husband, but toys with the idea of "teaching him a lesson" for his straying. But their typicality admitted, the twists and turns of their behaviour, their subterfuges and self-deceptions and conflicting impulses are traced with remarkable fidelity, by a method which completely excludes comment and interpretation. And again Green's attitude towards his characters is much more mature than one of priggish reproof or indignation; despite the illusion of self-withdrawal which Green conscientiously maintains, he does not merely "let his characters damn themselves with their own words",[7] as one reviewer asserted. The comment of V. S. Pritchett that, unlike an Evelyn Waugh or a Somerset Maugham, Green is "inside the human zoo, preoccupied with it, and occasionally giving a sad startled look at the bars he had momentarily forgotten"[8] is much nearer the truth. His compassionate fellow-feeling for these victims of middle age, who try desperately to ignore the inexorable march of the years is clear enough. (Perhaps *that* is why Green remarked of the book that "in fifteen years it will be thought quite soppy".) And for all the shrewdness of his portrayal of young Annabel (who provokes Arthur Middleton to exclaim in righteous indignation: "One thing you must agree, that they simply wave it about in front of one," and "She's simply destroying me, the little tart," and who is fully aware of what is expected in return for being invited out, "Why bed, of course"), there is also a strong current of sympathy for the predicaments of this generation in a society in which an old-established way of life has fallen to pieces. Altogether if this novel (like *Nothing*) reminds one of Restoration comedy, its affinities are with Etherege rather than with Wycherley, and with Congreve even more than with Etherege.

D

3

None of the characters so far mentioned is a really major figure—not even Amabel or Mrs. Weatherby. The method which Green adopts in his three upper-class novels (though the method of the two latest novels differs considerably from that of *Party Going*) scarcely permits the creation of major characters; or perhaps it is that these people, their interests and preoccupations are too trivial, their lives too shallow, for them ever to be made into major characters. Whatever the reason, none of the characters in these novels is as memorable and as fully-realized as at least five others who have not yet been discussed—Mr. Craigan (*Living*), Bert Pye (*Caught*), Charley Raunce (*Loving*), Charley Summers (*Back*) and Mr. Rock (*Concluding*). Even these characters are best considered not in isolation, but each in relation to at least one other character—Craigan in relation to Lily Gates, Pye with Richard Roe, Raunce with Edith, Summers with Nance Whitmore, and Mr. Rock with Miss Baker and Miss Edge (and with his grand-daughter Liz).

It is worth remarking that, as one method of characterizing some of these, his most important, creations, Henry Green has employed the simplest and one of the oldest of all devices— suggestive naming. The most obvious example is Mr. Rock, whose name gives an indication of his time-worn massiveness; there is something of the same suggestion of cragginess in the name of Mr. Craigan, who resembles Mr. Rock in many ways. Mr. Rock's antagonists are also appropriately named—the short and thin Edge is both on edge and the dangerous member of the partnership; the less hostile and unpleasant Baker is fat and short, as bakers always are in illustrations to "Pat-a-Cake Baker's Man". In *Caught* both Pye and Roe are suggestively named. The name Richard Roe, which is a legal fiction for an anonymous, unknown or even non-existent person, is appropriate for one who is so colourless and lacking in identity. Pye (or "pie") carries a suggestion of mediocrity, ordinariness, commonness; but more specifically a pie is a "dish of meat, fruit, etc. enclosed in or covered with paste and baked" (*C.O.E.D.*). One never quite knows what one will find when one cuts the outer crust of a pie; the classic pie is the one containing four and twenty blackbirds that was placed before the King. Considering Green's fascination with birds, a conjecture that he had the nursery-rhyme in mind when he named his sub-officer may not be fanciful; certainly what is revealed when Green cuts through Pye's outer crust is as unexpected as two dozen blackbirds. There is irony too in the fact that Pye ends in a gas-oven, and in the application to him of such phrases as "right as pie" and "apple-pie order". Similarly there is something about the name Raunce which suggests clownishness; perhaps it is partly the association with Launce, the comic servant of Proteus in *Two Gentlemen of Verona*.

Green's earliest major character is Mr. Craigan, the ageing workman in *Living*. Mr. Craigan is an admirable old man, the beau ideal of the nineteenth-century artisan. He had begun his working-life at the age of eight or nine, well over half a century before (about 1870, in fact), "and every day he had worked through most of daylight till now". He is a reserved, quiet, self-respecting old man who takes a great pride in his work, never interferes in any one else's business, is the most respected man in the works and is liked by everyone except the malicious and vindictive Tupe who sees in him everything that he himself is not. Bridges, the manager, considers him "the best moulder in Birmingham", but to young Dupret he is just another slow, useless old man to be got rid of as soon as possible.

Craigan has never married; having no family of his own he has virtually adopted Joe Gates and his daughter Lily, who over the years has grown to be far more his daughter than Gates'. He is undemonstrative, stoical and reticent (he tells Gates "You talk more than is natural in a man"), but his whole life is bound up with Lily, for whom he has a great, possessive love. It is partly because he wants to protect Lily from harm and hurt that he tries to make sure that she marries his dependable young work-mate Jim Dale rather than the unreliable Bert Jones, but it is mainly because he is desperately anxious to preserve the barriers he has built up against a solitary old age.

"Home was sacred thing to him. Everything, his self-respect was built on home. If he had no home to go back into at evening then he would have to move to another town where none knew him. As it was shame for the Hebrew women to be barren so in his mind was it desolation not to have people about him in his house, though he had never married" (p. 153).

Mr. Craigan is old-fashioned and intensely conservative. He has certain fixed principles and prejudices by which he lives, and from which nothing can budge him. "None of the women-folk go to work from the house I inhabit" is one of them. "If I had a son I wouldn't educate him above the station he was born in" is another; this is an indication not of a slave-mentality but of a conviction that money and responsibility only bring added worries with no real compensations. "In this 'ouse the wage-earners must 'ave hot meals every night bar Fridays. . . . On Saturdays there is to be two 'ot meals and one on Sunday" is another. There is no romantic nonsense about him: "Love's all right for them that 'as Rolls Royces but for the wives of working men it's the money that comes in regular at the end of the week that tells."

But for all his apparent sternness and inflexibility (as a youth he has determined never to enter a church again) and his massive gravity (he laughs only once throughout the novel), he is a courteous and kindly old man—dignified and courtly with the neighbour, Mrs. Eames, gentle and tender as any woman with Lily when she returns from her abortive elopement.

Perhaps the finest, most perceptive and most touching part of the characterization of Craigan is his gradual loss of grip after he becomes ill and has to stay in bed. "You will hear men who have worked like this talk of monotony of their lives, but when they grow to be old they are more glad to have work and this monotony has grown so great that they have forgotten it. Like on a train which goes through night smoothly and at an even pace—so monotony of noise made by the wheels bumping over joints between the rails becomes rhythm—so this monotony of hours grows to be the habit and regulation on which we grow old. . . . When men who have worked these regular hours are now deprived of work, so, often, their lives come to be like puddles on the beach where tide no longer reaches" (p. 204). The news that he has been dismissed, however, rouses him; he realizes that Lily is "indispensable to his being now he had to sit about". But Lily elopes; on her return Craigan cares for her, and for a while he seems to be the old self, of years before, when he was "secretary of the Club". He is in a pub with Joe Gates when Bridges and Tupe, both of whom have been sacked also, come in together. There is something almost Olympian in the derision of his unexpected laughter. "Then Craigan looked Bridges in his eyes. Mr. Bridges felt like he was being hauled up before someone and when Mr. Craigan looked at him he stepped forward like he was the next now. He felt frightened even" (p. 259). But this is the last flash of his old authority. Though he is not ill he takes permanently to his bed; he realizes that he is imprisoned, tied down by his love for Lily, and that his love for Lily also chains him to her father, but he does not care. Only he is gripped by the certainty that soon Lily will find another man, and will go off to marry him. So he is content to lie in bed—and to die before this should happen. "Mr. Craigan lay in bed in his house. . . . He thought in mind how he had gone to work when he was 8. He had worked on till no one would give him work. He thought what had he got out of 57 years work? Nothing. He thought of Lily. He thought what was there now for him? Nothing, nothing. He lay" (p. 267).

The characterization of Lily is equally real and living. Lily is essentially a very simple and ordinary young woman, whose whole motivation is summed up in the phrase "she wanted to better herself and she wanted a kid", but Green enters into the quality of her existence with sympathetic zest. She is very fond of and deeply respectful towards old Craigan, who has been father and mother to her, but, when the novel opens, is becoming rather restive under his authority. She would like to go out to work in a factory, instead of spending her life cleaning and polishing and cooking at home—for "things are different now". She likes Mr. Craigan's nominee for her hand, Jim Dale, well enough until Bert Jones comes along (though she finds Jim rather peculiar); but with Bert's advent she determines to resist Mr. Craigan's palpable design on her.

Lily likes her fun and her outings; she loves going to the pictures, even with Mr. Dale. (The book has dated so little in essentials that it is rather a surprise that they are silent pictures, with the band churning out suitably romantic music.) But she is no mere good-time girl; it is her whole life that she is planning. Her courtship with Bert Jones in the cinemas, parks and streets of Birmingham shows all of Green's flair for the inextricable blend of comedy and pathos in human relationships and emotions. He captures perfectly all of Lily's infatuation, her maternal longings, her ambitious hopes, her anxieties ("We won't be like the others shall we dear?"). For Lily is not blind to Bert's faults; she knows that he is an unreliable worker and lacking in initiative. So while they vaguely plan for departure she drives him off to night-school (which he soon gives up, but pretends he is still attending).

When they do finally elope, all of Lily's nervous embarrassment, self-consciousness and trepidation on the train journey are finely rendered; so too is the nightmarish quality of the search for Bert Jones' elusive and disreputable parents through the dark, forbidding streets of Liverpool, with the unaccustomed and unrespectable smell of the sea and the eerie wailing of ships' sirens, which culminates in Bert's sudden comic desertion. Equally convincing is the presentation of Lily's feelings on her return—her gratitude to Mr. Craigan for taking her back, her mingled shame and pride in her adventure. When Mrs. Eames calls to see her, Lily thinks that she must know about her elopement, and put the worst interpretation on it; she is shocked when Mrs. Eames, wrapped up in her own affairs, shows so little interest or disapproval; she is even rather irritated and bitter because she is not even to get a child out of the escapade. So life settles down again into the humdrum uneventful round—the same as before, only quieter. Lily is the first of Green's perceptive studies of young working-class womanhood, which culminate in the portrait of Edith, in *Loving*.

4

One of the centrally important relationships in *Concluding*— that between the old scientist Mr. Rock and his distraught grand-daughter, Liz—is similar to that between Craigan and Lily. As already suggested, even though Craigan is only an iron-moulder, a "sand rat" (who does, however, read Dickens and go to symphony concerts) while Mr. Rock is a famous savant, there are distinct affinities between them. For on the summer's day when we meet Mr. Rock, he has long since retired from science, and is leading an uneasy existence in a cottage in the grounds of the training-school, to which he has been granted a life-tenure for his services to the state; there is little indication that he has been a scientist, except his sudden outburst to Sebastian that if he were a younger man he'd "have a shot at this filth of a swine-fever".

Mr. Rock is an even more tired, lonely, hard-pressed old man than Craigan. All he asks is to be allowed to spend his last years in peace and quiet with his small household, consisting of his goose, Ted; his cat, Alice; his sow, Daisy; and, while she is on sick leave from the service to recover from her mental breakdown, his thirty-five-year-old grand-daughter, Liz. But the school principals, particularly Miss Edge, are unremitting in their hostility, their suspicion and their determination somehow to have him removed—not merely because they want his cottage for a furnaceman, but because to these civil servants, these automata in whom all human feeling has been withered by rules, regulations, directives, commissions and reports, Mr. Rock is (in Jean Howard's phrase) "an anachronistic incubus, a hostile Idea too big for their individual intelligences to deal with".[9] For them Mr. Rock is a relic of the bad old days, when independence of thought and speculation were considered valuable and desirable—not, as now, dangerous heresy; to justify their resentment and fear they pretend to themselves that Mr. Rock is a possible source of moral corruption to their charges.

Mr. Rock adores his grand-daughter, Liz; it is for her sake that he is determined not to be voted into "the hunt kennels for broken-down scientists". But she makes his position even more difficult and anxious by her violent and undisguised infatuation with the fat little economics tutor, Sebastian Birt. Mr. Rock even wonders, unjustly as it happens, whether the "Babylonian harlots", "those evil ninnies whose absolute power so absolutely corrupted them", have set Birt on to Elizabeth "to break a poor old fellow down by simply driving his sad girl out of her wits". On this day there is the added worry of the disappearance of the schoolgirl, Mary—a mystery which is never cleared up— whom he has seen driven to desperation by Baker and Edge. ("Only because they liked the colour of her eyes they pushed her unmercifully.") Whereas Baker and Edge are worried about Mary's disappearance only because of the possible repercussions on themselves, the necessity for reports and investigations, Mr. Rock's anxiety is the result of ordinary human feeling.

Mr. Rock is not at all idealized. At times he is self-pitiful; at times he is truculent and boastful about his achievements and his influential friends. He has been forced by circumstances to adopt various masks and poses; he is reduced to virtually begging his daily breakfast from the fearsome Mrs. Blain by plying the same time-worn jest. At times his slowness and his deafness, his misunderstanding of almost everything that is said to him make him a comic figure; moreover he has a senile vanity in his appearance of antiquated distinction. But the important thing is his humanity. Imperfect as he is, he is a civilized man, the last representative of humanism, the rebel against the inhuman system (to him even worse than swine-fever) which destroys all individuality, breeds suspicion and hysteria. He is the only adult figure, the only one with a developed sense of justice and human proportion, the last vestige of dignity and wisdom in a society of unhappy, frustrated megalomaniac spinsters, of the unbalanced, mentally shattered and neurotic, of poseurs and charlatans and feverish adolescents.

Mr. Rock's antagonists are not so fully presented, but they are sufficiently differentiated; Baker, less malevolent than Edge, exercises some restraining influence on her colleague. But in one of the most remarkable scenes in the novel, a scene which illustrates Green's feeling for the incalculable and the unpredictable in human temperaments and relationships, Miss Edge suddenly breaks through the limits of the type, which had seemed fixed and definite. The scene occurs near the end of the book when, in the middle of the "little jollification", the Founder's Day dance, Mr. Rock, shocked and upset by the girls' gossip about Liz and Sebastian, determines to leave at once, but is prevailed on by Liz to pay his respects to Miss Edge first. He finds her in the "Sanctum", enjoying her treat of the day, a cigarette. Under its mellowing, almost intoxicating, influence, she is in a state of heavenly lassitude, relaxed, gentle, dreamy and languorous; she finds that she now has only pity for the old man and she speaks to him in a tone of gracious, friendly deference. Mr. Rock, in the face of so much unexpected sympathy and respect, finds that he no longer hates the woman. During the few minutes that the truce lasts they chat together amicably and with apparent mutual understanding. But soon they are at cross-purposes; the old man is made angry and disgusted by a misunderstanding which shows, for all Miss Edge's air of lazy softness, the depth of her misjudgment and the perversity of her suspicions. He still finds that he can forgive the woman, when out of the blue, and even to her own half-amused, half-horrified surprise, comes her scarcely-veiled offer of marriage, which Mr. Rock takes in his stride as entirely understandable, "unthinkable of course, but not, in her pitiable circumstances, in the least surprising" and proudly ignores.

Miss Edge quickly recovers her grip and it is with tired venom
that she bids Mr. Rock farewell—a venom that is undoubtedly
increased by his one short, sharp laugh just outside the door.

5

Though Mr. Rock has some likeness to Mr. Craigan, his girl
Liz has no likeness to Lily Gates, beyond her infatuation with
Sebastian Birt. Lily has a successor, however, in Edith, the
housemaid in *Loving*. Like Lily, Edith elopes, with Raunce, in
the last paragraph of the novel; but unlike Lily she is not
deserted, for, as Green assures us in the last sentence of the
novel, "over in England they were married and lived happily
ever after".

It is no dashing fairy-tale prince that Edith elopes with.
Raunce is a man of over forty, easily old enough to be her father.
He has the unhealthy pallor of one who stays indoors for months
at a time; he has big protruding ears and odd eyes (one dark,
one light) with a fearful squint; he is prone to stiff necks and
dyspepsia, especially (so he maintains) if he ventures into
the open air. But though Raunce is, in some respects, a
comic figure, he is one of Henry Green's greatest triumphs of
characterization.

Raunce's moral standards are as peculiar as his appearance.
He is quite unscrupulous and dishonest in his attitude towards his
employers. He regards the defalcations and fraudulent tinker-
ing with the household accounts by his predecessor as perfectly
normal and natural; his first thought, after Eldon's death, is
to get hold of his notebooks so that he can study his methods
and master the technique. He would even take over Eldon's
blackmail of Captain Davenport, Mrs. Jack's lover, if he got
half a chance. He draws the line at stealing Mrs. Tennant's
lost sapphire ring, when it is found by Edith, but only because
it is too risky. But there is no more suggestion of moral condemnation in Green's portrayal of Raunce than in Chaucer's
portrayal of those other double-dealing servants, the reeve and
the manciple. Raunce is himself so untroubled by moral
qualms in his plundering (though just a little anxious at first,
since he is new to the game) that one feels it must be the traditional and accepted behaviour of butlers to drink their
employers' whisky and charge them double for articles that

have not been purchased, and that, therefore, no more blame attaches to Raunce for doing these things than for breathing.

Though Raunce is so little perturbed by his larcenies, he is, like so many of Green's characters, a harassed man. His uneasy place in the servant hierarchy is one source of worry. No sooner is Eldon dead than Raunce is interviewing Mrs. Tennant offering his notice; Mrs. Tennant takes the hint, however, and Arthur the head-footman (his name is really Charles, but all footmen in Kinalty Castle have been known as Arthur, since the first one, who was really Arthur) becomes Raunce the acting-butler (with no extra pay). Then comes the difficulty of making the other members of the hierarchy acknowledge his new status; when he nerves himself to take Eldon's place at the head of the servants' table, he provokes a storm of suppressed giggles from the under-housemaids and a tearfully angry protest from the head housemaid, Miss Burch. There is further trouble next day when he insists to Miss Burch that his early morning cup of tea must be brought by one of her girls, as it always was to Mr. Eldon, and not by his boy Bert. Throughout the novel he has to contend with the fluctuating hostility of Miss Burch, and the baleful animosity of Mrs. Welch the cook. With his underling, Bert, he finds it difficult to strike the right note. At times he treats him with condescending, avuncular familiarity, but occasionally, especially when he is annoyed by Bert's obvious infatuation with Edith, he bullies him and bawls him out—though he usually apologizes in the next breath, as in the following exchange.

" 'Because you're sweet on 'er, that's why,' Raunce said in a sort of shout. 'Holy Moses I don't know why I allow myself to get put out,' he went on calmer. 'But there's a certain way you have of looking down that dam delicate snotty nose you sniff with that gets my goat. Gets my goat see?' he added in rising tones.

'Yes Mr. Raunce.'

'That's all right then. Don't pay attention to uncle, at least not on every occasion. No you're going the wrong way about it with that toast rack,' he said as helpful as you please. 'Hand over and I'll show you.' And he proceeded to demonstrate" (pp. 70–1).

Another cause of worry is Raunce's obsession with an

impending invasion of Ireland by the Nazis or of Kinalty Castle by the I.R.A. Obviously this anxiety is not entirely genuine; it is partly to justify his presence in safe, neutral Ireland, while England is being bombed, that Raunce convinces himself that they are all virtually in the front line and talks melodramatically but with deadly seriousness of the guns and ammo in the gunroom and "a cartridge each for you ladies". Similarly it is very difficult to disentangle the real motivation for Raunce's decision, after he and Edith have carefully planned their marriage in Ireland and their after-life in a cottage in the grounds, that they must return immediately to besieged Britain. Do they really make their sudden, secret departure because his self-respect and his filial duty to his aged mother demand it? Or is it that he has so completely convinced himself that Ireland is unsafe that he is afraid to stay on? Or does he think that there is more to be made from "the lovely money in munitions" than from his petty pilferings in Kinalty? Or has Bert's abscondment, on top of Eldon's death, left him with more work than he cares for? Or has he been made thoroughly uneasy by the business of the missing ring, in which he and Edith have narrowly escaped having their fingers burnt? The point is, surely, that all these motives—patriotism, manly pride, fear, cupidity, laziness—are present together, and they are so inextricably tangled, that no one, least of all Raunce (who, like most of Green's characters, knows very little about himself), can say which is the "real", reason. Henry Green does not tell us; he is content to present only what Raunce himself says in all its contradictions, and to permit the reader to interpret for himself. James Hall has commented: "The desire to do as he is told and let someone else manage seems to triumph, yet at the end of the novel he is busy managing the clandestine trip. He accepts his public responsibility in wartime England, but by running away from the more immediate responsibility which has become too complex."[10]

Raunce's most constant preoccupation and his chief source of anxiety and emotional upheaval is Edith. The development of the prosaic little love-affair between this ridiculous, dyspeptic butler and his common but entrancingly beautiful little housemaid is the core of the novel. Our first impression of Charley's sexual morality is a low one, for he seems at first to be a thorough lecher—though his boastful tone makes us suspect

that he has not been as successful as he claims. His conversation
with Bert is full of sexy chatter and innuendo. ("Let me tell
you there was many an occasion I went up to Mamselle's
boudoir to give her a long bongjour before she went back to
France.") Perhaps he would, in the early stages, seduce Edith
if he got a chance; his approach is loaded with the clichés of the
self-confident wolf—"Come to father, beautiful", "With those
eyes you ought to be in pictures", "Here give us a little kiss".
But Charley is always acting, and this effrontery is only a mask;
as he surprises us in other ways so does he surprise us by his
capacity for love and loyalty. The focal episode in the novel—
Edith's discovery of Mrs. Jack in bed with Captain Davenport
—marks a crucial change in their relationship; Raunce, so far
from trying to take advantage of Edith's unusual state of
feverish animation, in which she positively forces her body on
his notice, is upset and embarrassed and ill-at-ease. It is not
long afterwards that Raunce admits that he has "fallen for her
in a big way"; and soon he makes his romantic proposal—
" 'Love,' he went on toneless, 'what about you an' me getting
married?' " From then on their relationship is a thoroughly
realistic blend of hard-headed planning and passionate love-
making—but always within respectable limits, for Edie is
"keeping herself for him on their wedding night", while
Raunce, who a few weeks before had been insisting that his
morning tea be brought by Edith, since this was traditional,
now shamefacedly entreats her not to continue the practice
because "it might lead to talk".

Raunce is a remarkable creation; in the hands of a writer
less gifted with intuitive sympathy than Green he might have
been no more than a comic lecher, buffoon and petty thief.
But Raunce is continually surprising us with new facets of
character—dignity, sensitivity, filial devotion, self-restraint.
The characterization is all the more remarkable since it is so
completely objective: Irving Howe has very well remarked that
Green does not bungle the unfolding of Raunce's character
"because he writes about the servants' life from a steady,
uncondescending distance. No nonsense here about the author
being a butler; the author has no obligation to identify himself
with his hero, he needs only to create him and in *Loving* the
condition for creating is distance maintained and measured."[11]
So in this novel, unlike *Living* (to which it is closest in tone and

spirit) Green carefully refrains from all interpretation of his characters (and all presentation of their thought-processes). He is content to let them be as they are, live in their own terms.

Edith is, if anything, a more profound creation than Raunce; it is even more difficult to dissect her temperament and to ticket and label her qualities, because she is still an unformed, contradictory bundle of moods and sensations. One can say that, like Lily Gates, she is a mixture of ardent warmth and hard-headed calculation; but she is a living person, seen whole, not an abstract construct, and like Lily she is to be apprehended in all her elations and embarrassments, her trepidations and triumphs, her cruelty and coquetry and craftiness, her bawdiness and her prudery, rather than comprehended and judged.

6

Caught is unusual among Green's novels in having two important male characters, whose strained and exasperated relationship provides the core of the book. It is not completely obvious whose story it really is. It appears at first to be Richard Roe's; at the beginning of the novel his is the mind we follow at close range. But presently Pye becomes prominent, and Roe seems to become merely an observer of Pye's disintegration, only to emerge again at the end as the presiding consciousness and even to some extent as the narrator. Mark Schorer is undoubtedly right in his comment that while "the mechanical plot has largely to do with Pye . . . the true plot pertains rather to the achievement of identity by Richard Roe . . ."[12] Although the novel is written in the third person it has affinities with such novels as Fitzgerald's *The Great Gatsby* and Warren's *All the King's Men*—particularly the latter, in which Jack Burden, while ostensibly telling the story of Willie Stark, actually tells the story of his own moral education.

Pye, nevertheless, is the more obviously interesting character; he is interesting not only as an individual but also as a social phenomenon seldom so acutely studied before. As with the other firemen in the novel, Stephen Spender's *World Within World* bears witness to his complete reality; Spender's sub-officer, Alfie, with his panicked, hunted look, who "lived in unceasing terror of getting into trouble with his younger, more efficient, jumped-up superiors",[13] reminds one inevitably of at least one aspect of Pye.

Pye is a perplexed, well-meaning but suspicious and confusedly radical proletarian, for whom the sudden access of responsibility and authority proves disastrous. Like Spender's Alfie he has been for years an ordinary fireman, accustomed only to obeying orders; when he finds himself in charge of forty men and women he is anxious to be efficient and to secure the comfort and happiness of his subordinates, to understand and be understood, but he is not equal to his new position. Resented by the old hands, like Wal and Chopper, with whom he has served in the ranks, despised (or feeling he is despised) by some of the amateurs, he fluctuates between *camaraderie* and officiousness, between laxity and strict discipline. Moreover he is demoralized by the new conditions—far more money than he has ever been used to, pretty women throwing themselves at his uniform, in the early days after war was declared, when raids were expected nightly and the Fire Service came after pilots with the public. His infatuation with the young woman, Prudence, who is soon bored with him, since they have "nothing but bed in common" causes him to neglect his duties more and more; he gets deeper and deeper into trouble and disgrace, until he is eventually driven, in sheer bewilderment and despair, to suicide.

So far Pye is a typical social phenomenon; if this were all of him, the characterization would be substantial enough. But Pye is also a specific individual; his bewilderment and despair are not caused solely by his change of status and inadequacy as a leader. Robert Phelps has claimed that "it is Pye's jealous relation to the widower Richard Roe which finally breaks him, aggravating his at-first hallucinatory and then real persecution and ending in his suicide".[14]

This comment does not seem to be quite accurate; it misplaces the emphasis, for Pye's "jealous relationship" to Roe, important as it is, is a symptom of Pye's trouble rather than the trouble itself. Pye's hostility arises out of the abduction of Roe's five-year-old son, Christopher, from a London toy-shop by Pye's half-crazy sister, which results in her being committed to an asylum. All this happens some months before the war, while Roe is still training to be a fireman, and is one of the group instructed by Pye. Every subsequent lecture of Pye's is loaded with veiled references to his sister's trouble, and with insinuations that she and he have been victimized for an unfortunate little kink, only because they are poor and obscure, while Richard is well-to-do and influential. When Richard, after the mobilization, by one of a series of fatal coincidences, is posted to the very sub-station which is to be commanded by Pye, relations between them are inevitably uneasy and embarrassed. Pye's sense of persecution is exacerbated when he is asked to contribute to his sister's maintenance. That, having been forced to add his signature to those of the certifying doctors, he should now be required to pay for her in her "prison", seems to him unutterably vile and unjust. But this alone, or even combined with the other factors already mentioned, is not enough to break Pye and drive him to suicide.

Far more crucial is the recollection of a moonlight night some thirty years before, the night when he had his first girl—a scene recalled with a startling sensuous vividness. Associated with this memory is another, of the same evening, of how, sneaking home afterwards, "he had seen another shadow moving in front towards their bit of garden . . . , creeping as he was but lower, more like a wild animal, heavier in shame because a woman, and, as he saw with a deep tremor, his own sister, out whoring maybe as he had been. . . . He called to mind how disgusted it had made him, the sight of his sister, like a white wood shaving, when she darted, huddled, across the last still stretch of moonlight . . ." (pp. 41–2). But it is not until Pye is questioned by the physician who is in charge of his sister in the asylum that these two memories coalesce, and Pye suddenly suspects, with frantic self-loathing, the shocking truth.

"Without any warning, and with a shock that took all his breath, Pye saw the dry wood shaving creep, bent in the moonlight, the back way to their cottage. He saw it again as though it was before his eyes. . . . He had never before thought of his sister's creeping separate from his own with Mrs. Lane's little girl. In a surge of blood, it was made clear, false, that it might have been his own sister he was with that night. So it might have been her voice, thick with excitement and fright and disgust that said 'Will it hurt?' So in the blind moonlight, eyes warped by his need, he must have forced his own sister. . . . And he had always known and never realized" (p. 140).

From then on Pye exists in an intermittent agony of doubt and remorse, unsuspected by Roe or anyone else, which keeps him awake at nights, horrified at the thought of his incest and of the irreparable harm he had unwittingly caused his sister. It drives him out, again and again (though only the last most fatal excursion is described) into the summer moonlight "to try once more to find how much he could recognize by this light in the bright river of the street", to try to convince himself that he could not possibly have been so fearfully mistaken. It is this (in Henry Reed's phrase) "emotional black hole of Calcutta",[15] this abyss of guilt and dread and apprehension, yawning beneath the mundane, plebeian surface of Pye which makes him a tragically individual figure, and not merely an acutely observed social type.

Richard Roe, the wealthy widower turned amateur fireman is, for most of the novel, a curiously blurred and indefinite figure, even though so much of the action and of the other characters comes to us through his eyes and mind, and even though we are given more frequent direct glimpses into his feelings and reactions than into those of anyone else, even of Pye. In the opening chapters all of Roe's feelings and reactions seem to be negative, muffled, stunted; there seems to be no warmth of life in him—he is an empty husk, grey, desolate, mournful, drained by the death of his wife ("his ever present loss") of all vital feeling. Even his regret for her seems only half genuine; he seems afraid to allow himself to feel deeply, and yet at the same time is aware of his emotional inadequacy. His achievement of identity, his re-integration with life is presented obliquely and unemphatically—through his involvement, against his will, in the life of the station and his affair with Hilly, Pye's driver. ("The relief he experienced when their bodies met was like the crack, on a snow silent day, of a branch that breaks to fall under a weight of snow. . . .") But, paradoxically, it is the blitz which almost kills him which really brings him back to life. It is only at the end, when he has been knocked out by a bomb that came too close, after nine weeks of nightly raids on London, in which he has been near death a hundred times, that he seems a really alive human being. His sister-in-law finds him greatly changed—"his face was thinner, while his neck had thickened. His shoulders were broader. He was much dirtier than he used to be . . ." But he has shaken himself clear of the irrecoverable past, his involvement in Pye's tragedy has developed his capacity for sympathy, he can now face life without sentimentality or self-pity or neurotic self-consciousness.

7

There are close affinities between Richard Roe and Charley Summers, the chief character of *Back*. Both are bereaved men, haunted by an irrevocable past to which they look back as a time of paradisial happiness and contentment, who do, however, eventually achieve a new adjustment to and a new acceptance of life. Summers' "case" is the more difficult; the process of readjustment is even more painful for him than for Roe, because of his obsession that the past is not really dead at all. His mistress, Rose (the wife of James Phillips), died while he was a prisoner-of-war in Germany. When he is released and returns to civilian life in the later stages of the war, he is distraught and psychologically disturbed by his experiences; when he encounters Rose's half-sister, Nancy, who closely resembles the dead woman, but whose existence he has never suspected, he is convinced that she is actually Rose herself, alive, and for some inexplicable reason pretending to be someone else. The action of the book is concerned chiefly with Charley's attempts, by various stratagems, to make Nancy confess herself as Rose. His pitiful search for this woman who meant love and warmth and peace before the war is a moving and absorbing psychological study.

Orville Prescott has asserted that "*Back* is a story about a potentially poignant and dramatic situation written in such a dry and fussy way that all the poignance and drama have been squeezed out of it".[16] This is a strangely imperceptive comment: the drama is there, though, as nearly always in Green's work, it is below the surface, muffled, inward, not a parade of tumultuous emotions; the poignancy is no less great because Charley is so blurred and inarticulate. It is not a just criticism to say, as Prescott does, that "Charley is as shadowy as the friend of a friend in a snapshot taken by an inexpert photographer on a cloudy day". Charley certainly is shadowy, but this is not, as Prescott's comment suggests, because of a failure on Green's part to render adequately and accurately the quality of his existence and experience, but because Charley has his being

E

in a misty region between sanity and hallucination. His monomania colours and distorts every thing he sees and hears; everything is immediately interpreted in terms of his obsession. Every chance occurrence of the word "rose", whether used as noun, proper noun, adjective or verb, sets his nerves jangling with expectation and apprehension. It is true that even when he is more or less restored to normality Charley is not (and there are frequent hints that he has never been) a vital, dominating, dynamic personality, despite his big, brown eyes; he is, in fact, passive, rather slow-witted and absent-minded, shy, self-distrustful and unassertive. He is not at all an extraordinary or impressive person—but he is a person, he is *there*; we cannot help believing in him.

One of the most penetrating remarks ever made about Green's characters is a comment by H. P. Lazarus in a review of *Back*. "Charley is typical of the characters in Mr. Green's novels. He moves through his solipsistic world discovering himself only when he meets the reality of other people's solipsistic worlds."[17] In the real, outer world inhabited by people like his boss, Corker Mead, his secretary Dot Pitter, his raffish acquaintance Arthur Middlewitch, his dubiously respectable landlady Mrs. Frazier, Rose's parents, Mr. and Mrs. Grant (Mrs. Grant is a civilian casualty—she has lost her memory as a result of the raids—but it is Mr. Grant who dies during the course of the novel) and Grant's illegitimate daughter, Nancy Whitmore (who was born within three weeks of the legitimate Rose), Charley gradually learns that obsessions like his are not so abnormal, that the world to which he has returned is itself crazy. As Lazarus remarks, "The recognition of mutual exclusion is the beginning of love, and salvation in this world is through love." It is not until Charley at last realizes that Nancy is a real person, with an independent existence, that she is not merely a part of a fantasy world of his own, that he can be saved.

Nancy Whitmore is one of the most attractive of all Green's women characters. She is not a romantically idealized figure, but she is a simple, straightforward, warm-hearted, charitable young woman. Having lost her pilot-husband after only a few leaves of marriage, she naturally resents and is upset by Charley's repeated intrusions into her private life, and his stubborn persistence in error. But she is secretly proud of her startling resemblance to Rose, she has a great maternal protectiveness, she is lonely; and so she is eventually won over by Charley's very helplessness. In this novel, as in others, Green's treatment of the emotional and sexual life of his characters is extremely fresh and authentic. In such scenes and episodes as that in which Charley, staying with Dot Pitter at James Phillips' house, lies in bed wondering nervously whether he should go in to Dot and eventually does so, more, it seems, because he feels it may be expected of him than because he wants to, only to discover her bed empty and her in the next room with James ("Of course he felt cheated, but he slept well for once"), or that in which he lies in the make-shift bed in the Grants' house, wondering whether Nancy really intends to visit him "with all that dying in bed going on above", or their "trial trip" on the book's last page, when the real Nance and the ideal Rose at last merge, one sees why V. S. Pritchett has claimed that Green "writes better than anyone living about sexual life".[18]

Green's characters may not be as large, definite and memorable as those of many nineteenth-century novelists, but then what contemporary novelist's are? And how can they be when the whole classical psychology on which such characters were based has been abandoned as false? It might seem that Green has not a high opinion of modern theories of depth psychology either (certainly his characters have not—Roe tells Pye: "As a matter of fact I'm very doubtful about these psychologists," Charley Summers remarks sourly of the Army doctors: "They're all trick cyclists now.") But James Hall's comment on this point is nearer the truth: "Green inherits and absorbs Joyce's use of modern psychology, though he transfers Joyce's view of the mind from the world of reflection to the world of behaviour. Like Joyce—and Freud—he treats the mind as a symbol-making agent ready to assimilate every object and experience to its main obsessions. But . . . his most visible talent is for a casual and cheery acceptance of the human nature which Joyce had to prove and Lawrence become prophetic about."[19] So, while Green has made comparatively little use of the interior monologue, it is clear that no more than Joyce and Virginia Woolf does he believe that human personality is something fixed, definite and static, something that can be reduced to a neat definition or formula. His characters, though always recognizably themselves, are in a state of flux; he never over-simplifies their conflicting impulses and prejudices, fears and desires. Many of his characters are neurotic, but the unusual thing about them is that they refuse to be overwhelmed by their neuroses, and often manage to enjoy life despite them. And although Green's characters are so diverse, one never feels that he has ventured beyond his effective creative range; none of them is pasteboard. If Green had done no more than create such characters as Craigan and Lily Gates, the party going abroad, Pye and Roe, Raunce and Edith, Charley and Nance, Mr. Rock and Miss Edge—not to mention the hosts of minor characters of all ages and classes—he would be an important novelist.

III

Methods and Techniques

If you want to create life the one way not to set about it is by explanation.
("A Novelist to his Readers", *Listener*, November 9, 1950, p. 505)

I

IN the preceding chapter Henry Green's characters have been discussed as though they were actual people, with only passing and incidental consideration of the methods employed to present and vitalize them. This, of course, is a quite arbitrary procedure. Every fictional character must inevitably be based, directly or indirectly, consciously or unconsciously, on people in real life (but the use of a single model is exceptional, and earlier fictional characters are also, in many cases, important models); nevertheless fictional characters are different from real life people, because they are shaped and moulded by one specific imagination, which is stirred into creative activity by only certain aspects of human experience, and also because, since they function in relation to other characters, plots, themes, etc., they have to adapt themselves, or be adapted, to the requirements of the novel as a whole. Hence the question, "What are the characters like?" is, if anything, less important than the other questions, "How do we know what they are like?" (or "How does the novelist enable us to know what they are like?") and "How important is their contribution to the total effect of the book?" In other words, characterization is only one aspect of the novelist's fundamental problem—which is to present an individual vision of life, an individual attitude to experience, with the greatest possible force and immediacy.

Henry Green has himself stated this fundamental problem clearly and simply. "What is the aim of the novelist? All artists mean to create a life which is not. That is to say, a life which does not eat, procreate or drink, but which can live in people who are alive. . . . Art is not representational. But if it exists to create life, of a kind, in the reader—as far as words are concerned, what is the best way in which this can be done?"

65

Throughout his career as a novelist he has been seeking the answer to this question, but it was not until 1950, almost a quarter-century after his first novel was published, that Green, in two B.B.C. talks[1] (the above quotation is from the first) and an essay[2] committed himself publicly to any fictional creed or programme. (Unlike many leading contemporary novelists, including Graham Greene and Elizabeth Bowen, Henry Green has never written reviews or critical essays on earlier writers which might shed some light on his views about the functions, methods or materials of fiction.) His manifesto is, however, in some respects at least, at variance with his previous practices.

Probably the most vehement attack on Green is that by Orville Prescott, who has recently dismissed Green, along with Elizabeth Bowen, Ivy Compton-Burnett and Graham Greene, as "Comrades of the Coterie".[3] Prescott maintains that, because these writers dislike the modern world intensely, "they retreat from direct communication with their contemporaries and write peculiar puzzles for their own amusement. Their creative gifts are real; but they find it more attractive to experiment with technique, to string together pearls of sensibility, rather than to interpret the main stream of life. . . . The novelist must be aware of the technique of his craft . . . but excessive concentration on method rather than on matter is highly dangerous. It can reflect a feverish revolt against traditional cultural forms, an effete and unhealthy reaction which seems not far from decadence. When technique ceases to be a means and becomes an end in itself something is wrong, either in the artist or in his society."

Apart from the complete fallacy on which this criticism is based ("A cruel chaos inhabited by unfortunate victims of forces too strong for them" is a thoroughly misleading definition of Green's vision of the modern world) it is, as Prescott admits, a matter of opinion whether Green, or any of the other novelists, actually sins in this fashion. It seems to me that it is only in the two novels published since his manifesto that Green can, with any justice, be accused of "*excessive* concentration on method". For these two novels—*Nothing* (1950) and *Doting* (1952)—were deliberately written in support and illustration of the fictional theory he had just stated. Green's answer to his own question: "What is the best way to create life in the reader?" is "By dialogue." The reasons he gives are that "communication between human beings has come to be almost entirely conducted by conversation", that "we get experience, which is as much knowledge as we shall ever have, by watching the way people around us behave, after they have spoken", that "it is only by an aggregate of words over a period followed by an action that we obtain, in life, a glimmering of what is going on in someone, or even in ourselves". Dialogue, however, must be "non-representational (that is, it will not be an exact record of the way people talk)". This leads him to an attack on traditional techniques in fiction. "Because art is not representational writers have taken to explaining what they think is going on in their dialogue, speaking directly to the reader. The kind of action which dialogue is, is held up while the writer, who has no business with the story he is writing, intrudes like a Greek chorus to underline his meaning. It is as if the characters were alone and a voice came out of the ceiling to tell us what they were like and what they felt. Do we know, in life, what other people are really like? I very much doubt it. We certainly do not know what other people are thinking and feeling. How then can the novelist be so sure?" Green is arguing then, that the traditional omniscient method of the eighteenth and nineteenth century—the analytical, interpretative, summarizing, reflective method of a Thackeray or a Trollope, in which the author stands between the reader and the action explaining things rather in the manner of the commentary accompanying a documentary film—is a presumptuous arrogation of knowledge and power which no one has in real life. Moreover it destroys the illusion of reality. "The moment the novelist does tell his readers, he enters into a pact with his audience. He is telling a story as a casual acquaintance in a pub might. What he tries to do is to set himself up as a demi-god, a know-all." But Green is also, by implication, arguing against the use of one particular character's eyes and mind as the point of view (as in *The Ambassadors* or *Lord Jim*) and against the most spectacular innovation in twentieth-century fiction, the stream of consciousness or internal monologue (defined by Dujardin as "the direct introduction of the reader into the interior life of the character, without any intervention in the way of explanation or commentary on the part of the author"[4]). This variety of omniscience he also apparently considers presumptuous, or at least obsolete, for he insists that "communication between the novelist and reader will tend to be more and more by dialogue". Another element of traditional fictional method which he now distrusts is description. The novelist, he contends, should be no more (or should create the illusion that he is no more) than a sensitive recording apparatus, watching, and, above all, listening to the characters and transmitting what he sees and hears without comment. "What I should like to read and what I am trying to write now is a novel with an absolute minimum of descriptive passages in it, or even of directions to the reader (that may be such as 'She said angrily') and yet narrative consisting almost entirely of dialogue sufficiently alive to create life in the reader." (Ivy Compton-Burnett had already published a dozen novels written almost entirely in dialogue but hers is a very special convention in which characters often speak not to be heard, often say unsayable things.)

Nothing and *Doting* carried out this programme to the letter, without achieving the stated aim of "creating life in the reader" —or at least without achieving this object as fully as earlier novels which were not written in conformity to such a rigidly restrictive formula. In reading these novels one feels that Green has deliberately strapped himself into a strait-jacket, that through rigorously denying himself the use of almost all the traditional methods of the novel, he has failed to make the most of his subjects. Green had claimed that another indispensable function of the novelist is "to quicken the reader's unconscious imagination into life", and in *Pack my Bag* had defined prose as "a gathering web of insinuations . . . a long intimacy between strangers with no direct appeal to what both may have known. It should slowly appeal to feelings unexpressed . . ." (p. 88). His earlier novels do succeed in establishing this intimacy and in quickening the reader's unconscious imagination into life, but *Nothing* and *Doting* do so only fitfully at best. By his exclusive concentration on the trivial surface of upper-class society, by his determination to present nothing but what his characters say aloud (and, unlike Ivy Compton-Burnett, by permitting them to say only what such people *would* say aloud) he prevents the formation of a "gathering web of insinuations". He presents characters who seem themselves to be so lacking in genuine feeling that they make little appeal to "feelings unexpressed". There are hints of important themes in these novels—the disintegration of what was once a dominant social class, the reversal of the traditional roles of parents and children—but his chosen method of presentation deprives them of much of their potential interest. One feels that in these novels there is a disparity between the seriousness of the issues and the mannered superficiality of the treatment; one feels, too, that Green's dialogue here is not sufficiently non-representational—it seems to be an exact record of the way such people talk. One can only conclude that Green's attempt at purification of the novel, in the interests of greater reality, has resulted instead almost in sterilization. It was perhaps worth trying once, as James tried it once, though in a less extreme form, in *The Awkward Age*, but, one feels, not worth doing twice. (Miss Compton-Burnett is exempt from the implications of this remark, because for her this method is not a deliberate, but an instinctive choice, as one sees from her "Conversation" with Miss M. Jourdain.[5]) Green possibly felt, however, that a sequence of such novels was necessary to give depth to his portrayal of a disintegrating "society".

But the fact remains that Green's earlier novels give a quite different impression. In reading them one does not feel that he has, with cold, academic calculation, chosen and insisted on a certain method; one feels rather that the method of narration has chosen him—or, if this seem to belittle him, one feels that he has been a sufficiently skilful and resourceful artist to adopt the method of presentation most suitable to bring out the potential values of his material. In at least some of these novels Green has attained the ideal, reached when form and content are interdependent and indivisible; when the story *is* the way it is presented.

2

In reading the work of the novelists whom Prescott calls "Comrades of the Coterie", one quickly notices that Green's novels are more varied in method and manner than those of the other writers. One soon discovers that they are less orthodox in their narrative methods than those of Elizabeth Bowen and also that they avoid the uncompromising but monotonous individuality of Ivy Compton-Burnett's strange conversation-pieces. More, perhaps, than any English novels since Joyce's, they demand close technical study.

Unfortunately, study of methods of presentation is the most neglected branch of fictional criticism. Phyllis Bentley has pointed out that "few critiques exist on general fictional topics comparable with those on the aesthetics and mechanics of drama and poetry. Many books have been written to discuss the achievements of individual novelists . . . but few mention his actual method of presentation, his narrative. . . . Indeed ignorance on the subject of fiction narrative prevails to such an extent that its terminology is as yet quite undetermined."[6] This is quite true: for example, one of the most important ingredients of fictional narrative is variously called "the panoramic method", "summary" and "generalized narrative". Miss Bentley's own contribution to the subject is interesting and suggestive, but she does not differentiate clearly enough the various elements of narrative. Whereas she recognizes only three main elements, it seems clear that, even in novels which have an external point of view (that is, novels in which the story is told by a narrator who is not a character in the story), at least six main elements must be recognized, if anything but the most obvious differences in narrative textures are to be revealed and analysed. These six elements may be called Scene, Summary, Description, Character Exposition and Revelation, Commentary and Variation of Point of View. But since there is no general agreement on terminology, some explanation of how the terms are to be used is necessary.

I. SCENE

(a) *Direct scene.* It is generally agreed that "scene" is the narrative method by which the novelist makes things happen before the reader's eyes. Pure scene presents specific action in terms of speech, gesture, facial expression, movement. (Miss Bentley is surely wrong in including "thought" as part of scene.[7] If unexpressed thoughts, sense-impressions, etc., are admitted as a normal part of "scene", the term becomes so general as to be meaningless: one is reduced to using the same term to describe a passage from *The Sun Also Rises* and a passage from *To the Lighthouse*.) The conversation between Philip Weatherby and Mary Pomfret already quoted (p. 44) is pure scene.

(b) *Indirect scene.* Robert Liddell has pointed out that there is "scene in indirect speech".[8] Sometimes the difference from direct scene is no more than typographical and grammatical, as, for example, in many passages of Green's *Living*. ("And Dale asked him why he went round with Tupe then and Mr. Gates said he never and Dale said he seen him and Joe Gates answered it might have been once", p. 29). More usually it presents the essence of a conversation without reproducing the actual words. "It appeared that Piper could not understand why Pye disliked him. Richard investigated, found the old man was ignorant of the effect his interruptions and echoing had on the lecturer. Roe left him in ignorance" (*Caught*, p. 39).

II. SUMMARY

This term is used (unsatisfactorily, as she admits) by Phyllis Bentley for "all condensations and integrations including not the minute by minute thoughts of a man but a summarized account of his gradual conversion to a new course of life".[9] Again it seems inadvisable to include these "inner" elements as part of summary. Robert Liddell's definition is more satisfactory. "Summary is that part of a novel in which the novelist says that things are happening, or that they have happened."[10] Summary is the method which relates action without dramatizing it or condenses habitual actions. (E.g. "There was often no real work went on in the Castle of an afternoon. Generally speaking this times was set aside so that Edith could sew or darn for Mrs. Jack whom she looked after, and for Kate to see to the linen", *Loving*, p. 35.)

III. DESCRIPTION

(*a*) *Description of surroundings and settings*. This element—the stimulation in the reader of sense-impressions, so as to make vivid the appearance and atmosphere of a place concerned in the novel—is far less easy to detach from other elements in the modern novel than it was in the eighteenth- and nineteenth-century novel. Description now is generally allusive, fragmentary and impressionistic, not detailed and straightforward. But this kind of description must be included.

(*b*) *Description of characters*. Here too it is necessary to include not only introductory descriptions of the physical appearance of people, but also specific notations of their appearance when they are involved in scenes. This is necessary, because in many modern novels, our impression of the physical being of the characters is based entirely on a series of swift, apparently casual, flashes of description.

IV. CHARACTER EXPOSITION AND REVELATION

This category includes all those sections of a novel which give information about the individual temperament or personality of a character, or which indicate his state of mind or emotional condition—all reference, in fact, to "mind stuff", to the inner world of mental processes, perceptions, ideas, thoughts, sensations, feelings, memories, impressions. Here too it is necessary to include not only separate, extended passages but brief notations of these "subjective elements" blended with dialogue. Two varieties have to be recognized.

(a) *Formal character exposition.* This term is used to describe those parts of a novel in which the writer analyses the temperament of his character, or the thoughts and feelings of a character in response to a particular event or situation, and organizes his findings in a coherent, expository manner, frequently using extended metaphor for more accurate definition. This is often used to report habitual modes of thought, or long periods of reflection. A good example is the analysis of Mr. Bridges, already quoted (p. 38).

(b) *Informal character revelation.* This, of course, is the attempt to record the thoughts, impressions, sensations, memories, etc., in their original state, as they flow through a character's mind. The extreme form is the "stream of consciousness", but the essential difference between formal exposition and informal revelation is that in the former the author translates and interprets, whereas in the latter the author merely presents without explanation. Brief indications of states of mind are classified as informal rather than formal exposition (e.g. "Charley felt everything was getting beyond him." "But he did feel somehow ashamed", *Back*, pp. 150–1). Informal character revelation is, therefore, the "inner" equivalent of scene, as formal character exposition is the "inner" equivalent of summary.

V. COMMENTARY

(a) *Particular or Interpretative commentary.* This element of direct commentary by the author on the characters and situations of his novel is seldom prominent in modern fiction. Modern novelists are so expert at implying and subtilizing their comments, their explanations that it is often impossible to isolate commentary from scene, summary and character exposition.

But traces of this element can still be detected in most novels if one looks carefully enough (e.g. "In his good nature, for he was a kind-hearted man", *Back*, p. 83). Also included in this category is information given by the novelist which cannot have been known to anyone else, including forecasts of future events (e.g. "She thought he would be O.K., though as yet she had, of course, no idea at all how, or how much", *Back*, p. 123. "Later on he carried out his promise. He was to regret it." *Caught*, p. 47).

(*b*) *General commentary.* General commentary includes all the observations made by the author about life, death, society, men, women, love, marriage, friendship, art, etc.—comments which may be provoked by the behaviour of particular characters, but which are not limited to them. Few modern writers are as ready to generalize and philosophize as Fielding or Thackeray or George Eliot. But even today there is wide variation in the willingness of novelists to use their characters' behaviour as illustrations of explicitly stated general "truths".

VI. VARIATION OF POINT OF VIEW

The use, in the same novel, of the various methods already listed obviously implies variation in point of view. When a novelist presents a pure scene, with no direct indication of what is going on in the characters' minds, his viewpoint is that which is commonly called "objective"; when he elects to plumb the depths of his characters' minds, to analyse their hidden motives, to summarize their past lives or to forecast their futures, his viewpoint becomes omniscient. In most novels there are frequent, though almost imperceptible, shifts of viewpoint, or focus, between these two extremes.

But in this category, account is taken of those sections of a novel which temporarily abandon the external for an internal point of view. *Bleak House*, with its oscillations between omniscient narration and the narration of Esther Summerson, who knows very little, is an extreme example. Far more usual is the introduction of diaries, journals and letters, in order to give the reader the illusion of a direct, uncensored and uninterpreted glimpse into the mind of one of the characters.

The possibilities of combination of these elements is infinite. Many passages of fiction are an intricate blend of several elements, and the transition from one to another is often practically

imperceptible. It is certainly not contended that these categories
are watertight, or that every sentence, or even every phrase can
be incontestably labelled as belonging to one or another. One
category merges into another—description into scene; exposition
into commentary. Even scene and summary, which are, in
theory, the two most different from one another, are actually
(in Miss Bentley's words) "not antitheses, but distant points
in a scale of subtle gradations".[11] Furthermore, the various
elements can be made to do one another's jobs. Informal character revelation (approaching interior monologue) can be used
(as by Joyce and Virginia Woolf) for description of settings and
characters or for summary. Even scene (conversation) can be
made to perform the function of summary. Many critics frown
on this practice, and it can be crude and clumsy; on the other
hand it has occasionally been demonstrated (e.g. by Elizabeth
Bowen in the opening chapter of *The Death of the Heart*) that, in
skilful hands, scene can be used in this way without provoking
Sneer's famous objection ("There certainly appears no reason
why Sir Walter should be so communicative").[12] But when all
these difficulties have been admitted, these categories remain
sufficiently precise to make possible more exact analyses than
are generally made of differences between the characteristic
methods of individual novelists, and of a single novelist's variations of method from novel to novel. Most comments on
fictional techniques are purely impressionistic; I do not know
of any estimate, based on thorough investigation, of the actual
proportions of scene and summary (or "pictorial" and "conversational" methods, or "dramatized" and "non-dramatized"
elements) in any single novel.

Such analyses can be made—but only by the arduous process
of random selection of sections or chapters scattered throughout
each novel, totalling at least half of the whole book (smaller
samples are invariably misleading), assignment of every line
in these sections to its appropriate category, and conversion of
the total entries in each category to percentages. All of Green's
novels, except *Blindness*, have been analysed in this way, and, for
purposes of comparison, the same process has been applied to
four of Elizabeth Bowen's novels and four of Ivy Compton-
Burnett's. The results, to the nearest percentage, are given in
the table on the opposite page. The novels are listed in chronological order.

	I		II	III		IV		V		VI
	a	b		a	b	a	b	a	b	
HENRY GREEN										
Living	57	13	4	2	1	4	17	1	1	—
Party Going	49	13	3	3	1	3	21	7	—	—
Caught	48	12	10	5	3	1	15	6	—	—
Loving	91	1	2	3	2	—	—	—	—	1
Back	70	4	5	2	1	—	16	1	—	1
Concluding	64	5	2	5	3	—	17	4	—	—
Nothing	94	3	—	1	2	—	—	—	—	—
Doting	94	3	1	1	1	—	—	—	—	—
ELIZABETH BOWEN										
To the North	39	8	12	6	3	8	15	8	1	—
The House in Paris	42	7	10	9	3	2	15	7	2	3
The Death of the Heart	42	10	9	7	3	3	7	5	3	11
The Heat of the Day	36	8	10	9	3	7	15	6	5	1
IVY COMPTON-BURNETT										
Men and Wives	96	—	1	—	1	1	—	1	—	—
A Family and a Fortune	85	4	3	—	2	2	1	3	—	—
Maidservant and Man-servant	84	3	3	—	2	1	2	4	—	1
Darkness and Day	97	1	—	—	1	—	—	1	—	—

Ia Direct Scene   Ib Indirect Scene
II Summary
IIIa Description of Settings   IIIb Description of Characters
IVa Formal Character Exposition   IVb Informal Character Revelation
Va Particular Commentary   Vb General Commentary
VI Variation of Point of View

3

Even when allowance is made for experimental error, this analysis shows that each of the women-novelists has a distinctive mode of presentation. The analysis of Miss Bowen's novels confirms the impression that, in her mature work, her narrative methods have been remarkably constant. Scene is always (as it almost certainly is in every novel ever written) the chief ingredient, but scene (even including "indirect scene") has never been more than half of the whole, and it is seldom pure; it is almost always interwoven with other elements—flashes of description,

swift insights into the characters' states of mind, interpretation and reflective generalizations. One observes that in *To the North* and *The Heat of the Day* there is a rather higher proportion of formal character exposition and analysis, mainly of a rather acid kind, verging on commentary. There is a gradual increase in general commentary, reaching its peak in her most "public" novel, *The Heat of the Day*, in which there is a corresponding decline in dialogue. But the main deviation from normal is *The Death of the Heart*, the only novel in which Miss Bowen has made extensive use of a character's journal. Here Portia's diary is used as a substitute for character exposition and commentary, which diminish correspondingly.

The analysis of the Compton-Burnett novels reveals a rather wider variation than one might have expected. Her method is so heavily weighted in favour of scene (dialogue plus stage directions) that even the small quantities of description, analysis and commentary in the middle novels come as a surprise. The novels selected cover a twenty-year period; the percentages suggest that Miss Compton-Burnett, beginning with almost pure conversation, yielded a little in the middle stages of her career to criticism of her methods and slightly diluted her dialogue with other elements, but that she has returned in later books to what is for her as natural a mode of presentation as Conrad's use of Marlow was for him. The complete absence of description of places shows why hers has been called "a country of the blind".

In both cases, it is possible to derive an average from which no single novel varies significantly. One can say with confidence that Miss Bowen's novels consist of (and predict with almost equal confidence that any future novels will consist of) approximately equal parts of scene (including scene in indirect speech) and other elements, of which character revelation is quantitatively twice as important as any other (Portia's diary can be so regarded), with description, summary and commentary also present in significant, and approximately equal, amounts. (The actual average percentages are: Scene 48; Summary 10; Description 11; Character Exposition and Revelation 21; Commentary 10.) One can say with equal confidence that the typical Compton-Burnett novel contains at least nine-tenths scene, with no more than traces of other elements. Her "formula" is 92; 2; 2; 2; 2.

In contrast, the statistical analysis of Henry Green's novels suggests that it is impossible to ascribe to him any standard made of presentation. When one obtains a theoretical norm (78; 3; 5; 12; 2) one finds that only one novel, *Back*, conforms, even roughly, to it. It is true that Green has always preferred to present experience mainly in terms of what the people concerned say aloud; thus scene has always been more dominant in his novels than it has ever been in Miss Bowen's, but the amount varies greatly from novel to novel. The extremes are *Caught* (which in this, and other respects, is not greatly dissimilar from a novel like *The Death of the Heart*) and *Nothing* and *Doting*, which have an obvious resemblance to the more extreme of the Compton-Burnett novels. Similarly the amount of scene in indirect speech varies from a very small quantity in *Loving* to more than one-eighth of *Living* and *Party Going*. Summary, constituting a tenth of *Caught*, disappears altogether from *Nothing*. There is always some description (though never as much as in any novel of Elizabeth Bowen); but there is four times as much in *Caught* and *Concluding* as in *Doting*. In *Party Going* character exposition constitutes almost a quarter of the whole novel, and it is very prominent in all the novels, except *Loving*, *Nothing* and *Doting*, in which there is virtually none. The amount of interpretative comment also varies greatly; it is an important element in *Party Going*, *Caught* and *Concluding*, but scarcely detectable in any other novel. As for general commentary, one can scarcely imagine a less didactic writer than Henry Green, or one more distrustful of generalization—except Miss Compton-Burnett. Since *Caught* Green has not ventured a general observation on any subject. One of the few generalizations he has ever made—"People, in their relations with one another, are continually doing similar things, but never for similar reasons" (*Party Going*, p. 114)—is itself an indication of why he so seldom generalizes.

Closer examination reveals, however, that while it is impossible to define any stock mode of presentation to which *all* of Green's novels approximate, it is possible to divide his work into two groups, each with something like a standard mode. The smaller group contains *Loving* as well as the two most recent novels, which have already been discussed; aspiring as it does to the condition of pure scene (96, 1, 3, 0, 0) this group represents Green's conception of what the novel should be. The other

F

group of five novels, not written in conformity with any ideal conception or theory, suggests that Green's "natural norm" is made up of about two-thirds scene, one-fifth character exposition, with the remainder fairly evenly distributed among summary, description and commentary (67, 5, 5, 19, 4).

Even within this group there is considerable variation— much more than in Miss Bowen's novels. Scene varies from 60 to 74 per cent (44 to 52 in Elizabeth Bowen), summary 2 to 10 (9 to 12), description 3 to 8 (9 to 12), character exposition 16 to 24 (17 to 23), commentary 1 to 7 (8 to 11). But in reading none of these novels do we feel that what is being presented is in any way at variance with the manner of its presentation, nor do we feel that the author has deliberately made things difficult for himself by refusing to employ any of the usual techniques of fiction. While dramatizing as much as possible, Green does not make a fetish of dramatization; whenever his material requires it he is ready to comment and analyse, to summarize and forecast, to dip into the minds of his characters and either reproduce or interpret whatever he finds there. That the proportions of the different elements vary widely is not the result of an interest in technical dexterity and resourcefulness merely for their own sake; it is due largely to the differences in subject-matter of his novels.

Just as the comparative uniformity of treatment in the novels of Elizabeth Bowen and Ivy Compton-Burnett reflects the comparative uniformity and homogeneity of their respective worlds (their scope, themes, preoccupations), so do the differences in methods of presentation in Henry Green's novels reflect the fact that in almost every book he has presented a different social stratum, a different order of experience. Thus, if one reads in succession several novels of Elizabeth Bowen or Ivy Compton-Burnett (and this, surely, is true of most novelists) one gains an enlarging impression of the same social, mental and emotional landscape; but if one reads in succession *Living*, *Party Going*, *Caught*, *Back* and *Concluding* one gains instead a series of impressions of entirely different social areas and entirely different countries of the mind and feeling. V. S. Pritchett has asserted that Green's is "the most curious imagination in the English novel during the last twenty years, for though Miss Compton-Burnett's dramatic confection of Greek tragedy and Jane Austen is stranger, it has never altered, whereas Mr. Henry Green's

aquariums always contain different fish. He changes the water, the greenery, the exquisite or the plain inhabitants, from book to book."[13] And—to modify the metaphor—the landing of these different kinds of fish has required the use of different kinds of equipment.

4

Scene, however, has always been of paramount importance in Green's work. Conversation has always been his chief instrument both for portraying his characters, and for developing the action. (Nigel Dennis quotes Green as saying, "Anything which has a voice is invited to use it".[14]) All of his novels shape themselves in basically the same way, through a series of dialogues in which people, usually unwittingly, reveal themselves as they try to deceive themselves and others. Green has insisted that to be effective dialogue must be non-representational, that it must not be an exact record of the way people talk. But his own dialogue is not as obviously non-representational as Ivy Compton-Burnett's. In reading her novels one's first impression (which fades with closer reading) is that all of her characters, whether male or female, young or old, masters or servants, speak with one voice. Another impression (which does not fade) is that no group of real human beings ever spoke with such cutting logic, such barbed wit, such polished epigrammatic eloquence as does the most casual assemblage of her characters. Green's dictum that "it is the writer's duty to meet as many pedestrian people as possible and listen to the most pedestrian conversation" has been quoted previously and, in contrast to Miss Compton-Burnett's, his dialogue captures faithfully all the banality and fatuity of ordinary conversation, all of its desultoriness and haphazardness and repetitiousness, all of its concealments and evasiveness, all of its misunderstandings and parallel progression. Green's dialogue has all the muddled syntax, the lost threads, the broken sentences, the lame conclusions that we hear (and most of us perpetrate) every day in real life.

Green has also claimed that "dialogue should not be capable of only one meaning or mood", that "it is the tone in dialogue which carries the meaning, as in life it is what is left unsaid which gives food for thought".[15] So his dialogue is seldom (as real life conversation is seldom) a clear transparent medium through

which we can look directly into the speakers' minds; rather it
is a prism through which the characters' real thoughts and
feelings are refracted. What they really think and feel we have
to deduce for ourselves, sometimes with, sometimes without
their creator's assistance. Not only do his characters generally
say only what they don't mean, but if they do try to say what
they mean or feel (or think they feel) they usually are not
listened to or not understood. Robert Phelps has very well said:
"What makes the dialogue in his books so moving and real is
just the fact that . . . [it] often stands still, or blurs, because the
people who speak so rarely understand, much less acknowledge,
what is in turn being said to them. Almost invariably there is
some loss, some ambiguity, which then breeds the suspicion,
fear and aloneness in which most people live."[16]

These more subtle uses of dialogue are not much in evidence
in *Living*, where dialogue is much supplemented by other
methods. Here the dialogue is notable chiefly for the freshness
and fidelity with which it captures the talk of the workers. For
some of them, especially Jim Dale, monosyllabic grunts are the
chief vehicle of self-expression. But often their talk is picturesque in its exaggeration, its real or sham violence. (E.g. Gates
on Tupe—" 'Elp that carcase. It was as much as I could do
not to wipe me boots on 'is lying mouth. I'll be —— before I
'elp 'is kind." Or Tupe on Craigan—"Deceitful old bleeder,"
he said. "Enough to make you go bald 'eaded just seeing 'im go
up the street.") But it captures with equal nicety the self-conscious efforts of works and departmental managers, who have
risen from the working class, to speak correctly—Tarver, with
his habit, which is so perplexing to young Dupret, of addressing
his superiors as "Colonel" or "Squire". ("And he said, speaking
refinedly, 'Top hole. What about you Colonel?' "); Bridges in a
constant frenzy of anxiety, suspicion and self-pity ("John, I
don't know what's the matter with me but I feel like someone
had given me a cut over the brow with a $\frac{5}{8}$ spanner. Worry,
I've 'ad enough of that washing about in my head to drown a
dolphin. . . . Anyone else'd be dead in my place."). Less prominent, but equally well rendered, is the pompous "educated
jargon" of young Dupret ("Mr. Bridges," said he, "we've got to
have what the French call a little explanation") and the empty-
headed inanities of the young upper-class people whom Dupret
meets at balls and dinners and house-parties. This chit-chat

becomes the staple of *Party Going*. For several hours the group of three young men and five young women talk about one another, play up to one another, score off one another, exploit one another, lie to one another, vie with one another for the centre of attention, try to save their faces and to justify themselves. Unlike *The Way of the World*, *Party Going* has no developed plot; but as in Congreve's masterpiece there is no clearcut division of forces. Each is for himself (and especially herself) first, last and always, but there is a constant formation and dissolution of uneasy alliances among these elegant, beautifully dressed, exquisitely made-up, soulless females. Unlike the Millamants and Harriets, the Dorimants and Mirabells of Restoration comedy, none of these modern people of fashion ever says anything at all witty or memorable. Their interests are of the most trivial kind. They spend a great deal of time speculating whether Embassy Richard, a young man of their circle, who joins the party at the last moment, really sent to the London newspapers, for publication in the court columns, the notice that he was unavoidably prevented from accepting some Ambassador's invitation, or whether someone else had sent it, and, if so, who? Another subject of aggrieved discussion is the sudden mysterious illness of Miss Fellowes, the aunt of one of them, which, it is feared, may further upset their plans. But though no one cares whether they ever go to France (one is more likely to wish them further), one cannot deny that they are alive, and that each of them is perfectly distinct. It is not entirely through their conversation, however, that they are brought to life, and scene is only one of several important elements in the complex total effect of this untrivial treatment of triviality.

Similarly in the other three novels dialogue is important, but not all-important. In *Caught* it is almost entirely through their speech that Green presents the subordinate characters. The language of Wal, Chopper, Shiner, Piper and the rest carries immediate conviction; this, we feel at once, is the authentic speech of real people. Shiner's talk is often odd and extravagant, as when he philosophizes to Richard—"It's muckin' awful, ain't it, the first few days, the conga little place you've left, the little woman there, eh, it's like the first days at sea. Sitting on the old rail where they can't see you, the old ship trembling under your arse, and that mucking awful sea for miles. Then you kind of

fall in with it and everything's conga. But stone me up a bloody gum tree, thank God I got a job on land" (p. 65). The infuriating old Piper comes to life almost entirely through his talk —his "While I was in Africa . . ." (he usually forgets the point before he reaches it), his "oh mother", his habit of addressing himself as "you silly old sod, you". Even Pye makes his impression very largely through his speech—through his lectures, always interlarded with muddled "leftist" ideas, through his "man-to-man" talks with Richard, through his well-meant, but unappreciated and misinterpreted, attempts to be helpful to the ladies on his establishment, through his hypocritical comments on the night-clubs to which he takes Prudence nightly ("Champagne pressed out of the skin of the grape by the feet of starving peasant women, boy. Drunk to the accompaniment of music made by tubercular niggers tempted away from the climate their bodies is acclimatized to by luxury wages", p. 107), through his desperate attempts to keep Prudence entertained by lurid stories of peace-time fires, through his unhappy interviews with superiors and subordinates. But there is much more to Pye than we learn from his talk. The dialogue of *Back* captures perfectly the absent-mindedness, the mental confusion, the fear of life of Charley Summers, the robust good sense and good feeling of Nancy, the easy-going good nature of James Phillips, the care-free, self-confident pose of Arthur Middlewitch; the dialogue of *Concluding* depicts equally adroitly the vinegarish malevolence of Miss Edge, the empty charlatanism of Birt, the dignity and pathos of Mr. Rock, the shattered mind, the half-despairing sensuality of Liz. But both books would have been greatly impoverished if Green had insisted on using scene to the exclusion of all other methods.

5

The next matter to be considered is the various ways in which Green has adapted his basically scenic method to the demands of different subject-matters. In *Living*, one notices, four elements are more prominent than usual—scene in indirect speech, summary and both kinds of character revelation. The high proportion of indirect scene is not of much significance; as already mentioned there is little real condensation—in almost every case the characters' full speech is given, with no more than

changes of tenses and persons. Often there is alternation between direct and oblique discourse in the same paragraph, as in the following exchange between Craigan and one of the boys in the foundry. "Craigan said how would he like piece of cake and while boy ate piece of cake he said it was easier for boys in foundries now than when he started. Boy said it may have been but all the same wouldn't have been a misery like Craigan in any iron foundry, not to touch him, not since they started. Mr. Craigan said in his young days you could never have said that to a moulder when you were core boy. 'You would say worse' boy said and Craigan said this one would never make a moulder" (p. 23).

The rather high proportion of summary is due mainly to the fairly protracted time-scheme of the book. The action occupies almost a year, and there are some episodes which could not be effectively dramatized—notably the illnesses of Dupret senior and Craigan. Also there is some retrospective summary of Craigan's earlier life; and near the end there is a good deal of summary of the Craigan household's gradual establishment of a new pattern of living, after the dislocation caused by the sacking of Craigan and Joe Gates, Lily's elopement and return, Jim Dale's departure and Gates' ten days in gaol.

But the most important non-scenic element is that of character exposition and revelation. The percentage of formal exposition is higher in this novel (four per cent) than it was ever to be again. It is, however, quite novel and unconventional; Green on several occasions uses ingenious extended conceits to define the mental or emotional condition of his characters and the relationships between them. There is the metaphor of the sunken submarine (p. 93) to describe the condition of old Mr. Dupret as he gradually sinks towards death, that of the liquid metal leaking from the moulding box to describe Mr. Bridges (p. 113), that of the ship, the tropical birds and the flying fish to define Hannah Glossop's emotions when she is rebuffed by Tom Tyler (pp. 156 and 168), that of the piece of metal to be worked on the lathe to express the relationship between Bert Jones and Lily Gates (pp. 195 and 234). Of great importance, thematically, is the constant use, in the later sections of the book, of the image of homing-pigeons for the feelings of Craigan and Lily Gates. It is to be regretted that Green, after this novel, abandoned this rather Jamesian method of character

delineation, presumably because it conflicted with his theory that "the one way not to set about [creating life] is by explanation".

The proportion of informal character-revelation, generally moment-by-moment interior monologue, often prefaced by such phrases as "He cried in mind", is also extremely high. There are two good reasons for this. In the first place, one of the characters (Dupret junior) is a young man of Green's own age and social class. His position as the boss's son is much the same as Green's would have been, when he went into his father's Birmingham factory, if he had not chosen to work his way through the various departments; it seems likely that Dupret was fashioned partly out of Green's own self-awareness. This is not to suggest that Dupret is a self-portrait of Green, any more than Geoffrey the pilgrim is a self-portrait of Chaucer the poet. It is rather that Green subjected himself to a merciless scrutiny and recognized in himself certain tendencies; he then set out to show how these tendencies (to suspiciousness, bumptiousness, vanity, self-glorification, arrogance) in a young man in a similar position, but lacking his intelligence and individuality, could affect the lives and livelihoods of many other people. Dupret's self-deceptions and self-dramatizations are extremely important in the action of the book, and we are given ample opportunity to observe them. ("Intrigue he cried in his mind, still sitting in private room in London office, intrigue and how horrible people are. Of course Archer was working against old Bridges for Bridges ignored Mr. Archer and only dealt with him through old Walters. Both these were old, old. How horrible they all were and everyone too for that matter, loathsome the people in buses, worse in trams of course:- he faintly smiled.")

The other, and more important, reason is that the sensibilities and ideas of industrial workers like Craigan, Tupe, Dale, Jones, Gates and his daughter were, in 1929, as foreign to most English novel-readers as Sanskrit. If these people had been presented only through their actions and words they would have seemed queer and incomprehensible. It is largely because Green, without anger or sentimentalism, recreates and interprets for us their vague, wordless longings and desperations that they come to life and do not seem freaks or oddities. A typical example is this glimpse into Lily Gates' maternal yearnings. "And then in bed, after, rigid, she cried in her, I, I am I. I am

I, why do I do work of this house, unloved work, why but they cannot find other woman to do this work.

"Why may I not have children, feed them with my milk? Why may I not kiss their eyes, lick their skin, softness to softness, why not I? I have no man, my work is for others, not for mine.

"Why may I not work for mine?" (p. 109).

Philip Toynbee has commented on *Living*: "As all in this writer's novels, the characters appear at first to be moving in an odd and unfamiliar way, their motives and their conduct seem to be just out of focus, just to one side of centre. . . . At some point in this book a reader may find that the characters and the actions are suddenly in focus; that they have found their centre. And in the same moment he will understand that it is not the characters and the actions which have shifted, but the focus and the centre. In other words what has happened is that Green has succeeded in imposing his peculiar vision on the reader."[17]

This is an interesting comment, but it does not indicate how this feat is performed. It would be truer to say that the conduct of the characters in the early sections of the novel seems to be "out of focus" because their motives and attitudes are unfamiliar, and that their conduct comes into focus as Green gradually takes the lids off their minds and lets us see how their conditions of living affect their way of looking at everything. Statistical analysis shows this very clearly: in the first third of the novel, character exposition and revelation amount to only nine per cent (while scene is no less than eighty-four per cent); in the central third "characterization" rises to thirty-one per cent (and scene drops to sixty-two); in the final third this element remains constant, while scene diminishes further (to fifty-six). Thus in this novel it is not so much that Green imposes a peculiar vision on us, as that he convinces us of the truth of his portrayal. He could not have done this—or at least not so effectively—by a presentation, however adroit, of the surface alone.

In *Party Going* Green's method is not radically different, despite the difference of subject-matter, and despite the unity of time and place in the later novel. The amount of scene in indirect speech is even greater than in *Living*: though much of it is simply the recording of the actual words in *oratio obliqua*, as in *Living*, there is also a good deal of genuine compression. The reason for this, presumably, is that the conversations of this

Mayfair crowd are utterly banal for the most part; Green
sensibly recognized the limits of the reader's patience with a
literal transcript of their talk and tactfully distilled much of it.
E.g. "Both exclaimed aloud at the beauty and appropriateness
of the other's choice, but it was as though two old men were
swapping jokes, they did not listen to each other they were so
anxious to explain. Already both had been made to regret they
had left such and such a dress behind . . ." (p. 29). Two other,
non-scenic, elements are more prominent in this novel than they
were ever to be again—informal character revelation and particular commentary—and they are almost inextricably entwined with one another. This, indeed, is the most omniscient
of all Green's novels; it shows quite conclusively that "explanation" is not necessarily fatal to the creation of life. We
have an almost constant double view of the characters, which
is almost indecent, for it is as if these members of the *beau monde*
were all sitting about naked, without knowing it. Not only do
we hear what they say, but simultaneously we are told what are
their motives for saying it, what they hope to get out of their
present attitude, what, in fact, their game is at the moment.
In the following paragraph all three of these elements are
blended:

"Claire, who did not care for silences, she thought them
unnatural, took up what Amabel had said about this room.
While she went rattling on, blaming the directors for allowing
decorations such as these and saying she could not think what
Julia's uncle was about in letting them do such things, Amabel
wondered again how Max would be and what he had on with
Julia. She had expected to find him with these others and when
she had opened the door she had been braced up to meet him.
She was like someone who opens his front door expecting to
step out into a gale of wind and then stays bent although he
finds he has no wind to lean against, although it is still whining
in the chimney and rattling windows. She knew well she could
deal with Max but he was always escaping. It was while he was
not there that she felt anxious and that was one reason why she
has made up her mind to come along" (p. 147).

Party Going is also the most satirical of Green's novels; although there is no trace of acerbity or acrimony in Green's
attitude, the cool dispassionate interlinear commentary underlines the horrifying futility of these lines dedicated to party

going. It is, however, in a two-page-long passage of interior monologue of Alex Alexander's (the longest uninterrupted unspoken soliloquy that Green has ever written—pp. 195-6) that Green brings together the various themes of the book.

Another element which is slightly more noticeable in *Party Going* than in *Living* is description. In his descriptions of the railway station, so ordinary yet so strange and mysterious, and of the fog (as previously in his descriptions of the foundry) Green shows his poet's eye for beauty in unexpected places. ("Coils of it reached down like women's long hair reached down and caught their throats and veiled here and there what they could see, like lovers' glances", p. 199.) This strong visual element (stronger than the percentage figures indicate, for sensuous awareness of their surroundings is part of the consciousness of some of the characters) is one notable difference from the method of *Nothing* and *Doting*.

In *Caught* the percentage of every element except that of direct scene is above average. The proportion of summary is far higher than it is in any other novel; the amount of description of characters also reaches its peak, while description of settings is equalled (actually slightly surpassed) only by *Concluding*. Particular commentary is second only to *Party Going*, indirect scene is still much in evidence, and informal character revelation, though below any of the other four books, is also extremely important. The amount of summary can be explained partly by the fact that *Caught* covers a longer period of time— about two years—than any of Green's other novels; through the memories of Pye and Roe it reaches much further back in time than that. It can also be explained partly by the documentary aspect of the novel; the action of the book is linked with contemporary history—the phoney war, the invasion of the low countries, Dunkirk—which is briefly sketched in at intervals. Though this one fire-station is the constant focus of our attention, we are made aware of the general atmosphere, the loosening of standards under war-stress. ("This was a time when girls, taken out to night clubs by men in uniform, if he was a pilot she died in his arms that would soon, so she thought, be dead. In the hard idiom of the drum these women seemed already given up to the male in uniform so soon to go away, these girls, as they felt, soon to be killed themselves, so little time left, moth deathly gay, in a daze of giving", p. 49.)

Some of the description and commentary is also documentary in character—it sketches the conditions of the life in the A.F.S. posts, it indicates what sort of people the amateur and professional firemen were and what they looked like. There is more specific detailed description of some of the characters— notably Pye, Piper, Shiner, Mrs. Howes—than in any other novel. In *Living* the appearance of none of the characters is specified in anything but general terms ("Plump she was"), but here we are told of Piper, for example, that "he had a narrow, dark face, not healthy, and coloured as is the sole of a shoe after walking dry streets in summer, whether by dirt, or ill-health, or both, it was hard to tell . . . He had thick dark eyebrows, with a yellow white moustache. His hair was short, so that the skin, dry and pied, and as though travel stained with dust, came through in places" (pp. 20-1).

But much of the description is poetic and atmospheric rather than documentary. One of the most brilliant single passages is the account of the kidnapping of Christopher (presented partly as his father imagines it some months later, partly through parenthetic omniscient narration) from a toy shop, which is like something out of fairy-land. "The walls of this store being covered with stained glass windows which depicted trading scenes, that is of merchandise being loaded on to galleons, the leaving port, of incidents on the voyage, and then the unloading, all brilliantly lit from without, it follows that the body of the shop was inundated with colour, brimming, and this colour, as the sea was a predominant part of each window, was a permanence of sapphire in shopping hours. Pink neon lights on the high ceiling wore down this blue to some extent, made customers' faces less aggressively steeped in the body of the store, but enhanced, or deepened that fire brigade scarlet to carmine . . ." (pp. 12-13). But even more spectacular are the descriptions of the first fires of the blitz, in the last section of the book. They present with a shocking vividness the horrifying beauty of a city aflame. E.g. "They saw the whole fury of that conflagration in which they had to play a part. They sat very still, beneath the immensity. For, against it, warehouses, small towers, puny steeples seemed alive with sparks from the mile high pandemonium of flame reflected in the quaking sky. This fan, a roaring red gold, pulsed rose at the outside edge, the perimeter round which the heavens, set

with stars before fading into utter blackness, were for a space a trembling green" (pp. 176–7). Green's painter's eye for colours, and, more important, his ability to render lyrically and yet exactly the quality of sensuous experience, are nowhere seen to better advantage than in this novel.

None of these other elements, however, is permitted to distract attention from the real subjects of the book—Pye's disintegration, through a combination of internal and external causes, and Roe's achievement of identity. Again and again we are made co-partners of their thought and feeling; it is as much through their unexpressed meditation, memory, reverie, apprehension, regret and despair as through their spoken words that we come to know them. When one remembers that the novel was written and published so soon after the blitz, one must admire Green for resisting the pressure of public events, for his concern, at a time when many writers were content with journalism, with permanent truths about human character, and for utilizing so skilfully the transitory and abnormal circumstances of the war years as catalysts rather than as principal elements.

One unusual feature of the technique of this novel is Green's practice of interpolating, in parentheses, omniscient comments, indicating the inadequacy of the character's reactions, or the imperfectness of his knowledge. Thus Richard's description of the dock-fire is halting, tame, prosaic; Green's own, side by side with it, is vividly impressionistic. The passage already quoted, for example, is followed by: "'I almost wetted my trousers,' he said, putting into polite language the phrase current at his substation." The most important of these interpolations is the only clear evidence that Pye's suspicion of his incest was justified. "(What he did not know was the year after year of entanglement before her, the senseless nightingale, the whining dog, repeating the same phrase over and over in the twining briars of her senses)" (p. 42).

Back, in technique, is almost a bridge between the two groups of Green's novels. As already mentioned, it is the only book that is at all close to the theoretical norm obtained by averaging the percentages of all eight novels. The proportion of scene is a good deal higher than in *Living*, *Party Going*, *Caught* and *Concluding*; conversely, the proportions of the other ingredients, except summary, are lower. Summary here consists partly of

retrospective glimpses of Charley's past life and his relationship with Rose, partly of bridge-passages between the discriminated occasions, which are quite natural since the action occupies over six months (June 13th to Christmas Day). Although the actual quantity of description is so low, its effect is greater than the figures suggest; it is concentrated mainly in two important passages—the description, in the opening pages, of the cemetery where Rose is buried, with its mournful cypresses entwined with roses in the summer rain, and the description, near the end of the book, of the blitzed autumnal rose-garden, where Charley first kisses Nance Whitmore (or, to be exact, she kisses him) and life begins again for him.

But this book certainly belongs with the four just named, not with *Loving*, *Nothing* and *Doting*. Although Green was now trying more deliberately to dramatize, to use dialogue as much as possible, he does not avoid the inner view. There is no formal character exposition, but informal revelation is scarcely reduced. Indeed, in the allocation of psychological space to individual characters, it is higher than ever, for here it is concerned almost exclusively with the confusions and uncertainties, sorrows and delusions of one character. Green keeps close throughout to Charley's nerves and consciousness; we follow at close range his half-comprehending, half-suspecting daze, his slow, incredulous acceptance of reality, his rapturous rediscovery of love. Green's method fully creates Charley—inarticulate, bemused, unable to feel anything except as it is distorted by his self-pitying obsession. *Back*, in fact, is the nearest that Green has ever come to a novel in which the viewpoint is that of a single character, of, to use James' term, "the fool". It is perhaps the most remarkable of Green's many *tours de force*, because although so much of the novel consists of scene, the reader sees always through the eyes of Charley, and (to adapt Chapman's phrase about Emma Woodhouse) the reader's "vision is distorted by Charley's faulty spectacles".[18] As Philip Toynbee puts it: "Charley's obstinate error of mistaken identity so colours his vision that the whole panorama of post-war [*sic*] England is seen from a strange and hallucinatory angle . . . When Charley observes the world through the [rose] coloured spectacles of his obsession, his creator is also behind those spectacles, sharing and encouraging that peculiar but illuminating vision."[19] There is, of course, a suggestion of Kafka in Charley's search for the real rose

through a frightening maze which reflects his own neurotic state. But the novel is far more convincing than the novels of avowed English imitators of Kafka like Rex Warner, Edward Upward, William Sansom and (in some novels) F. L. Green.

In *Concluding* the proportion of scene is almost as high as in *Back*, but other elements which are extremely important are informal character revelation and description. In this novel Green exercises his right of entry at will into any of the characters, and he requisitions for use the memories, sensations and thought-processes of several—not only of Mr. Rock, but of Liz, his grand-daughter, her lover, Sebastian Birt, of Miss Baker and Miss Edge. Green frequently uses preceding dashes to indicate unspoken thought, as in the following passage (p. 34): "—Well, Mr. Rock, she'd say, and am I to congratulate you, or some such phrase, the smarming harpy, after which, if he knew he had been elected, he would have to smirk thank you, yes, they've put me in, I'm delivered over to their charity now all right. Or, on the other hand, if they had not elected him, was he to eat humble pie, tell her that young men whose work he despised had not thought him worth the candle, after all he'd done—— Never, he told himself, never, he'd take the money. . . ." In many scenes the counterpointing of the spoken word with the unuttered reaction gives a greater psychological richness, depth and complexity than is possible in "pure" scene. It is the constant dipping into the consciousness of the characters, particularly of Mr. Rock, with his massive, ancient, pragmatic humanism, which makes *Concluding*, despite the inconclusiveness and mystification of its "plot", so absorbing a study of (or so haunting a poem about) the individual's resistance to the dehumanizing effects of the institution, and so impressive an allegory of civilization on the verge of darkness.

The quantity of description of settings is slightly higher in *Concluding* even than it is in *Caught*. One cannot help feeling, however, that "description" is an inadequate and even rather misleading term for Green's poetic evocations of the clouds of fog hanging over the woods in the early morning, of the sunshine blazing through the thickets in the heat of the day, of the unearthly, bewildering moonlight through which Mr. Rock and Liz wade homeward, of the girl-students, all in white, sensuously whirling to waltz-strains.

"At this instant, like a woman letting down her mass of hair

from a white towel in which she had bound it, the sun came through for a moment, and lit the azaleas on either side before fog, redescending, blanketed them off again; as it might be white curtains, drawn by someone out of sight, over a palace bedroom window, to shut behind them a blonde princess undressing" (p. 7).

"A great beech had fallen a night or two earlier, in full leaf, lay now with its green leaves turned to pale gold, as though by the sea. . . . The wreckage beneath standing beeches was lit at this place by a glare of sunlight concerted on flat, dying leaves which hung on to life by what was broken off, the small branches joining those larger that met the arms, which in their turn grew from the fallen column of the beech, all now an expiring gold of faded green. A world through which the young man and his girl had been meandering, in dreaming shade through which sticks of sunlight slanted to spill upon the ground, had at this point been struck to a blaze, and where their way had been dim, on a sea bed past grave trunks, was now this dying, brilliant mass which lay exposed, a hidden world of spiders working on its gold, the webs these made a field of wheels and spokes of wet silver" (pp. 54–5).

This element, whatever it be called, is chiefly responsible for the strange beauty of the book, a beauty that is all the more radiant because it is set against, crossed and chequered by evil and sterility.

In all of these five books Green seems to be writing naturally and instinctively, employing any method that will best serve his purpose of the moment, not fussing with rules or theories, commandeering any character's vision as his point of view, surreptitiously commenting, explaining, interpreting, sometimes even flouting the tenet of objectivist theory that the author must never anticipate what lies ahead. This he does not only in *Caught* with its rather Conradian dislocation of normal chronological sequence, but also occasionally in *Living* (when the lavatory attendant returns the tulips to Bert Jones—" 'Maybe, again, you'll forget 'erself', he said, more to himself than to Mr. Jones, turning prophetic", p. 214) and *Back* ("So it was the same night, under Mr. Mandrew's roof, that he went to her room, for the first time in what was to be a happy married life", p. 208). In these novels he seems to write with a technique so spontaneously casual that he appears to have abandoned all

technique; his methods are not spectacularly novel, but he uses all the traditional methods with complete freedom and freshness —and he does not seem to be at all concerned about concealing the means by which he achieves his effects. In these books he does succeed in what he considers the novelist's chief duty— that of "setting the reader's imagination to work, of so ordering what he is putting down that by evocation, by memory, by the mysterious things we all share, which is another set of words for the lone word 'life', he may create life in the mind of the reader".[20] This, it has already been suggested, he does not achieve so completely in the two most recent novels, *Nothing* and *Doting*, which were written to a formula.

6

One other novel, however, has not yet been considered, a novel which, in technique, is far closer to *Nothing* and *Doting* than to Green's other books, even though it was written several years before them—*Loving*. *Loving* is crucial in any discussion of Green's methods; while it is generally considered that *Nothing* and *Doting* are inferior to the other five books that have been discussed (and that they are inferior, partly at least, because of their technique) *Loving* is often regarded as the peak of Green's achievement to date. Robert Phelps seems to have overlooked the significance of *Loving* in his strictures on the two later books. He asserts "That some relation exists between Green's insistence on so debilitating a technique and the triviality of what, in a book like *Doting*, it allows him to say, seems obvious. When an artist's vision is truly and intensely upon him he creates without *a priori*, wrong-headed purification of his means. He is as 'impure' as he needs to be. . . . It is only as [Green's] vision has relaxed that he has begun to fuss with rules and devise theories which conveniently *prevent* his writing what, apparently he no longer can or wants to write."[21] It is true that when Green wrote *Loving* he had not publicized any theories he may have formulated, yet (at least according to the statistical analysis) it was virtually the same technique that he employed. This raises several questions—Had Green's vision already "relaxed" when he wrote *Loving*? Or is Phelps mistaken in his view that this "debilitating technique" is capable only of representing "triviality"? Or is he wrong in considering the

G

technique debilitating? Or is the statistical analysis inaccurate or misleading?

In the first place, while I do not think that Green's vision has relaxed in *Loving*, this novel is not, it seems to me, his most important or most impressive novel. It is a masterpiece, but it is a minor masterpiece; it may be the most perfect, the most completely harmonious of Green's books, but it lacks the depth of psychological insight, the emotional resonance of *Caught*, *Back* and *Concluding*. Moreover, after several readings of both novels, I am not convinced that *Loving* is a finer work than the earlier study of working-class life, *Living*. Although *Loving* is clearly a much more important novel than *Nothing* and *Doting*, the fact that Green's vision in *Loving*, as in the other two novels, is essentially comic, suggests that, for Green at least, the conversational method is viable only for not necessarily trivial, but certainly for un-tragic material and experience.

In the second place, while the statistics (I hope) are not inaccurate, they can, like all statistics, be misleading unless very carefully interpreted. One thing to be stressed is that a difference in scene of five per cent is far more noticeable and significant in the ninety per cents than in the sixties. The difference between *Loving* (92 per cent scene) and *Nothing* (97) is greater than that between *Concluding* (69) and *Back* (74). As in *Nothing* and *Doting*, there are in *Loving* only infinitesimal traces of character exposition and commentary, but there is a little summary, and, more important, there is three times as much description of settings as in the later books (only *Caught* and *Concluding* have more). In *Nothing* there is only one substantial passage of description—that of the private room in the "great hotel" where Philip Weatherby's absurd "twenty-firster" is held; in *Doting* there are only the descriptions, in the opening and closing sections, of the two night-clubs. But in *Loving*, which strictly preserves unity of place, we are always aware of Kinalty castle. We may not attain a mental picture of this "great Gothic pile" as a whole, but many sections of it become quite familiar to us—the servants' quarters behind the green baize door; the pantry connected by a stone passage with a vaulted ceiling to the servants' hall, with its red mahogany sideboard; Charley's room decorated with its purloined prints and photographs; the attic bedroom shared by Kate and Edith. More important, we know the morning room, with its six tall

french windows with Gothic arches; the Red Library, with its
deep armchairs in purple leather, its walls covered in green silk,
its desk with a flat, sloping top of rhinoceros hide supported on
gold pillars of wood; the Blue Drawing Room, with its vaulted
roof painted to represent the evening sky, its Gothic imitation
hammock fashioned of gold wire, slung between four marble
columns, its milking stools, pails and cow byre furniture in
gilded wood, its sandalwood fly whisks, its white marble mantel-
piece; the disused ballroom with its five great chandeliers; the
imitation Greek temple sculpture gallery; Mrs. Jack's bedroom,
with its boat-shaped black and gold bed, with a gold oar at the
foot, and pink silk sheets. Outside the castle we know the
rutted gravel drive; the artificial, carefully ruined Greek
temple; Paddy O'Conor's lamp room, divided from the next
room, now given over to the peacocks, only by a vast glass-
fronted cupboard; the tower of Pisa dovecote. Though there
are few lengthy descriptive passages, the constant reference to
this background of obsolete, functionless, prodigal splendour is
of great importance in the total effect of the book. Moreover
many of the scenes and tableaux in these settings—the game of
blind man's buff in the sculpture gallery; the housemaids
waltzing in the deserted ballroom; Paddy O'Conor snoring on
his bed of ferns, with spun-gold spiderwebs in his hair, watched
by the ruby-eyed peacocks—are poetic in their perfection of
design and vividness of imagery.

This suggests an obvious and undeniable limitation of
statistical analysis—it is purely quantitative, not qualitative.
It can define the proportions of the various elements, but it
cannot indicate for what purposes and with what effects they
are used. So, while this analysis records the very high proportion of scene it does not indicate the masterful authenticity
with which Green captures the cadence of working-class conversations. His dialogue is never more exact than in *Loving*;
Rosamond Lehmann has a fine comment on "the choppy stream
of dialogue". "On the servants' Hall's side [there is] the class
language of circumlocution, ambiguity, rhetorical flourish, of
devious sly approach to the end in view; all the verbal taboos
['Miss Burch fixed a stern eye on Kate so much as to say a
minute or so ago just now you were about to be actually
coarse.'] and traditional tags and saws. [' "No' me," he went
on, "I take things to 'eart. . . . When I feel whatever it is I feel it

deep." ' 'No it was everything got me down all of a sudden.'
'That's a fine way to start bein' married, to throw good money
down the drain.'] On the drawing room side [there is] the habit
of incoherence, tentativeness, over-emphasis, the obsessive
modish portmanteau words. ['My dear it was quite fantastic.'
'I know it's an absurd thing to expect . . . but Eldon with all
his faults always had a word of comfort when there was a
disaster.'] . . . *Loving* correctly shows the drawing room worn
down and losing out, its command of a vocabulary disintegrating along with its mastery of the situation." [22] Two other important features of the technique of *Loving* are not caught by the
coarse net of statistical analysis. One is the way in which the
servants' idiom is used to present their movements and their
appearance, so that almost the whole book is permeated by their
collective consciousness. The other is the extent to which "stage
directions" are used. This is one of the most crucial differences
between the still natural technique of *Loving* and the artificially
bare method of *Nothing* and *Doting*. Nigel Dennis has commented
on *Doting*: "Though no single character is described, each builds
a lifelike portrait solely by speaking. To each of us certain ways
of speech suggest certain shapes of flesh, which, as in a telephone
conversation with a stranger, we automatically construct around
the shapeless voice", and he quotes Green as saying of this novel,
"Let each middle-aged gentleman with a roving eye colour and
shape the creature out of the aching shallows of his own
experience." [23] Apart from the fact that in *Loving* there is more
specific description of the characters (Raunce's greenish hue,
Edith's magnificent eyes, Paddy's tangled, matted hair, etc.)
there is a continual insistence on appearance as a clue to feeling.
Green, while almost always preserving the point of view of a
detached and impartial but intelligent bystander, with no
greater knowledge of the characters than the reader possesses,
constantly uses the device of the tentative comment; there is
a very high incidence of verbs like "seemed", "looked",
"appeared", "might have", "could have been," of adverbs like
"apparently", "obviously", "probably", "possibly", "plainly",
"presumably" and of phrases like "as if" and "as though".
(E.g. "He said, obviously putting on an act", "she added, as
though confidentially", "Her daughter-in-law's silence seemed
to imply".) This constant interweaving of stage directions and
veiled comments with the dialogue is mainly responsible for the

difference in narrative texture between *Loving* and the later books.

One becomes more and more painfully aware of the limitations and inadequacies of this kind of analysis when applied to a novelist like Henry Green. It would undoubtedly go much further towards defining the individuality of many novelists than it goes towards defining his. Such analysis does at least suggest that Green's individuality of technique consists partly in his encouraging every novel to set him a different problem of method (at least up to and including *Concluding*, after which the method has come first and the material been squeezed into a predetermined mould) so that he has no fixed, stable method. But this kind of analysis, in Green's case, cannot be more than a useful preliminary investigation, for it allows too much to slip through unnoted—notably his highly individual handling of language and his poetic use of colour, imagery and symbol to suggest the underlying, never explicitly stated theme. These elements will be discussed in later chapters.

IV

Stories and Structures

Where and how he places his characters in fiction is for the writer the context of his story. The superimposing of one scene on another, or the telescoping of two scenes into one, are methods which the novelist is bound to adopt in order to obtain substance and depth.

("A Novelist to his Readers", *Listener*, March 15, 1951, p. 425)

I

THE most obvious difficulty in discussing the work of Henry Green is one which also confronts the critic of Virginia Woolf—that the venerable stand-by of fictional criticism, the plot-summary, serves even less purpose than usual. Green, in this respect, is at the opposite pole from his near-namesake, Graham Greene, whose books—at least up to and including *The Power and the Glory*—can be read, without regard to their philosophical and religious implications, their austere and fastidious distaste for the shoddy materialism and spiritual poverty of contemporary civilization, simply as quickly-moving, incident-packed, constantly surprising action thrillers. Story is not eliminated from Henry Green's work, but it is deliberately underplayed; one imagines him sighing with E. M. Forster—"Yes—oh dear yes—the novel tells a story . . . and I wish that it was not so, that it could be something different —melody or perception of the truth, not this low atavistic form."[1] Hence his work can never have much appeal for readers whose interest is held only by the unexpected twist of plot, the multiplication of incident, the decisive resolution. But even the more sophisticated reader, who is actuated by something higher than a primitive curiosity to know what will happen next, is likely to be exasperated at times by Green's determination not to be a traditional teller of tales, his careful avoidance of conventional climax.

Some of Green's novels suggest that he shares Henry James' view: "Catching the very note and trick, the strange irregular rhythm of life, that is the attempt whose strenuous force keeps fiction upon her feet. In proportion as in what she offers us we see life *without* rearrangement do we feel that we are touching the truth; in proportion as we see it *with* rearrangement do we feel that we are being put off with a substitute, a compromise or convention."[2] But in other novels he deliberately uses "re-arrangement" (especially in the forms of coincidence and an artificially symmetrical grouping of characters). In fact, as with other aspects of Green's work, generalization here is impossible; structurally his novels vary from something approaching a breadthwise *tranche de vie*, an almost plotless spatial cross-section in *Living*, to the complex "comedy of manners" intrigue of his two latest novels, *Nothing* and *Doting*, in which a few characters are moved about like chessmen. In this chapter such "story" element as Green's novels possess will be outlined, and an attempt made at an analysis of the various methods he has used to give shape, unity and coherence to his subject-matter.

2

The completely commonplace and unspectacular story on which *Living* is based has already been outlined. The centre of the novel is Dupret's factory in Birmingham; for every character in the book living is inextricably bound up with its progress, its curtailed production, its rules, restrictions and policies. The factory's policies are the outcome of a fluctuating struggle for power between the contending forces of youth and age, which ends eventually in the triumph of youth. For when the callow young Dupret, who has been dominated all his life by a father half-a-century older than himself, and who is determined to forget his infatuation with Hannah Glossop in "work", succeeds to the managing directorship on his father's death, he self-consciously assumes the role of the new broom sweeping clean, and, ostensibly in the cause of increased efficiency, proceeds to take his revenge on "horrible" old age by sacking all employees old enough for the pension, from the works manager down. One of the victims of the reorganization is the novel's most important character, the old moulder, Mr. Craigan, who, by dint of staying single and saving most of the wages of fifty-seven years, owns his own house, and is concerned above all, to hold together the small household he has gathered, and to ensure its permanence by the marriage of his "daughter", Lily Gates, to the dependable man of his choice, Jim Dale.

How this plan is frustrated by Lily's infatuation and elopement with Bert Jones has been mentioned. The book ends in an uneasy equilibrium, with Craigan more emotionally dependent than ever on the returned Lily, but fearful that she will marry soon and leave him.

Although the personal drama of Craigan and Lily Gates comes eventually to engage most of the reader's attention, it is not at once obvious that they are the novel's leading characters. They slowly move to the front of the stage out of the crowd of people associated with the Dupret factory. In the early chapters Green's method is decidedly cinematic. Each chapter (the chapters—seventeen of them—are numbered in this novel, but in no other) is divided into a number of smaller sections and sequences, and the camera constantly moves from one group of characters to another. Almost the whole of the first chapter is shot in the Dupret factory: First we see and hear Mr. Bridges, the works manager, talking to Richard Dupret; then Joe Gates is overheard gossiping with some of his cronies in the lunch-hour; we cut back again to Dupret and Bridges and follow them in their tour of inspection from the engineers' shop to the foundry; back again to Gates wasting time nattering to the storeman, Milligan; then we are given a private view into Dupret's mind as he romantically declaims to himself about the wild beauty of the machines; we watch Tarver, the chief designer, furtively following Bridges and Dupret round the factory, and seizing an opportunity to buttonhole Dupret and surprise him with vague accusations against Bridges; we hear Bert Jones in mild altercation with the old trouble-maker Tupe. The chapter ends with a brief glimpse of Bridges at home worrying over the implications of Dupret's visit. In this chapter Craigan has been mentioned and observed by other characters, but has not yet stepped into the foreground. The second chapter gives a series of swift shots covering more than a week (as we deduce from the two Friday nights); first Bert Jones and 'Erbert Tomson discuss, in a street, the latter's intended emigration; we get our first glimpses of the Craigan household, and of the Eames family who live next door; we see Lily at the pictures with Jim Dale and talking in a shop with Mrs. Eames, and her father in a pub with Tupe; we return to the factory to see Bridges and Tarver in temporary truce, and Craigan giving one of the core boys a piece of cake. In the fourth chapter the ripples from the centre spread wider, reaching the London house of the Duprets, where Richard and his mother leaf through their engagement books to find when they can dine quietly at home together (impossible for two weeks, it seems), and the home of the Tarvers, where the bumptious designer plots to write to the firm's headquarters to complain about Bridges. The book generally proceeds in straightforward chronological sequence, covering about a year in all, from the spring of 1927 to the spring of 1928; but we have our first glimpses of the Dupret *ménage* on the evening of Richard's return from his first visit to Birmingham, while the shots of the Birmingham characters which precede and follow them are a couple of weeks later in time; there seems to be no significance in this slight temporal dislocation.

So the book proceeds, interspersing scenes in the Birmingham factory and the London office of the firm with incidents in the private lives of many of those connected with the firm, from the Duprets down through the Bridges and the Tarvers, to Craigan, the Gates and the Eames. In the central third of the novel we see the development of two similar triangle situations, both of which are of great importance to Mr. Craigan, though he is aware of only one of them. He knows that his girl Lily, whom he wants to marry Jim Dale, is attracted by the "flashy card" Bert Jones, and that his whole future happiness depends on the outcome of this situation; he does not know that he is pensioned off partly because Richard Dupret has lost the girl he is in love with (Hannah Glossop) to another flashy card, Tim Tyler, who quickly tires of her (just as Bert Jones is to desert Lily). The "repetition with variation" in the unemphasized parallelism between these two affairs is an important means of giving shape and unity to the novel.

Living, in fact, is a very satisfactory compromise between the social documentary and the novel of personal relations. Its structure and method are designed to illustrate—and they are unusually successful in illustrating—the inter-penetration of working lives and private lives and the inter-relationships between widely disparate social groups.

3

Plot in *Party Going* is of less importance than in *Living*. It is
scarcely an exaggeration to say that nothing happens at all.
The party of wealthy young socialites gathers at a London
railway-terminus on a foggy afternoon. They adjourn to the
station hotel where they establish themselves in slightly frowsy
comfort; eventually after a few hours' delay the fog lifts
sufficiently for the trains to start running again. When the
books ends they are about to depart—the party now one
female and one male larger than originally planned.

Party Going is unusual (though certainly not unique) in its
strict observance of unity of time. What A. A. Mendilow calls
"the chronological duration of the reading" ("the length of
time as judged by the clock which the reader takes to read a
novel") is approximately equal to (and, if anything, a little
longer than) what he calls "the pseudo-chronological duration
of the theme of the novel"[3] (that is, the time involved in the
action—or, in this case, inaction—of the novel). Mendilow
remarks that "where very brief periods of fictional time are
covered, it must be remembered that this short reckoning is
made on one of the time-planes involved only, for the whole
life of the protagonists is brought into that period by the use of
various devices such as the flash-back, the stream of consciousness and the time shift".[4] In *Party Going*, however, these devices
are not much used. There is nothing that can be described as
a flash-back or a time shift. There is one parenthetic passage
summarizing the *cause célèbre* of Embassy Richard; there are a
couple of pages of commentary on the way of life of people like
Max and Amabel. But no episode prior to this single foggy
afternoon is "dramatized" (i.e. treated as a fictive present).
From the moment when Miss Fellowes stops to pick up her
dead pigeon, until the moment when Embassy Richard agrees
to join the party ("I can go where I was going afterwards", he
said to all of them and smiled) we are constantly (except for
occasional brief deviations to the servants) with one or more of
these bright young things, listening to them talk, and watching
their wheels go round. But although there are several interior
monologues, the characters' minds are usually more occupied
with thoughts about the present situation and the behaviour
of the others than with memories of the past. Most of the

information we do get about their past is given by the dramatic method, through conversation. Almost every moment seems to be accounted for; everything they do, every word they utter, every thought and feeling they have seems to have been recorded. This, of course, is not really so; Green has not really abandoned selection. But he does appear to give a transcript of the process of living, in a restricted period of time, as recorded by some super-sensitive apparatus.

The first four of the nineteen (unnumbered) chapters, in which we accompany in turn the various members of the group—on foot, in taxis or in private cars—to the station, are again reminiscent of film technique. But much of the book, particularly after the party has taken possession of half the hotel, is more analogous to ballet. The characters are constantly forming groups and tableaux, going through their paces, breaking up and recombining in different sets. David Garnett made the pertinent observation that the novel's "construction reminds . . . of that of a ballet such as *Les Sylphides*. The subsidiary figures are grouped elegantly in the wings while two of the leading female dancers each does her solo, or they do a *pas de deux* together, until they are quite out of breath. Not till halfway through does the leading star, Amabel, appear, dazzling us by a technique and a beauty far exceeding all that has gone before."[5]

The novel, although so lacking in plot in the traditional sense, has several elements which bind it together on the narrative level. The most important of these is the fierce subterranean competition between the ostensible friends Julia and Amabel for possession of the leading man, Max Adey—with the reserve Angela Crevy, waiting hungrily on the sideline for her chance to join the fray. Another is Embassy Richard who appears in person only in the last two pages, but who is argued and speculated about throughout the whole novel—"Did he send the notice to the papers, himself? If not, who did and why?" Another is the peculiar behaviour and mysterious illness of Miss Fellowes, which is also a fruitful topic of conversation and speculation. This was the first of those queer and inexplicable happenings that were to become part of the usual pattern of Green's books—the intrusions of the abnormal on the normal. Here this element is not quite so skilfully integrated into the structure of the book, as it was to be in *Caught* and *Loving*. It seems too arbitrary; but it does, at least, show Green's talent for strange juxtapositions of people, situations and emotions, his ability to create an effect of livingness through incongruities.

4

Austen Warren has discussed an important distinction made by the Russian formalists between the "fable" (the temporal-causal sequence which, however it may be told, is the "story" or story-stuff) and the "sujet" (or the narrative structure). "The 'fable' is the sum of all the motifs, while the 'sujet' is the artistic-ally ordered presentation of the motifs. . . . 'Sujet' is plot as mediated through 'point of view', 'focus of narration'. 'Fable' is, so to speak, an abstraction from the 'raw materials' of fiction (the author's experience, reading, etc.); the 'sujet' is an abstraction from the 'fable'; or better, a sharper focusing of narrative vision."[6]

In *Living* the "sujet" differs little from the "fable"; after the first few chapters, which give a general impression of the characters and setting, there is a clearly defined story, treated in straightforward chronological sequence. *Party Going* is virtually all "sujet"; it can hardly be said to have a "fable", since the sequence of its groupings and re-groupings is not temporal-causal, but "temporal-casual". *Caught* would probably have appealed much more to such formalists as Shklovsky who laid great stress on *ostranenie* (estrangement), the deliberate effort at strange and difficult form, "in order to increase the difficulty of receptivity and its duration".[7] *Caught* is, in narrative structure, by far the most complex of all Green's novels, the only one in which there is any important temporal displace-ment, backward and forward movement in time or shift in point of view. Giorgio Melchiori has remarked that Green in almost ever chapter "devises new ways of linking and alternat-ing and non-parallel actions. . . . The sense of the present is so bound up with past and future that the temporal sequence is abolished."[8]

The book's "fable" concerns a well-to-do widower, Richard Roe, who, a year before the outbreak of World War II, joins the Auxiliary Fire Service and trains every Tuesday night until the service is mobilized a few days before the declaration of war. The sub-officer commanding the station to which he is posted is his former instructor, a recently promoted fireman, Albert Pye, whose unbalanced sister some months before had briefly abducted Roe's five-year-old son. Against the background of petty intrigues in the station we are shown the various stages in, and the causes of, the disintegration of Pye culminating in his suicide, and in the reintegration of Roe. The book ends with an account of the first fires of the blitz, some months after Pye's death. Even though much of the novel is concerned with a period of waiting, boredom and nervous strain far more protracted than in *Party Going*, it does not drag, because the inner drama of both Pye and Roe is of absorbing interest; Green ensures that their inner lives remain in the forefront of the reader's attention by constant re-arrangement of the temporal-causal sequence (which results occasionally in confusion between historical time—as indicated by developments in the war—and the "private life" time of the characters). A synopsis of the various chapters of the novel is necessary to bring out the difference between the "fable" and the "sujet", the number of time-planes on which the novel proceeds, the surreptitious and distributed exposition through the characters' streams of consciousness and through omniscient retrospective (and anticipatory) flashes, and the confusion between the different orders of time.

The novel is divided into fifteen (unnumbered) chapters. *Chapter 1* begins with a brief summary of war-time conditions as they affect Roe (two days on duty, one day off; no public holidays; trains too slow to permit him to visit his son, Christopher, in the country) during the first three months of the war (September–November 1939). The bulk of the chapter describes Roe's first two-day leave with Christopher, "after three months of war and no raids"—presumably in mid-December 1939. This sad, wet, wintry day establishes the emotional tone of the novel.

Chapter 2 ostensibly covers only the few hours of Roe's return train-journey to London after his first leave. But through his memories much of his life is brought in. His recollections include a visit to Tewkesbury Abbey when he was sixteen, presumably about 1920 (Roe's age is never given, but one can certainly assume that he is, as Green was when writing *Caught*, in his mid-thirties) and the early days of his training as a fireman (in late 1938). But much of the chapter is taken up with his

imaginative reconstruction of Christopher's abduction from
the toy-shop by Pye's sister (elaborated and corrected in
omniscient parenthetic narrative), and the rest by his recollections of the differences in tone of Pye's instructional lectures to
the group of which he was a member, before and after the
abduction.

Chapter 3 gives an account of Roe's second forty-eight-
hour leave, "seven weeks after he had first been home", on
Christopher's birthday—presumably in late January 1940.
There is also a brief flash-forward to "the height of the first
blitz"—in August 1940.

Chapter 4 begins with a brief summary of the fluctuations in
Roe's feelings, mainly about Christopher, from his first joining
the service (September 1938) until the blitz (August 1940).
Most of the chapter concerns Roe's five-day leave soon after
the previous one ("he was to be back in a day or two")—
perhaps in early February 1940. ("The weather was so cold.")
Roe's return to the house where he had been brought up stirs
memories of his own childhood, of his dead wife and of
Christopher's abduction.

In these four chapters, then, despite a few passages of
retrospective summary and a number of glimpses into Roe's
past life through his memories, we have advanced in time about
two months, from early December 1939 to early February
1940. We have come to assume that December 1939 is the
point of reference, from which (as Mendilow puts it) "the
fictive present may be considered as beginning". Dr. Mendilow,
the first critic to attempt a thorough and methodical treatment
of the problem of time in the novel, comments that in most
novels "the reader translates all that happens from this moment
of time onwards into an imaginative present of his own and
yields to the illusion that he is himself participating in the
action or situation, or at least is witnessing it as happening, not
merely as having happened. Everything that antedates that
point . . . is felt as a fictive past, while all that succeeds it,
as for instance . . . anticipatory hints . . . are [*sic*] felt as future.
Verbally all may be equally past; psychologically, once the
point of reference has been established, each event presented
in its time-order constitutes a point in the past series considered as a now, and whatever is out of sequence in relation
to that series of points is considered as relatively past or

future."[9] In each of Henry Green's other novels the opening chapter does establish such a point of references. But in *Caught* we find that this is not the case; in Chapter 5 we are taken back to an earlier point in time, which is treated, and felt by the reader, not as a fictive past, but as another fictive present; it is many chapters before we again reach the point in time at which the novel opened.

Chapter 5 begins with Roe talking to Piper (who has accidentally heard of Christopher's abduction) on "the evening of the second day in the sub-station"—September 1, 1939. There is a brief flashback describing the mobilization on the previous day, but most of this chapter proceeds in straightforward chronological sequence. Pye and Roe have a man-to-man talk; Pye, before he goes to sleep, recalls the first girl he had known nearly thirty years before, and his sister (now in an asylum) creeping home on the same evening, after being "out whoring maybe as he had been". The rest of the chapter (except for another brief flash-forward to "months afterwards, when the blitz began") concerns the first few weeks of the war (though the Auxiliaries are too tired to notice when war is declared). The two girls, Prudence and her Norwegian friend, Ilse, make their first appearance; Roe tells Pye that they want advice about sand-bags.

Chapter 6 is given over entirely to a flashback to "one evening before the war". We glimpse old Piper's "home", and see him in conversation with his friend Mary Howells, the char, making his first suggestion that she should join the A.F.S. as a cook. We also see an encounter between Roe and Hilly, the "short, fat, fair girl" who is also training, as a member of the W.A.F.S.

It is impossible to assign a certain date to this chapter. It takes place either in September 1938 or February 1939. There are conflicting indications. One is a comment that Roe "was not to know what real smoke was like for another eighteen months"; this can only be a reference to the blitz (August 1940), and it would place this chapter in February 1939. The other is the opening sentences of Chapter 7—"It was on a morning twelve months later. Just three weeks after mobilization . . ." This would place Chapter 6 in late September 1938. The former seems more likely; Chapter 7 should probably begin "It was on a morning *six* months later".

Chapter 7, except for another brief "atmospheric" passage

on the war-time relaxation of moral standards, and Roe's sensuously vivid reminiscence of the first visit of his wife to his parents' country place (in July 1930), is concerned entirely with station incidents of "these first weeks of war". Mary Howells, now the third cook, worries about her daughter Brid; Eileen, the cook, and Hilly gossip in the kitchen and are visited by Pye; Roe and Shiner Wright talk about girls.

Chapter 8 is devoted to an account of the farewell party for the Regular Fireman, Wal, attended by all the firemen, Ilse, Prudence and Hilly. No indication is given of the date, but it is probably October.

Chapter 9 is quickly placed in time. "The month was November." Much of it concerns the events of one day; Mrs. Howells' daughter, Brid, turns up, with her baby, having left her soldier-husband; the action has its first (civilian) alarm and the crews disgrace themselves by rushing into the wrong house; Pye is dressed down by District Officer Trant; Mrs. Howells, thoroughly upset by her daughter's troubles, is offered a few days' unofficial leave by Pye, but not understanding, plans confusedly to go to Doncaster to confront her son-in-law without telling anyone; Pye in bed, worries about tomorrow's first visit to the asylum. The following day Pye goes off duty a little early, is "covered" by Chopper when Trant rings up, and at the asylum finds things "simpler, but more horrible than he had dreamed." Next day Mary Howells is missing, Trant turns the station out and finds dirt under Roe's bed.

So far the time-scheme of this chapter is clear enough; we have had the events of three successive days. But then it becomes a little uncertain. We are told: "Richard did not feel the backwash for several days. . . . But Richard bought his way back into favour with free beer, plus extra housework. Before he managed, however, he . . . sought advice from Hilly." Their conversation is reported; their differing opinions about the capabilities of the Regulars provide the occasion for a fairly long (three-page) flash-forward to a night blitz incident "almost twelve months to a day after this conversation" (that is, in November 1940), during which we learn that Pye is dead.

In *Chapter 10* it seems that Green has (temporarily at least) lost control of the time-sequence. The chapter begins "Three weeks later Richard asked Hilly out for a night". These three weeks, together with the "several days" mentioned in Chapter 9, would place the chapter in December (or late November). But during the conversation between Richard and Hilly, it emerges that Mrs. Howells is still missing. Later (in the next chapter) we find that she was away for only four days altogether. In other words, by some magical feat, four days for Mrs. Howells have been equal to four weeks for Richard. This is perhaps no more than an unimportant accidental slip, like the one in Chapter 6. There is no obvious reason for the completely blank three weeks. If the chapter began "Next day", the time-sequence would be straightened out—temporarily at least. This chapter, whatever its exact location in time, is concerned with one day. It cuts back and forth between Richard and Hilly in the evening, first in a restaurant and later in a night-club, Piper talking to Trant as he whitewashes the ceiling in what was to be the Trants' bedroom (in the morning), and Pye talking to one of the firemen (in the afternoon).

Chapter 11 clearly begins in November 1939, on the second day of the three-day sequence in Chapter 9. We accompany Mrs. Howells on her fruitless trip to Doncaster; she returns to the sub-station two days later. Then follows an intricate piece of *montage* in which we cut back and forth between Mrs. Howells pouring out her troubles to old Piper in the sub-station kitchen, Roe and Hilly, on leave, in bed together "for only the second time", Pye with Prudence in the same night-club to which Roe had taken Hilly, Brid in her mother's room crying for her Ted, District Officer Trant talking to the Chief Superintendent, Dodge, about Pye's sub-station, and the Auxiliaries discussing Roe and Pye round a barrel of beer. We move on then to the next evening; Piper talks to Richard about Mrs. Howells in the pub next door, while at home Mrs. Howells finds her daughter even more unbalanced; then Richard angrily discusses the Howells affair with Hilly. This leads naturally ("If he could only have witnessed the appearance Mrs. Howells made before the Superintendent he would not have excited himself.") to the scene of Mrs. Howells' "trial". This can only take place at the end of November; earlier in the chapter Trant has been ordered by Dodge to "have her up before me at the end of the month".

Chapter 12. It is in this chapter that we become aware of something very odd in the time-sequence. The chapter begins

"Soon after Mrs. Howells had been before Mr. Dodge . . .
Trant came down to give Pye a shake up". This must be in
early December. Then, following a paragraph giving Pye's
reactions to his dressing down, we are told that "he was too
disturbed to notice the invasion of Norway"—which did not
begin until *April 9, 1940*. Somehow four months have evapor-
ated, leaving no trace! There follows an account of Pye's
tightening of discipline, and of a deputation to him about
Piper's privileges. Then comes another contradictory indication
of time—"Coming back from his second spell of leave,
Richard . . ." This we have established was in *late January 1940*.
Pye decides to investigate the complaint about Piper's special
treatment, with the result that Eileen gives notice. And "the
news from Norway was worse" (*April again*). Pye is again
summoned to the asylum; but before he can make arrange-
ments to pay this visit he is summoned to appear before Trant.
"It was some days after he had been told off by the D.O. at
the sub-station" (*December again*). "Next day he went down to
the asylum." It is still winter ("He had to remind himself afterwards it was a false spring, just one of those days come much to
early . . ."). It is during this interview that the shocking truth
of his incest forces itself into Pye's mind. From him we cut to
Prudence and Ilse—"it might have been the same day". If it is,
it is a strange day, located in both December 1939, and April
1940. For Ilse "had been complaining. The war with Finland.
The invasion of Norway." The chapter ends with a passage of
summary covering an indeterminate period. "So it came about
that Prudence went off Pye"; and Pye begins to make recognition experiments at night, in an endeavour to reassure himself
that he could not have been so fatally mistaken thirty years
before.

Chapter 13. In this chapter the time-sequence straightens
itself out again. It begins "About this time", and it becomes
apparent that the private time of the characters has now
synchronized with historical time. Richard's sister-in-law brings
Christopher to look over the sub-station, and they accidentally
encounter Pye. The same day Pye rings Prudence and gets his
marching orders; immediately afterwards he reprimands Hilly
for not drawing a double line in her log book after the entry
on the last day of the month. This should be April 1940, for a
little later (after a summary of the spread and expansion of

the abduction story from Piper's hints, and of the men's changed attitude towards Roe) we are told that "the invasion of the Low Countries had begun" (May 11, 1940). The men's attitude towards Piper hardens until another deputation goes to Pye "about the time of Weygand's stand" (the end of May or early June). The same night Pye and Roe again talk in the pub about Pye's sister; Richard is alarmed by Pye's assertion that he is only thirty-five years old.

Chapter 14 continues on the same evening. Pye truants in the warm, vast, moonlit night. He is unlucky again; Trant rings him and finding him absent, comes round to turn the station out. It is then that we learn that "the evacuation of Dunkirk was on" (May 30 to June 4). Next morning Trant 'phones to tell him that he is to be charged.

Chapter 15 jumps forward in time to "some months later, after nine weeks of air raids on London"; this should be late October 1940, though it appears to be later, as "the ground was under snow". Roe, having been knocked out in a raid, is sent home to recuperate. The whole long chapter consists of a conversation between Roe and his sister-in-law, in which Roe describes at length the first night of the blitz; during the conversation we learn of Pye's suicide in the gas oven two months before the blitz (in June).

The novel, it can be seen, falls into three distinct blocks, each beginning at a different point in time. The first part (Chapters 1 to 4) covers, with some backward glances, the months of December 1939 and January 1940, concentrating, however, on half-a-dozen days scattered throughout this period; the bulk of the book (Chapters 5 to 14) covers, again with retrospective and anticipatory glimpses, a nine-month period from the beginning of the war in September 1939 to the evacuation of Dunkirk, but concentrating almost entirely on events in four of these months (September, November, December, May); the third part (Chapter 15) is retrospectively concerned with the beginning of the blitz (August, 1940).

The book's structure may be described as dialectical. The first part is concerned mainly with Roe's private life away from the sub-station; in these chapters we see his loneliness and self-consciousness, his sense of inadequacy and deprivation and bereavement, made more acute by his uncertain, disappointing relationship with his son, with whom he is unable to communicate. In the second part (three-quarters of the book) the sub-station is the centre, and usually the setting; here, in contrast to the early chapters, we see Roe in his relationships with other people—with Piper and Shiner, more importantly with Hilly, and most importantly in his awkward and difficult relationship with Pye, who, indeed, comes to seem the novel's central character. But, as suggested in an earlier chapter, Pye is no more the book's chief character than is Willie Stark, in Robert Penn Warren's *All the King's Men*, who also dies violently, and whose death is an important stage in the moral education of his less spectacular henchman, the narrator Jack Burden. That *Caught* is essentially Roe's story is proved in the last chapter. Here we have the synthesis—Roe again in his parents' country home with his son and his wife's sister, but now developed, matured, educated by his experience. He is now a human being, not the drained husk of the beginning of the book. As he himself says, describing the first night of the blitz: "After twelve months there we suddenly were, men again, or for the first time." For him, however, it was not "for the first time". He became a man two months before. "No, what I mean is, we were suddenly face to face with it, as I was with Pye two months before when I pulled him out of the gas oven."

Even if this interpretation is correct—that Green wished to show first the isolated Roe, then Roe being forced back into participation in life, and finally Roe shaken but made whole by his experience—the time-scheme of the book is not fully explained. Why begin the novel in December, and then, a few chapters later, begin again in the previous September? No doubt this can be explained partly on factual grounds; it is probably quite true that members of the A.F.S. were not given two-day leaves until three months after the beginning of the war. More important, however, is the "seasonal structure" of the book. It is aesthetically right that these first leaves of Roe's should be in mid-winter. It is as much through carefully chosen descriptive detail—the misty rain, the bare, dripping oaks, the coughing deer, the silence broken only once by a low-flying plane (on the first leave); the dead soiled swans of snow (on the second); the bitter cold, the ice covering roadway, pond and moat (on the third)—as by direct character revelation, that Roe's desolation, his state of frozen death-in-life is conveyed. It is equally right that the book should end as it begins; Jean Howard has a fine comment on the "difficult fires flaring out of the darkness of *Caught*, all dying away to the strange and touching image of Hellebore and snow, Pye's death and his sister's monstrous defloration composed now and settling to winter in Roe's convalescent mind".[10] That Roe knows nothing of Pye's incest, and that the Hellebore is figurative only do not invalidate the comment; it does at least suggest the difference in emotional quality between this winter and the winter in which the book begins.

Similarly it is artistically right that Pye's life (as far as his actual appearances in the novel are concerned) should end in the "deadly moonlight", of summer. Green's evocation of the moonlight ("the milk moon stripped deep gentian cracker paper shadows off his uniform. Then the next building, in a line as acute as its angle to the moon, laid these back on as he went") is one of the most wonderful things in the book, but it is not merely a passage of bravura. It is connected with that other moonlit night so long ago. When Pye "once was full in it, in the radiance, against which, on the other side, were triangular dark sapphire shadows exactly laid by houses", he recalls (and the reader recalls) "that winding lane between high banks, in moonlight, in colour blue, leaning back against the pale wild flowers whose names he had forgotten her face, wildly cool to his touch, turned away from him and the underside of her jaw which went soft into her throat that was a colour of junket" of thirty years (and 120 pages) before. It was then that Pye made his first terrible mistake; it is right that it should prove fatal on an identical night.

There still remains, however, the peculiar double chronology of Chapter 12 to be explained. It seems unlikely that Green was unaware of the anomalies in this chapter. Since he began to write the book in June 1940, about the time of Dunkirk, he could hardly have forgotten that Norway was not invaded until April and the Low Countries not until May 1940. So one assumes that what he did in this chapter was deliberate. But what was its purpose? This question also can be answered in terms of the seasonal structure of the book. Green apparently wanted to do two things; he wanted to place the crisis in Pye's life in mid-summer (and to connect it, by implication, with the British retreat), and he wanted it to follow quickly, and without any apparent gap in time, on what had already

happened. Up to this chapter the stages in Pye's ruin have
followed one another in rapid succession; Green obviously felt
that it would have been an artistic mistake to leave the
characters frozen in static immobility while he jumped forward
four months in time. It was indeed a situation which could not
possibly have remained static for four months. So Green, in
this chapter, while placing the events in the characters' lives
in winter, immediately succeeding what has gone before, unobtrusively introduces references to later events in the war to
prepare the reader for the transition to summer and Dunkirk.
It is for the same reason, no doubt, that Pye's second visit to the
asylum is on a day of false spring. Logically the chapter is all
to pieces, but that it succeeds in its purpose is suggested by the
fact that no one (so far as I know) has detected the anomalies
(or, at least, no one has attempted to explain them).

5

There are no problems of this kind in *Loving*. In this romance of
the servants' hall the time-sequence is fairly simple and
straightforward. Some of the events (and particularly some of
the conversations) of seventeen separate days are selected for
presentation in the twenty-one unnumbered chapters. Only
one date is mentioned (May 18th, in the ninth chapter), but
since most chapters begin with an indication of their relationship in time to previous events ("Next afternoon", "It was
some days later") it is easy enough to deduce that the action of
the book occupies about two months—May and June. This is
confirmed, in Chapter 13 (no more than three weeks from the
end of the novel), by a reference to one of the opening incidents
of the novel as having happened, "It must be six weeks since",
and by a comment in Chapter 17 that "the evenings were fast
lengthening". (The same paragraph contains a back-reference
to an incident in Chapter 7 as having happened on "the first
day of spring", which does not seem to be reconcilable with
other time indications.)

Most of the chapters consist of a series of four or five dialogues.
It is as though every room in the castle has a concealed micro-
phone and Green switches them on in irregular rotation,
allowing us to eavesdrop. Usually a single day is treated in a
single chapter: except in very brief summary no chapter deals

with more than one day, but four of the selected days require
two chapters each (4 and 5; 6 and 7; 10 and 11; 20 and 21).
The stream of consciousness method is not employed at all,
and there is only one brief flashback in the whole novel—when
talk of Captain Davenport's search for treasure in the bog
reminds Edith of Mrs. Jack's last visit to Clancarty, on a wet
afternoon, from which she returned "without her drawers".
So, even more completely than in *Party Going*, what we get to
know about the past lives of the characters (and it is very little
indeed) is conveyed through their talks; and we are never quite
sure that such information is to be relied on. We pick up such
snippets as that Charley Raunce has not been outside the castle
for several months (he says since Christmas; Kate says three
years—but we learn that she has been in Kinalty only sixteen
months), that Mr. Jack has made passes at both Kate and Edith,
that Mrs. Tennant is constantly losing track of her possessions,
that Eldon, the late butler, had been blackmailing Captain
Davenport. But we remain, almost exclusively, within the time-
limits of these two months of late spring and early summer.
Even more completely we remain within the space-limits of
Kinalty Castle and its grounds. The Tennant ladies cross over
to England, but we do not accompany them; our furthest
excursions are with them on their daily walks to the artificial
ruin, and with the younger servants and the children to the
beach for a picnic. The book is, indeed, as Rosamond Lehmann
remarks, "a trifle claustrophobic".[11]

The core of the novel is the development of the love-affair
between the somewhat grotesque Raunce, the forty-year-old
"butler", and the beautiful under-housemaid, Edith, who is
young enough to be his daughter, but who, nevertheless, "could
open the veins of her right arm for that man". It is this faithful
love of "an immoral hobbledehoy for a wayward chit"[12] (as an
American reviewer called them) which gives shape and point
to a series of inconsequential episodes and banal conversations.
For between the death of the butler, Eldon, followed by the
partial promotion of Raunce to succeed him (which begins the
book), and the elopement, without a word to anyone, of Raunce
and Edith (which ends it) only half a dozen quite trivial things
happen. Edith steals some "peacock's" eggs from their Irish
guardian, Paddy, and from Mrs. Welch ("Don't call her cook;
she doesn't like it") steals a quart of waterglass in which to

preserve them, as a beauty preparation and love-charm; both
thefts are discovered and have repercussions. The cook's eight-
year-old nephew, Albert, on the first day of his visit, strangles
a peacock which is rash enough to peck at him; the corpse gets
no rest—buried by Mrs. Welch, it is rooted out by Mrs. Jack's
greyhound, Badger (Does Green intend an allusion to "The
Burial of the Dead" section of *The Waste Land*?

> That corpse you planted last year in your garden,
> Has it begun to sprout? Will it bloom this year?
> Or has the sudden frost disturbed its bed?
> Oh keep the Dog far hence, that's friend to men
> Or with his nails he'll dig it up again!"[13])

is hung by Raunce in the outside larder, and stuffed by Mrs.
Welch in Albert's boiler. Mrs. Tennant mislays her sapphire
cluster ring; after she has gone to England Edith finds it and
plants it in a chair in the Red Library; she and Charley
consider keeping it, but decide against it as too risky; unfortunately she tells Miss Moira where it is, and through Moira Mrs.
Welch's Albert gets hold of it; just at the moment when the
insurance investigator is questioning the servants about the
ring and Raunce's Albert is making his unpremeditated "confession", the other Albert is hiding it under half an empty eggshell and swearing the two girls to secrecy; it requires great
diplomacy on Edith's part to get it back again. On the morning
of May 19th, Edith surprises Mrs. Jack in bed with her lover,
Captain Davenport. Henry Reed exaggerates a little when he
maintains: "It is round this bedroom scene that the book, at
once comic and pathetic, revolves. In despondency and amaze-
ment, the scene is spoken of, retold, doubted, asserted, imagined, and talked, talked, talked about. It is the point on which
are centred all the emotions of Edith and of the others who are
loving her."[14] This *is* one of the chief catalytic incidents; it does
speed up the romance between Raunce and Edith. But at least
as important is the enigmatic earlier incident of the mouse
caught by the leg in the gear-wheels of the wind-vane. The sight
causes Edith to faint slap into Raunce's arms; the incident is
vital to Raunce's first awareness of Edith. Moreover, after the
first shock of Mrs. Jack's adultery has passed, the bedroom
scene is absorbed into the texture of the servants' lives and soon
is less spoken of than other things that have happened (especially

the disappearance of the ring) and others that, so the servants fear or pretend to fear, may happen (especially the destruction of the castle by the I.R.A., or the invasion of Ireland by the Jerries). For them almost everything that happens or might happen is equally important.

Just as Pye's accidental incest recalls certain similar fatal situations in classical myth and mediaeval romance (for example, King Arthur's unwitting incest with his sister, Margawse, the fruit of which was Mordred, who eventually gave the king his death-blow), so do several incidents and situations in *Loving*—Edith's "love potion", the mystery of the lost ring, with their attendant false suspicions; and indeed the whole entranced atmosphere of this incredible castle—remind one of legend, fairy-tale and (Irving Howe remarks[15]) Shakespeare's comedies. But it seems unlikely that Green, in either of these novels, was deliberately attempting a detailed parallel with any single myth, legend, romance or fairy-tale (as Joyce used the parallel to the *Odyssey* in *Ulysses*) as a means of organizing his observations and interpretation of contemporary life. He is content with "overtones from some lonely world unknown",[16] with hinted parallels, which, oblique, fragmentary and shadowy as they are, have the effect of enlarging his commonplace, contemporary characters by connecting them with a past at once more romantic, glamorous and magical and more heroic, terrible and horrifying.

6

The same is true of *Back*. It has previously been remarked that *Back* is a modern *Romance of the Rose*, but this is intended to suggest only a basic similarity in theme to the mediaeval romance, not a parallel in details. Like the romance, Green's novel is concerned with the quest of a Lover (Charley Summers) for his ideal love, symbolized not as a Rosebud, but as the woman Rose. But *Back* is no simple allegory in which the Lover is assisted by such personified abstractions as Pity and Frankness (though Pity, to be sure, does prove a powerful ally to Charley Summers), and thwarted by Danger, Shame, Scandal, Jealousy and Fear; Charley's enemies are more subtle and insidious, and more difficult to overcome—delusion, obsession and self-pity. For, before the war, he has found his Rose;

now that he is back from a prisoner-of-war camp, knowing that she has died during his imprisonment, he meets her half-sister, who closely resembles Rose, and is convinced that she is Rose herself. He cannot regain love until he can conquer this delusion. Actually it is possible to find closer parallels than that with *The Romance of the Rose*. There is, for example, a curious similarity between the dilemma of Charley Summers and that of the legendary hero, Tristan—with the obvious difference that Charley's dilemma arises, not from two women of the same name, but different appearance; but from two women of similar appearance, but different names. Margaret Reid summarizes this episode in the Tristan story (from Ulrich von Türheim and Heinrich von Freiburg): "Tristan, who had gone to help the Duke of Arundel in war, met his son Kahedin and his daughter Iseult of the White Hands. Her name and her beauty called up old memories and he was strangely torn between two desires." She quotes from Jessie L. Weston's *Gottfried von Strassburg* (Vol. ii, p. 144), the following passage, which is startlingly close to a description of Charley's state of mind. "And he said in his heart 'Yea God how the name doth lead me astray! truth and falsehood betray alike mine eyes and my soul. "Iseult" rings laughing in mine ear at all times, yet know I not who Iseult may be—mine eyes behold her and yet they see her not. Iseult is far from me and yet she is near. . . . I have found Iseult yet not the fair-haired Iseult who was so cruelly kind. The Iseult who vexeth thus my heart is she of Arundel, not Iseult the fair: she alas! mine eyes behold not. And yet she whom I now behold, and who is sealed with her name, her I must ever honour and love, for the sake of the dear name, that so oft' hath given me joy and gladness unspeakable.' " And Margaret Reid adds, almost prophetically, "This is a complicated situation even for the modern psychologist and novelist."[17] Green, of course, makes the situation even more complicated by having his "Tristan" mistake the second "Iseult" for the first. But though mistaken identity is a time-honoured comic device, *Back* is no comedy, despite its happy ending. It is, as C. J. Rolo puts it, "a new rendering, immensely of our time, of the old fable of love's victory over an evil spell".[18]

Philip Toynbee, after briefly describing the "plots" of *Caught*, *Loving* and *Back*, remarks "From these descriptions it might be supposed that *Caught* was the most conventional of the three books, since its plot, though unusual, is at least describable in other than the book's own terms".[19] Actually the comment seems to apply much more to *Back* than to *Caught* with its intricate interweaving of two stories, its complicated flashbacks (and flash-forwards), its elaborate *montage* effects. *Back* is much more conventionally constructed around a single central character, who is always present (except for one brief scene between Nancy Whitmore and Arthur Middlewitch, in which he is the sole subject of discussion). The sequence of events is straightforwardly chronological (except for a few apparently accidental and careless slips), though through Charley's memories, and through the conversations, the importance of the past in shaping the present is made plain. But the action (essentially inner action, of course) is fairly easily summarizable through Charley's first partial reintegration with life, based on acceptance of the fact that Rose is dead, which is shattered by the apparent rediscovery of her alive and deceiving him, and the gradually dawning realization that this is not really Rose but Nancy, and that it is, after all, possible (and necessary) to live without Rose. The most unusual structural feature of the novel is Green's introduction, exactly in the middle, of a "short story", which not only purports to be, but in fact is, a translation of an eighteenth-century French memoir and which, with a reversal of sex (so that it is a woman who falls in love with the half-brother and double of her dead lover) elaborately parallels Charley Summers' situation. This parallel, like the legendary overtones, has the effect of universalizing the novel's central situation, of making it seem, not something merely bizarre and unlikely, but an archetype of human experience. It is used, like Eliot's evocations of the past, as a means of suggesting at once contrast and continuity with the past; as Melchiori remarks, "the central evasion into a pre-romantic setting contrasts with, and at the same time enhances, the shabbiness of the contemporary world in which the main action is set".[20]

Back is the only one of Green's novels in which both the beginning and ending are exactly dated. There can be no doubt that its action covers the last half of 1944. But between Charley's visit to the rose-overgrown cemetery to look for the grave of his dead love (on June 13) and his "trial trip" with Nance, in old Mandrew's house (on Christmas Day), there is, as already mentioned, some uncertainty and confusion in the time-sequence. In the third of the twenty-seven unnumbered chapters Charley runs across "a man by the name of Middlewitch whom he had met, in July, at the centre where he had been to have his new leg fitted". The wording indicates that July is past, that it is now at least August. But there is a conflict with Chapter 1; there a telegram is quoted, instructing Charley to report to Officers' Rehabilitation Centre for his new leg, on June 12. He is already a day late, but it seems unlikely that even Charley would wait until July. So it can probably be assumed that the quoted sentence should read ". . . whom he had met in June . . .", and that this second meeting with Middlewitch takes place in July. This seems to be confirmed in Chapter 4 (subsequent to Chapter 3, since the meeting with Middlewitch is referred to); in this chapter Charley talks to his landlady Mrs. Frazier (or, more accurately, does not listen to her talking). Mrs. Frazier mentions "the new bombs he's sending over". The flying bombs began on June 12. One would think they would have been more likely to be described as "new bombs" in July than in August. (By July 6, 2,754 had already been launched and 2,752 people killed; by August 2, 5,735 had been launched and 4,735 people killed.[21]) So it seems safe enough to assign these two chapters to the beginning of July.

In Chapter 5 there is a more misleading indication of time. This chapter, which introduces Charley's new assistant, Dot Pitter, covers an indeterminate period of time, during which Charley begins to be erotically obsessed by Dot, while she is gradually enslaved by his complex card-index system. The process seems to occupy only a few weeks, and we are rather startled when a crisis in the office occurs, because an order received "September the 10th" has not been recorded in the card-index. But we accept the date as accurate; there are sufficiently clear indications that the next nine chapters occupy about two weeks, so we assume, in Chapter 15, that we are now in late September. At this point, however, the time-structure of the novel collapses like a house of cards, for Charley receives a letter from James Phillips, asking him down "over the August holiday". So we are presumably back in late July, and can only assume that the date specified in Chapter 5 was a careless mistake; apparently it should have been, not September 10, but July 10.

Perhaps even to notice these slips is to condemn oneself of an incurable literal-mindedness. It is not suggested that they seriously damage the novel. But they are irritating. One feels that, if Sterne in *Tristram Shandy*, Emily Brontë in *Wuthering Heights*, and Faulkner in *The Sound and the Fury* could handle their infinitely more complicated time-sequences with complete certainty, Green should have been able to handle a straight-forward six-month period without these annoying confusions. It is not suggested either that a novelist may not legitimately tinker with chronology; but here, unlike in *Caught*, there seems to be no purpose whatever. Green seems merely to have tossed in a date at random and not to have realised that it conflicted with every other time-indication in the novel. That Dos Passos (in *U.S.A.*) and O'Neill (in *The Great God Brown*) have done worse things (as anyone who tries to keep track of the ages of J. Ward Moorhouse and Dion Anthony discovers) is not sufficient excuse.

From this point on, the time indications are clear and certain. Chapters 16, 17 and 18 are in August; 19 and 20 in September; 21 to 24 in October; 25 in October and November; 26 and 27 on Christmas Day.

Coincidence is employed by Green even more lavishly in *Back* than in *Caught*. The whole plot, of course, is based on the accidental likeness between two half-sisters born a few weeks apart, and on the verbal coincidence that the name of the flower, rose, is also a woman's name, a colour adjective, and the past tense of a common verb. As James Hilton remarks, "the whole story is a half-nightmarish play on the word 'rose' ".[22] As well as this, there is a whole series of apparently less central coincidences, involving the father of Rose and Nancy, Gerald Grant, Charley's landlady, Mrs. Frazier and, especially, his fellow-amputee, Arthur Middlewitch. Wherever Charley turns he finds Middlewitch. He accidentally encounters him first at the Officers' Rehabilitation Centre where they have their artificial limbs fitted. Soon after their first lunch together Charley discovers, in conversation with Mrs. Frazier, that Middlewitch had previously been the tenant of her bed-sitting-room, and that he had been recommended to her, as Charley himself had been, by Mr. Grant. Charley had not known that these two were acquainted, and the discovery makes him deeply suspicious—he does not know of what. When he first visits Nance he discovers that Middlewitch lives "across the landing";

Middlewitch is actually quite unaware of any connection between Nance and Mr. Grant, but Charley cannot believe this. He is convinced that they are all involved in some sinister and deplorable plot—that Rose has dyed her hair, gone on the streets, and that both Middlewitch and her father are sharing in her immoral earnings.

Green uses these coincidences with complete deliberation. So far from trying to disguise them, he underlines them in Charley's talk with Mrs. Frazier. (" 'What is there strange in that?' Mrs. Frazier enquired, irritable still. 'Once you start on coincidences why there's no end to those things.' ") They do not have the same effect as the coincidences in, say, *Jane Eyre* or *Oliver Twist* where the reader experiences only disbelief, while the characters either accept them as quite natural or express naïve wonderment that such things should happen. Here where the coincidences are admitted and stressed the situation is reversed; the reader accepts the coincidences as possible, while Charley, who, in the prisoner-of-war camp, has come to mistrust everything, invents, from a series of quite innocent and unconnected circumstances, what V. S. Pritchett aptly calls "a frightening, pathetic, imbroglio".[23] There seems less point, however, in the revelation that "old Ernie Mandrew", with whom Middlewitch professes to be so pally, is a bookie for whom Nance's airman-husband, Phil White (who "got his at Alamein") used to work in peace-time. But even this has a point. When Nance asks Charley to stay with her over Christmas at Mandrew's (it is a further coincidence that she uses "almost exactly the same words he had used to Dot Pitter on a previous occasion"), he again suspects a trap of some kind. But it is a sign of his regained normalcy that, feeling sick though he does, he accepts her explanation of how she comes to know Mandrew and agrees to go. These coincidences are best regarded as a series of tests, important not as elements of a complex plot, but for Charley's response to them.

7

There is little to be said about the narrative structure of *Concluding*, for the organization of this book is lyrical or musical, rather than dramatic or narrative. Among Green's novels it comes nearest to *Party Going* in achieving unity of time (a single summer day sometime in the future) and nearest to *Loving* in achieving unity of place (an English mansion and its grounds, converted into a training-school for girl civil-servants). The novel is given a roundness and shape, a simple natural rhythm by the slow passage of this long day from the fog-shrouded early morning, through the noonday heat to the sun's late setting and the strange, bewildering moonlight of the late evening. But to many readers it is more exasperating in its in-conclusiveness and mystification, its complete abolition of plot, than any of Green's other novels. For here not only are we left in doubt about what is to be the outcome of the antagonism between Mr. Rock and the school-principals, but we are even left in doubt about what has already happened. The mystery of the missing schoolgirls (which has the same kind of structural importance as Miss Fellowes' dead pigeon and undiagnosed illness in *Party Going*; the abduction of Christopher in *Caught*; the discovery of Violet in bed with her lover and the missing ring in *Loving*) is still unsolved. We do not know why or how Mary and Merode have vanished, whether they went together or separately, why Merode has been found and Mary has not, whether Mary is alive or dead. Nigel Dennis's comment that Green is "like a detective story writer . . . except that he does not provide a full explanation of his mysteries in the last chapter"[24] is most obviously true of *Concluding*.

Concluding is unlike any of Green's previous novels, except *Blindness*, in being divided into three distinct parts. These, unlike the parts in the earlier novel, are not named or even numbered; there is merely a blank page at the end of each, like the curtain at the end of an act of a play, to indicate a lapse of time. Part I is concerned with the events of the morning from (so it seems) about six-thirty to lunch time; Part II with the late afternoon from tea at five until the beginning of the Founder's Day dance; Part III with the evening and the dance. Each part is further divided into chapters (seventeen, twelve and ten re-spectively); most of these are single scenes involving two or three people, but in a few (notably the first chapter of the central part) Green chooses a single point in time and cuts from one character, or group of characters, to another. *Concluding* is quite different from *Back* in that there is no single character who is continually present (as Charley Summers is, except for one brief scene); Mr. Rock is so much the most memorable of the characters that it is a surprise to discover, on investigation, that he actually appears in only seventeen of the thirty-nine chapters (in only six of the seventeen in Part I, and in only four of the twelve in Part II); his chief antagonist, Miss Edge, appears in the same number (and her fellow-principal, Miss Baker, in eleven); his grand-daughter, Liz, and her lover, Sebastian Birt, in fifteen each (usually, but not always, together). There are five chapters in which none of these leading characters appears. As these figures suggest, *Concluding* is a *Lear* rather than a *Hamlet*; the conflict is not primarily internal, but one between implacable enemies, which, although it never flares into open, malevolent hostility and is left unresolved, is coldly remorseless. The parallel with *Lear* is not as remote as it might first appear; although Baker and Edge are not Mr. Rock's daughters, they belong to a younger, dehumanized generation which regards him and all he stands for with suspicion and enmity. Certainly if *Concluding* is to be compared with any drama, it must be with poetic drama, for its controlling ideas are expressed at least as much through its poetic logic, its images, as through its episodes (its narrative logic). This is better left for consideration in the next chapter.

8

It has previously been suggested that if Green's two latest novels, *Nothing* and *Doting*, are to be compared with any form of drama, it is not with Shakespearean tragedy, but with the comedy of manners of Etherege and Congreve. More than any of Green's previous books—even more than *Loving*—these two are, in conformity with Green's new theory of the novel, conversation-pieces. Even so the comparison cannot be pushed too far, because, whereas the dialogue of Etherege and Congreve is remarkable for its sustained vivacity, wit and epigrammatic sparkle, the dialogue of *Nothing* and *Doting* is generally banal in the extreme—full of clichés and conventional gush. It is quite lacking in the verbal brilliance, the hypnotizing snake's eye glitter of Ivy Compton-Burnett. It is difficult to agree entirely with Melchiori that the dialogues "acquire a rarefied brilliance through their very realism".[25] What *is* brilliant is the ironical contrast between the plight of these characters, the last anachronistic, moribund vestige of the privileged classes, and their bland ignoring of their situation, and the building up of these dialogues, each futile and inconclusive in itself, into a shapely structure. Such beauty as the books possess results from the delicate precision of the architecture, not the rarity of the building materials.

The action of both books is worked out with an almost mathematical exactitude. There are, in *Nothing*, four central characters, symmetrically grouped—the widow, Jane Weatherby, and her son Philip, who celebrates his twenty-first birthday in the course of the novel, the widower, John Pomfret, and his daughter, Mary, who is a little younger than Philip. Years before (in the twenties) Pomfret and Mrs. Weatherby have had a violent affair, but at the beginning of the novel Pomfret has another mistress, Liz Jennings, who belongs to the intermediate generation, while Mrs. Weatherby has a devoted admirer in Dick Abbott.

The novel, like *Concluding*, is divided into three "acts". (It is not, like *Concluding*, "set in the future",[26] as Melchiori asserts; it opens with the words "On a Sunday afternoon in nineteen forty-eight . . .".) In the eleven chapters of the first part we have a series of thirteen dialogues (two of the chapters have two each, one immediately following the other) between various pairs of characters on seven separate days scattered over an indeterminate period. (A check of introductory time-notations, combined with back references to previous events suggests that it is only three or four weeks, but Liz, in Chapter 6, refers to an incident in the opening chapter as having happened "about nine weeks ago"; one wonders again whether Green considers that consistency in these mundane details would be fatally damaging.) In this part, mingled with other matters, including the emotional effects on Philip's six-year-old sister Penelope of her "mock-marriage" with John Pomfret, and talk about poor Arthur Morris's misfortune, we are shown the contrasting attitudes and ways of life of the two generations; the attraction (very different from that between their parents twenty years before) between Philip and Mary, and their—particularly Philip's—concern that they may be half-brother and sister; and the prejudice of each parent against the other's offspring. Eight of the fifteen chapters of the second "act" are devoted to Philip's pretentious and absurd twenty-firster, which is really his mother's show, attended almost exclusively by her

I

contemporaries, until he steals the thunder by announcing his engagement to Mary. In these chapters the rigid pattern of successive tête-à-têtes is broken down; there is slightly more fluidity and flexibility in the grouping and re-grouping of the characters which is checked, however, by the fact that it is a formal dinner-party, in which the guests are seated at tables for four. None of those present, except the six characters already named, emerges from anonymity for more than a moment at a time. In the subsequent chapters, covering a few more weeks, the tête-à-tête method is again resumed, and it becomes increasingly clear that Mrs. Weatherby will stop at nothing to prevent the marriage and that John Pomfret's support is half-hearted at best.

In the last act, again through a series of (seventeen) conversations *à deux*, we see the concurrent breaking off of the engagement of Philip and Mary, the belated engagement of their parents, and the coming together of their parents' discards, Liz Jennings and Dick Abbott.

The development of the action of the book can, in fact, be almost exactly represented in a series of three diagrams, each corresponding closely to one part.

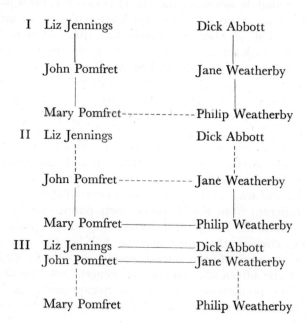

The construction of *Doting* is as rigidly schematized as, but slightly different from, that of *Nothing*. *Nothing* can be envisaged as a stream of conversation flowing into the mild whirlpool of the dinner-party and then out again. In the central section all the characters appear together, and while one set of relationships is apparently being established, the seeds of another, disruptive of the first, are being sown. In *Doting* there are two such party scenes, one at the very beginning, the other at the very end of the book—the first to celebrate the homecoming, the second the imminent return to school of the seventeen-year-old Peter Middleton, who is not, however, one of the major characters. These two scenes are connected by a long series of (no less than forty-six) dialogues, covering in time the couple of months of Peter's vacation, in which almost every possible combination of the five main characters is taken two at a time. The intricate pattern of doting, cross-doting and counter-doting involving these five characters—Peter's parents; their contemporary friend, the widower, Charles Addinsell; and two young girls—can be represented geometrically. Beginning as a triangle, it becomes a parallelogram made up first of two, then of four, triangles, and finally a quadrilateral involving no less than six triangles. It only requires Arthur Middleton to make a pass at Claire Belaine for the figure to be complete.

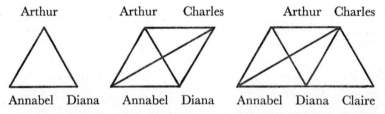

Despite the angular diagrams, it could be argued that this novel, rather than its predecessor, should be called *Nothing* (o). In *Nothing* something does happen, however unimportant it may be, and at the end the relationships between the characters are different from what they were at the beginning. But the movement of *Doting* is almost perfectly circular. At the end we are exactly where we were at the beginning, especially as the two additions to the original party have united and departed. But this is not final. In the book's last sentence we are assured that "the next day they all went on very much the same".

In these two most recent novels Melchiori sees Green aiming, like the Cubists in painting, at "complete abstraction—a pattern of rigid geometrical figures creating abstract emotions through the intellect rather than the heart". He suggests also that in these novels, where Green builds up "a perfect structure, beautiful in its delicate sequence of scenes, held together by a constant rhythm . . . the final impression is similar to that of a Mozart opera: a musical edifice made of elegant nothings, but endowed with a strangely pathetic poignancy", and that an even closer musical equivalent can be found in Schoenberg, whose work reached its final stage in the atonal method, "the affirmation of an abstract classicism based on pure form". The "abolition of common human values", the " 'dishuman' aloofness", the "isolation from reality" [27] in these books are not, I consider (and have previously maintained), as complete as Melchiori contends, but it is undeniable that in them Green's interest in structural precision and technical adroitness outweighs his interest in his subject-matter. Whether this "abstract art" is to be the final stage in Green's development or whether in future novels (if there are to be any) different subject-matter will require a different attitude and method, only the future can tell.

V

Themes and Symbols

The truth is, these times are an absolute gift to the writer. Everything is breaking up. A seed can lodge and sprout in every crack
and fissure.

(Quoted by Rosamond Lehmann, "An Absolute Gift",
Times Literary Supplement, August 6, 1954)

As these birds would go where so where would this child go?

(Epigraph to *Living*)

I

JAMES HALL has recently remarked, a little inaccurately:
"Although Henry Green has been writing for twenty-five
years and has been famous for at least ten, no one writes articles
on him." Hall suggests that this is "a symptom of modern embarrassment in writing about comedy".[1] There have been more
articles about Green's work than the remark suggests, but it is
true that few of them have paid much attention to Green's
claims to be one of the great modern writers of comedy. Green's
ability as a comic writer has also probably been taken too much
for granted in the preceding chapters, but it is doubtful whether
any contemporary novelist has created more scenes and episodes that are hilarious in their credible absurdity than he has.
Living is full of laughable scenes, ranging from the introduction
of the "courtesan" into Mr. Dupret's bedroom in an effort to
reawaken the old man's interest in life, while his son stands
outside in an agony of embarrassment, to Bert Jones' difficulties,
in his elopement with Lily, with the tulips and the lavatory-less
train, and Lily's first meeting with Mrs. Eames after her return
when Lily is shocked because Mrs. Eames is not. *Party Going* is
such an unbroken sequence of funny scenes that it is difficult to
choose examples, but who will forget the unidentifiable little
man with his repertoire of accents, whom Alex mistakes for the
hotel detective, or Amabel having her bath, with Angela
misled into thinking Alex is "helping" (while "actually most
elaborate precautions were taken"), or Angela reducing her
young man to crawling abjectness? In the sombre *Caught* a good
deal of comedy is provided by Piper, Shiner, Chopper and the
other professional and auxiliary firemen—Piper painting the

Trants' bedroom for the tenth time, being told it is still not right
and thinking: "A shade too yellowy, the tight-fisted bastard";
Aggie Howells travelling all the way to Doncaster to give "the
son-in-law" a piece of her mind, and then getting so absorbed in
gossip that she lets him go without a word; and later, at her
"trial", exchanging gossip with Mr. Dodge about the things
child-birth does to women. Almost every page of *Loving* is
funny, from Raunce's assumption of Mr. Eldon's "throne",
through the Nanny's fairy-story to the children and the servants' farcical interview with the lisping insurance investigator
(suspected of being an I.R.A. man) to the long conversation,
full of double meanings and innuendoes, between the two Mrs.
Tennants, in which almost every utterance of the elder lady
makes her daughter-in-law fear that her adultery is known or
suspected. Even *Back* and *Concluding* have their amusing moments—such as when Charley Summers, after nerving himself
to visit Dot Pitter in her bedroom, finds that the bird has flown
to the fat arms of James Phillips, or when he lies awake, in a
tumult of expectation, apprehension, hope and misgiving,
waiting for Nance to come to his improvised and noisy bed, or
when he is advised to marry by Corker Mead, who, at the same
time, is embroiled in a savage telephone quarrel with his wife;
and such as when Mr. Rock, his empty belly rumbling in protest, waits huffily to be invited to breakfast by the cook, or when
he is initiated into the girls' secret society in the basement, or is
proposed to by Miss Edge.

Yet none of Green's books is comedy pure, simple and
unalloyed. David Garnett's reaction to *Party Going*, when that
novel first appeared, must surely be the reaction of many
readers to this and other novels. "As I read the book aloud [a
practice Green deplores, incidentally] we were continually held
up because it was so funny: almost every page sent us into fits
of laughter. Yet an hour afterwards none of us remembered the
book as comic."[2] In many of the scenes and episodes that I
have mentioned there is as much pathos as comedy, and in at
least three of the novels—*Caught, Back* and *Concluding*—the
comic element is of comparatively minor importance. It is as
much a mistake and as much an injustice to Green to regard him
merely as a funny-man, as it is to ignore his great comic gift.

What, then, are Green's novels really about? The answer is
not easy because as a novelist Green is completely undidactic;

he undoubtedly shares Virginia Woolf's view that "when philosophy is not consumed in a novel, when we can underline this phrase with a pencil, and cut out that exhortation with a pair of scissors and paste the whole into a system, it is safe to say that there is something wrong with the philosophy or with the novel or with both".[3] In a previous chapter the scarcity of commentary of any kind—whether moral precepts, ethical judgments, philosophical dicta, or even social or psychological generalizations—in Green's novels has been noted; it is even more difficult to extract from his novels than from those of Virginia Woolf any easily formulable body of belief, any explicit system of values, any precise message. Even in his autobiographical "self-portrait", *Pack My Bag*, where one might expect some statements of belief, there is scarcely a trace of any concern for ideas, religious, philosophical, social or psychological; there is only a nostalgic, elegiac, narcissistic, yet strangely detached recreation of small incidents.

But no novelist can create characters, place them in relationship to one another, and let them live and act and speak, without giving some indication of the things he considers important, and those he considers of no account, the ways of living and the attitudes towards life that he considers desirable and undesirable. "Considers" is probably the wrong word, since it suggests conscious deliberation and reflection, whereas, in fact, no novelist ever really chooses his range or angle of vision. Certainly in Green's case it is far more a question of an emotional, instinctive apprehension of the world and humanity —a question of vision and intuitive response—rather than of intellectual evaluation and rational judgment. It has been suggested in an earlier chapter that, despite Green's refusal to pontificate, despite his conscientious objectivity in the presentation of diverse subject-matter, despite the illusion of self-suppression and withdrawal that his novels deliberately foster, all of his novels are recognizably his own, the products of a highly individual sensibility. His novels, like all novels of any consequence, are not mere records, documents or case-histories; they are a symbolic presentation of an attitude towards experience, a concrete embodiment of a special and highly selective interpretation of life. This selection is based on the bent of his whole temperament, in which the imagination, the senses and the emotions are all at least as important as the intellect. It will be the purpose of this chapter to define some of the chief elements in Green's vision of the world, some of the intuitions and predilections, the conflicts and tensions that his novels embody. This chapter will also attempt to illustrate some of the means which Green, like other modern novelists, has borrowed from poetry—allusion, symbolism, patterns of colour—to support, and sometimes, indeed, to carry, his principal meanings.

One of Green's best critics, Mark Schorer, has maintained that "Green's work from the beginning has been concerned with the theme of dissolution".[4] In a sense this is true, but taken alone and without qualification, the comment is as misleading as Orville Prescott's previously quoted attempt at definition of the "somewhat similar reaction" of Henry Green, Ivy Compton-Burnett and Elizabeth Bowen to the modern world. Green's novels are undoubtedly a more telling representation of an age of decay and disintegration in society and morality (not in religion, because religion simply does not exist in Green's world) than all the tedious naturalistic chronicles which laboriously document every fissure and false note. But Green is not a naturalist, and he is not predominantly a satirist; he is far too interested in the queer individuality of the most common-place people, and has far too much sympathy and respect for them, to reduce them to the passive, will-less automata of the naturalist, or the grotesque stereotypes of the satirist. He has a tender solicitude for his characters in their loneliness and their perplexities; he never sneers at them or condemns them, never under-rates them or over-simplifies them, and he never uses them as pegs on which to hang an argument, or as mouthpieces of attitudes. They are very ordinary people, narrow, limited and often self-deceived; they do not expect much in this life, and they have no conception of any other. But what they do seek— often without knowing what it is they seek—is happiness. Hence it would be far more accurate to say that his novels have from the beginning been concerned with the problem of the attain-ment of happiness in a disintegrating world. Dissolution and chaos and upheaval are always there in the background, but Green's unintellectual and self-centred (yet generally unin-trospective) people are aware of it and concerned by it only as it affects them immediately. They are preoccupied with their own affairs, with the attempt to create for themselves oases of

peace and security and contentment. And surprisi.
their efforts, blind and groping as they are, are succ
C. J. Rolo has remarked; "Green has found a stance .
has enabled him to rescue the 'happy ending' from the sh.
literature."[5] The happiness which his characters somet.
achieve is partial, incomplete and chequered, but at least it ι .
possible and believable condition, a happiness based on a
recognition of life's limitations and inadequacies. The maturity
and responsibility of Green's response to life—his refusal
equally of defeatist despair and sentimentality—is neatly
summed up in the comment with which *Back* concludes: "It
was no more, or less, really, than she had expected."

It would not be a gross over-simplification to say that the
basic theme of Green's work is that of love versus loneliness.
The lonely man—the man for whom the inescapable solitude
of the human condition is accentuated by age or bereavement
or inarticulateness or ugliness or neurosis—is as constantly
recurring a figure in Henry Green's fiction as is the hunted man
in Graham Greene's. Again and again in Green's novels, we see
his people yearning to escape from their solitary confinement,
striving to share their existence with others and to share in the
existence of others, but frustrated, more often than not, by the
extreme difficulty of communication between human beings.
But they are not always frustrated; occasionally two of his
people do make contact and escape out of loneliness into love.
Love is the great positive principle in Henry Green's world, but
it is not an ideal, transcendental emotion or relationship, nor
has it any of Lawrence's biologico-mysticism. It is sensual, but
never merely sensual; it is a liberation of the spirit, a haven
from the grimness and confusion of modern life.

Three comments on Henry Green's vision of life seem to me
especially apt. The first is made by Robert Phelps: "Human
existence consists of being born into a sense of belonging; of
falling into a sense of aloneness that can only rarely be allayed;
and then, if you are lucky, of eluding that knowledge and slip-
ping back into a sense of belonging."[6] The second is by V. S.
Pritchett who defines "the intention of Green's novels" in this
way: "To gather together all the human resources of people of
which their sickness, their pain and their mischievous unconscious must be considered a vitally important part in defense
against the cold orderly brown-house inhumanity of the

modern world."[7] The third is by James Hall: "From his first
novel [Henry Green] has been trying to prove that people who,
by some going standard, ought not to be enjoying life are enjoying it and that other people who ought to be enjoying it are
not. Paradoxes in the conventions of pleasure and pain are his
specialities. . . . He wants . . . to find the unexpected pleasure
amid anxiety, exasperation, pain, moral stasis."[8] The ensuing
discussion of the individual novels will largely be elaboration
and illustration of these comments.

2

Philip Toynbee expressed a commonly held opinion, when he
remarked, of *Living*: "It is at least arguable that in this book
Mr. Green (an old Etonian as well as a capitalist) has written
about the proletariat with more insight than has any contemporary writer of proletarian origin."[9] The quality of Green's
insight ensured that *Living* is not a proletarian novel in the
technical sense. According to Philip Henderson, although
"that which is known as proletarian literature deals, perforce,
largely with the misery and wretchedness of the poor and their
struggle for a better life", and "by its very nature must be a
literature of conflict and bitterness", it is "a mistake to confine
the term 'proletarian' to novels which deal exclusively with
working-class life: it should refer to the key and vision in which
a work is conceived just as much as to its subject". It "begins
with a conception of society as divided against itself in the
struggle of the classes".[10]

Living is certainly not dominated by a dynamic revolutionary
idea; Green was aiming not at any propagandist effect, but at
conveying the "feel" of working-class life. There is very little
suggestion of class struggle; there are no strikes and no revo-
lutionaries and there is very little emphasis on the misery and
wretchedness of the poor. Most of the workers Green presents
seem to be satisfied with, or at least resigned to, their lives. They
do plenty of complaining; they grumble when one man is sus-
pended from work and another is not, after both have been
caught committing the same breach of the rules, more when a
man is posted at the lavatory door to time them in and out,
more when a wire rope breaks and almost decapitates Mr.
Craigan. But they are not stirred into impassioned denunci-

ations of the iniquities of capitalism, and the thought of concerted action never seems to occur to them. Some of them, like
Joe Gates, profess to wish " 'Tis 'Im" (Bridges, the Works
manager) dead, but this arises not from any general political
principle, but from mere personal animosity, which is directed
much more against Bridges' toadying informer, Tupe. A few
younger men, like 'Erbert Tomson (who emigrates to Orstrylia,
where he doesn't do very well) and Bert Jones (who plans to
take Lily to Canada), are vaguely discontented with England
(" . . . this be a poor sodding place for a poor bleeder") but
most regard the idea of emigration with suspicion, trepidation
or derision. For the most part they are content to stay put, take
life as it comes and get quite a lot of fun out of it.

The Dupret factory, which, no doubt, can be taken as
standing for more than itself, is going through a period of un-
settlement and difficulty and curtailed production; the book
reflects the breakdown of the old paternalistic industrial
organization and the substitution of a system less human and
personal. But to say, as Mark Schorer does, that "*Living* is *based*
[italics mine] in the disintegration of industrial relations at about
the time of the General Strike",[11] is to exaggerate the importance of these elements in the pattern of the novel as a whole. It
is, after all, called *Living*, and Green's titles are never random.

One thing that the novel does convey effectively, however,
is the monotony of the workers' lives. Young Dupret, in a fit
of romantic despair, asks himself what is the use of living, but
recognizes (or imagines) how much better his lot is than theirs.

"And what was in all this, he said as he was feeling now, or
in any walk of life—you were born, you went to school, you
worked, you married, you worked harder, you had children,
you went on working, with a good deal of trouble your children
grew up, then they married. What had you before you died?
Grandchildren? The satisfaction of breeding the glorious
Anglo Saxon breed?

". . . But these people, how much worse it was, he at least,
he thought, had money. These people . . . had really only
marriage and growing old. Every day in the year, every year,
if they were lucky they went to work all through daylight. That
is, the men did. Time passed quickly for them, in a rhythm.
But it was the monotony, as one had said to him" (p. 187).

Bert Jones, on one occasion, finds himself unable to work.

"Were days when he could not work, his mind was not in it. It was not that he couldn't concentrate because he was thinking of something else, but rather as if his mind was satiated by the trade he worked at, as if he had reached saturation point as day by day, year by year, he did very much the same things with almost identical movements of arms and legs" (p. 149).

This very monotony of work, however, becomes eventually a necessary condition of living. "And as women who have had knits [sic] in their hair over a long period collapse when these are killed, feeling so badly removal of that violent irritation which has become stimulus for them, so when men who have worked these regular hours are now deprived of work, so, often, their lives come to be like puddles on the beach where tide no longer reaches" (p. 204). So, after he has been sacked, Mr. Craigan, except for one brief period of activity, stays in bed and meditates gloomily on the wasted futility of his life. But his misery is due, partly at least, to the fact that he has not even had marriage and children of his own, and the fear that his "foster-daughter", Lily Gates, will marry soon and leave him. He and his young mate, Jim Dale, who longs for Lily with such wordless passion, are the first of Green's lonely men.

It would, however, be no more accurate to define the book's theme as "the monotony and loneliness and futility of living" than as "the disintegration of industrial relations". The theme is exactly what the title, *Living*, indicates. Old age and death are part of it, but so are infancy and youth; loneliness is part of it, but so are love and companionship; monotony and weariness are part of it, but so are novelty and gaiety and excitement. *Living* is the only one of Green's novels which has an epigraph; it is characteristic of this determinedly unliterary author that it is not a quotation from Dante or Donne, Heraclitus or Heidegger, but a sentence taken from near the end of the book itself, a reflection of the pregnant Mrs. Eames, who lives next door to the Craigan-Gates household—"As these birds would go where so where would this child go?" "This child" is only a few weeks old at the end of the novel, so presumably the epigraph is to be taken as referring to her, not as a specific individual, but as a representative of humanity generally. The book, then, asks the question "What is it to be a human being?"

The sentence occurs in the novel (as Green's thematic statements have a habit of doing) in a mildly ironical, depreciatory context. "Is nothing wonderful in migrating birds but when we see them we become muddled in our feeling, we think it so romantic they should go so far, far. Is nothing wonderful in a woman carrying but Mrs. Eames was muddled in her feeling by it. As these birds would go where so where would this child go? She thought this and Lily in her thinking now was simpler still . . ." (p. 246). But it is not by accident that the reflection is attributed to Mrs. Eames. When one realizes that this novel is concerned with the whole cycle of human life from infancy to age (as is implicitly stressed in its last words, spoken by Mrs. Eames to her young son—" 'You're too young, that's too old for you,' she said"), the importance of the Eames family in the pattern of the book as a whole becomes more apparent. The Eames are a thoroughly ordinary and average pair. The short-sighted Mr. Eames works in his garden in the evenings, does his job conscientiously and efficiently, minds his own business, is quite aware of, but temperate in his criticisms of, the vagaries and mismanagement of the factory; he is slow to anger, but one feels that he is far more to be reckoned with than loud-mouthed malcontents like Gates. He is a responsible, sensible, serious-minded, right-thinking young man; he dislikes the toadying Tupe and despises Joe Gates for associating with this vindictive enemy of Craigan's; he has Bert Jones summed up (" ' 'E seems like a lot of the other young chaps, you know, he don't seem to have much interest in nothing. . . . 'E's one of them that are always smoking cigarettes.' " p. 164). Mrs. Eames, absorbed in keeping house and looking after her husband and children, is fond of gossip, a little inclined to nag, but, on the whole, is cheerful, placid and devoted. They have little to do with the plot of the novel, but we are always aware of them in the background, living out their unheroic and circumscribed, but decent and industrious lives. They are indeed Mr. and Mrs. Everyman. It may be accidental, but it is certainly appropriate that their name suggests "Ems", the typographical units of measurement, for their quiet, sedate, self-absorbed, contented domesticity and parenthood are the norm, against which the various forms of loneliness of the other characters—Craigan, Jim Dale, Dupret, even Hannah Glossop—are (quite unemphatically and unobtrusively) contrasted, and the condition to which Lily aspires. ("She wanted to better herself and she wanted a kid.") Mrs. Eames' acceptance of living, with all its imperfections and disappointments, in her early-morning monologue to her baby son is the real spirit of the novel, not the "Nothing nothing" of Mr. Craigan, or Dupret's elaboration of the

> Birth, and copulation, and death.
> That's all, that's all, that's all, that's all . . ." [12]

of Eliot's *Sweeney Agonistes*.

" 'And when you're grown you'll marry and we shall lose you and you'll 'ave kiddies of your own and a 'ouse of your own, love, we'll be out in the cold. Why do we bring kids into the world, they leave you so soon as they're grown, eh? But you don't know one of these things yet. But sure as anything you'll leave us when you're a man, and who'll we 'ave then, eh cruel? Sons and daughters why do we bring them into the world?' She was laughing. 'Because, because' she said laughing and then lay smiling and then yawned" (pp. 24–5). Marriage and "the satisfaction of breeding the glorious Anglo Saxon breed", that young Dupret despises, may be all they have, but to them it is enough. Indeed the yearning for, and joy in, parenthood is a dominant theme of the book; it is almost "epiphanized" in one of the most poetic episodes of the novel.

"Then, one morning in iron foundry, Arthur Jones began singing. He did not often sing. When he began the men looked up from work and at each other and stayed quiet. In machine shop, which was next iron foundry, they said it was Arthur singing and stayed quiet also. He sang all morning.

"He was Welsh and sang in Welsh. His voice had a great soft yell in it. It rose and rose and fell then rose again and, when the crane was quiet for a moment, then his voice came out from behind noise of the crane in passionate singing. Soon each one in this factory heard that Arthur had begun and, if he had 2 moments, came by iron foundry shop to listen. So all through that morning, as he went on, was a little group of men standing by door in the machine shop, always different men. His singing made all of them sad. Everything in iron foundries is black with the burnt sand and here was his silver voice yelling like bells. The black grimed men bent over their black boxes. . . . Still Arthur sang and it might be months before he sang again. And no one else sang that day, but all listened to his singing. That night son had been born to him" (pp. 89–90).

It is peculiarly appropriate that Green's only epigraph should mention birds, for the most casual reader must notice that his are bird-haunted books. Pigeons, starlings, sparrows, doves, owls, geese, rooks, gulls, blackbirds—even peacocks—appear again and again, both in descriptive passages and as the vehicles of metaphor. Looking back, it is not surprising that one of the things most regretted by John Hay, the blinded semi-autobiographical schoolboy of *Blindness*, is that he is "never to see a bird again". Nearly thirty years later Rosamond Lehmann, discussing *Loving*, commented that "One is struck, as usual, by the prevalence of birds . . . as ornamental objects, and, in some unresolved sense, as symbols in the author's private landscape and mythology".[13] It would probably be impossible for Green to write a novel without a bird in it somewhere. Even in *Back* Charley Summers is compared to "a magpie with a broken wing", and Mr. Pike to "an owl in daylight"; and even in *Doting*, on the first page, we are told (for no discernible reason) that when, several weeks later, Peter Middleton would catch the last train back to yet another term, "he was to carry a white goose under one arm, its dead beak almost trailing the platform!"

In reading Green's novels one's mental state is likely sometimes to resemble that of the undergraduate Stephen Dedalus, as he stood on the steps of the library, leaning wearily on his ashplant, watching the flight of unidentified birds and through his mind "there flew hither and thither shapeless thoughts from Swedenborg on the correspondence of birds to things of the intellect . . . A sense of fear of the unknown moved in the heart of his weariness, a fear of symbols and portents." [14] For Green's birds provoke the same questions. Is there any correspondence between them and things of the intellect? Are they symbols and portents? And if so, of what? Giorgio Melchiori appears to be the only critic who has given any attention to these questions so his remarks will be given in full. Melchiori quotes the description of pigeons in flight in *Living* (p. 199), and comments: "One senses a hidden allusion in the sloping flight of the pigeon. . . . And the impression is strongly confirmed by the rest of the novel, and by the later novels of Green's where these images recur insistently, apparently carrying some sort of message, never fully revealed. The pigeon, like other birds in Green's prose, reaches at times the intensity of a symbol, but lacks all precision of reference and consistency, two essential qualities of symbols. And indeed Green's are not symbols: they are rather those sudden images recurring in the works of poets and marking the high points at which the strength of their feeling finds release in visual terms. Visual images without an abstract counterpart in the realm of thought ['a correspondence to things of the intellect'] or a definite reference to known facts or persons are the expression only of a mood, of a condition of the author's mind, so individual that it can be communicated only through this visual embodiment." [15]

There are some qualifications to be made to this analysis, suggestive as it is. In the first place, Melchiori, in insisting on "precision of reference and consistency", appears to be limiting the term symbol to the fixed symbol, to what E. M. Forster calls a "banner" ("such as we find George Meredith using—a double-blossomed cherry tree to accompany Clare Middleton, a yacht in smooth waters for Cecilia Halkett" [16]). He is using the terms "image" and "symbol" in much the same way as Cecil Day Lewis does when he asserts that "an intense image is the opposite of a symbol. A symbol is denotative; it stands for one thing only, as the figure 1 represents one unit." [17] This is an arbitrary limitation; as well as the fixed symbol there is what E. K. Brown calls the "expanding symbol", which, like the echo in *Passage to India*, slowly and irregularly accreting meaning from its recurrence in a variety of contexts, is a suitable device for (in Brown's words) "rendering an emotion, an idea, that by its largeness or its subtlety cannot wholly become explicit". [18] It is, it seems to me, more satisfactory to regard the birds of several of Green's novels (especially *Loving* and *Concluding*) as "expanding symbols" which provide a complementary expression of meaning, which indeed come to represent a complex structure of feeling and values that are of great importance in the total structure of the novels, than as randomly recurring and "meaningless" visual images.

In the second place, whatever may be the case in the later novels, it seems quite wrong to deny to the pigeons of *Living* "all precision of reference and consistency". *Living* is a "young" novel, in which many of Green's characteristic devices and stratagems are present in relatively crude form. He was experimenting, not only with language and with structure, but also with various novel methods of conveying the quality of his characters' experience. One method has previously been mentioned—the elaborate metaphor, which has affinities with both

the expanded conceit of the metaphysicals and the epic simile.
One of the most spectacular of these is the recurring metaphor
of tropical birds, flying fish and islands to define the feelings of
Hannah Glossop when she has been jilted by Tom Tyler. Here
Green carefully explains just what he is doing. "But stretch this
simile, and, having given Tom Tyler one island, make archi-
pelago about him,—though each day she circled farther from
Mr. Tyler yet she did not draw any nearer to where Dick
lay" (p. 168).

But this exotic imagery is exceptional. More frequently
Green uses the familiar features of his characters' daily life and
environment to interpret their emotions and attitudes. For
example, since the mind of Bert Jones, a fitter, is saturated with
his trade, it seems perfectly fitting that Green should translate
his perplexity in his relationship with Lily into visual images
derived from the lathe. "And now for Mr. Jones his position
was this: that as it might be foreman had given him a job out of
which, if he did it right and it was not easy to do, would come
advancement and satisfaction for him. . . . He said in mind
he had to go on and do the job right. He poised before it, tool
in his hand and it might be the sense of power he had and
which he felt for the first time, to make waster out of that bit of
steel or a good job out of it it might be that kept him still
undecided" (pp. 195–6).

The pigeons are pressed into service for Lily and Mr.
Craigan in much the same way as the lathe for Bert Jones (and
the moulding box for Mr. Bridges). It is surprising that a critic
of Melchiori's perceptiveness did not observe the process by
which these simple "objects" are converted into symbols. The
pigeons make their first appearance, early in the book, in a
simple and apparently casual description. "A man next door
to them kept racing pigeon and these were in slow air" (p. 13).

They are not mentioned again until nearly two hundred
pages later in a passage, part of which is quoted by Melchiori.
"Here pigeon quickly turned rising in spirals, grey, when clock
in the church tower struck the quarter and away, away the
pigeon fell from this noise in a diagonal from where church was
built and that man who leant on his spade. Like hatchets they
came towards Lily, down at her till when they were close to
window they stopped, each clapped his wings then flew away
slowly all of them, to the left" (p. 199).

K

This passage clearly is more than a vivid pictorial image: as Melchiori remarks, it carries "vague undertones which place it in a sudden deep perspective of feeling and meaning". But the undertones are not quite as vague as Melchiori suggests, as a glance at the context of the passage indicates. At this point Lily is on the verge of elopement with Bert Jones; the pigeons are implicitly connected with her own projected flight. What Melchiori has not observed, however (or has not commented on) is that this passage is only an intermediate stage. In several later passages the pigeons become much less enigmatic and mysterious, as Green virtually provides an arrow pointing from the thing observed to the meaning (the "reference to the known facts and persons" of the novel).

In the following passages it is easy enough to trace the gradual expansion of meaning. First we have a specific comparison with the movement of Lily's thoughts on a specific occasion shortly after she has observed the diagonal flight of the pigeons. "So, as pigeon when she had watched out of kitchen window had flown diagonally down in a wedge and then recovered themselves, as each one had clapped his wings and gone slowly away, so she drew back from him, her mind unbound, and said to him: 'Why, look it's raining' " (p. 206). A few pages later, while Lily and Bert are eloping in the train, there is a more general comparison between the circling of Lily's thoughts and their constant return to one point, and the flight of homing pigeons. "For as racing pigeon fly in the sky, always they go round above house which provides for them or, if loosed at a distance from that house then they fly straight there, so her thoughts would not point away long from house which had provided for her" (p. 217).

After her return the simile is extended to include Mr. Craigan, and, indeed, given a general application. "As pigeon never fly far from house which provides for them . . . as they might be tied by piece of string to that house, so Mr. Craigan's eyes did not leave off from Lily where she went. We are imprisoned by that person whom we love. . . .

"For now, wherever Miss Gates went there Mr. Craigan followed with his eyes. . . . He was not watching, it was like these pigeon, that flying in a circle always keep that house in sight, so we are imprisoned, with that kind of liberty tied down" (p. 250). Through the use of the pigeons as metaphors to render the quality of the thought and feeling of the chief characters, by the end of the novel they have attained a "precise" and "consistent" reference. Just as the migrating birds invoked in the novel's epigraph symbolize the longing to escape from the endless miles of mean dirty streets to "a golden land" bathed in "a golden light" (p. 189), so the pigeons symbolize the attachment to all that is known and loved, the impossibility of escaping from the places and the people that have become part of us. And the pigeons, reintroduced in vivid description in the last page of the book, as if to assert the reality of their existence, independently of any symbolic function, dominate the closing scene. In this picture of the Eames' baby (which, before its birth, provoked the reflection used as the novel's epigraph) in its pram, surrounded by pigeons, watched adoringly by Lily, who "wanted to better herself and wanted a kid", the themes of the novel are concretely embodied.

3

There is only one definitely identified pigeon in *Party Going*, but this perplexing bird winds its way ludicrously yet alarmingly through the whole novel. *Living* ends with a shot of a healthy, happy working-class baby gurgling in rapturous delight at a very live pigeon fluttering in winter sunshine round her pram; *Party Going* begins with a shot of an elderly, mysteriously ill upper-class woman compelled by some obscure impulse to pick up the body of a pigeon that falls dead at her feet in dense fog. The two scenes suggest some of the differences in tone and theme between the two novels.

Like every other feature of the book, the title of *Party Going* is more enigmatic than that of its predecessor. Obviously, on one level, the book is about a party of young socialites going somewhere or nowhere. (It makes little difference to them, and less to the reader, whether they go or stay.) Also, as Arnold Kettle has remarked, "*Party Going* is not a tract . . . but if a tract were made out of it, it would be a tract, quite simply, on party-going."[19] This is true enough, for there seems to be nothing in the bored and futile lives of these people except a monotonous round of parties, from which they have ceased to derive any real pleasure. They are far too self-centred and far too mutually suspicious to enjoy one another's company, but the craving for social prestige keeps them endlessly on the tread-mill, perpetually trying to raise themselves higher in the social circle by being seen, apparently having a wonderful time, in the company of the best people. This is the chief attraction that Max and Amabel have for the lesser lights—not their personal qualities, but the fact that they are so wealthy and well known that to be admitted to their circle is a hallmark of social success. "So that to be with her [Amabel] was for Angela as much as it might be for a director of the Zoo to be taking his okapi for walks in leading strings for other zoologists to see or, as she her-self would have put it, it was being grand with grand people" (p. 140). ". . . Evelyn, when she found herself agreeing, as she did almost automatically, despised herself for playing up to her. It was a question of prestige, she thought" (p. 146). The importance of Embassy Richard, the professional party-crasher, who appears only in the last few pages, but who is eagerly dis-cussed throughout, is clearly that he represents this fatuous and futile existence in its most blatant form.

But there is even more to the theme of the novel, and to the implications of the title, than this. The novel obliquely ques-tions the ultimate destination of this party. There is no sugges-tion of any religious scale of values, but if one wished to furnish the novel with an epigraph it would be easy enough to find one in the poetry of T. S. Eliot. One that suggests itself is the line from "Burnt Norton", "Distracted from distraction by dis-traction" for to read section III of the first of the quartets is to be strongly reminded of *Party Going*.

> Here is a place of disaffection
> Time before and time after
> In a dim light: . . .
> . . . Only a flicker
> Over the strained time-ridden faces
> Distracted from distraction by distraction
> Filled with fancies and empty of meaning
> Tumid apathy with no concentration. . . .

Perhaps even more apposite would be a quotation from *The Hollow Men*—

> Our dried voices when
> We whisper together
> Are quiet and meaningless
> As wind in dry grass

or

> In this last of meeting places
> We grope together. . . .

For the impression is irresistibly, though half whimsically, conveyed that this fog-bound railway terminus is "death's dream kingdom", a limbo out of space and time, a place of living death. This impression is conveyed mainly through the book's imagery. In the early pages the images of death and burial are thickly clustered—"the *pall* of fog", "the huge *vault* of glass", "the thin *wreath* or two" of the dead pigeon's blood in the hand-basin, the "two nannies dressed in *granite*". Later in the novel the scene is again and again explicitly compared to a graveyard or to the ruins of some forgotten civilization. "Again there was so much luggage round about in piles like an exaggerated grave-yard, with the owners of it and their porters like mourners with the undertakers' men" (p. 40). "They were like ruins in the wet, places, that is where life has been, palaces, abbeys, cathedrals, throne rooms, pantries, cast aside and tumbled down with no immediate life and with what used to be in them lost rather than hidden now the roof has fallen in" (p. 201). ". . . they were like the dead resurrected in their clothes under this cold veiled light . . ." (p. 203).

The characters themselves sometimes feel that they are dead. ". . . he likened what he saw to being dead and thought of himself as a ghost driving through streets of the living . . ." (p. 37). "She thought it was like an enormous doctor's waiting room and that it would be like that when they were all dead and waiting at the gates" (p. 59). ". . . for now that he was trying to get out of this hotel, and it was like trying to get out of one world into another . . ." (p. 174). And always in the background is Miss Fellowes, with her dead pigeon, stricken down by her undiagnosed illness, her mind wandering deliriously: "It might have been an argument with death. And so it went on, reproaches, insults, threats to report and curiously enough it was mixed up in her mind with thoughts of dying and she asked herself whom she could report death to" (p. 125).

Giorgio Melchiori has pointed out a number of probably unconscious borrowings from "The Fire Sermon" section of *The Waste Land* in *Living*, notably the river scene (pp. 114–15), in which, Melchiori claims, "Eliot's river images fuse with the

mechanical sound of the typist's gramophone, the music creeping upon the water, Elizabeth's pleasure barge and the narrow
canoe on the Thames, . . . to form Green's picture, a picture
like Eliot's of lassitude and emptiness." [20] But it seems that the
connection of *Party Going* with *The Waste Land* and *The Hollow
Men* is even stronger than that of its predecessor. This is natural
enough since Dupret, the spectator in the river scene, one of
Eliot's "loitering heirs of city directors", is a comparatively
minor figure, while almost all of the characters in *Party Going*
belong to Dupret's class.

But if one notices similarities with Eliot's poetry one is equally
struck by differences. The differences are, no doubt, to some
extent inherent in the nature of the different literary forms, but
they also reflect the differences in spirit between Eliot and
Green. The essential difference is that the people of *Party Going*
are not, after all, merely "hollow men, leaning together, head-
piece filled with straw"; they are specific individuals—not despised and undifferentiated nonentities. Judged by any religious
scale of values, they may be spiritually dead; nevertheless they
are very much alive, with their own queer little quirks of personality, and their own special memories, which, trivial and
childish as they may be, are treated by Green with tenderness.
"Memory is a winding lane and as she [Julia] went up it,
waving them to follow, the first bend in it hid her from them
and she was left to pick her flowers alone.

"Memory is a winding lane with high banks on which flowers
grow and here she wandered in a nostalgic summer evening in
deep soundlessness" (p. 198).

It is through the memory of Julia that some of the important
symbols of the novels are introduced, which to some extent
counteract the effect of the recurrent images of death and burial.
There is her memory of the clump of bamboos (or perhaps they
were only overgrown artichokes) in the kitchen garden of
Robert Hignam's parents, which to her and Robert as children
had been a place of romance and mystery and buried secrets.
One is reminded by their persistent recurrence of a sentence
from Walter de la Mare's Introduction to Frank Kendon's
The Small Years: "Like runes scribbled on some grey old
mouldering pre-historic stone, [the things seen in childhood]
had a secret meaning, though what precisely that meaning was
we may not be able to say." [21] And there are the three seagulls

which fly through the span of the bridge she is crossing on her way to the station, which become confused in her mind with two doves which had flown under the bridge when she first met Max, and which in the last page seem to have been transformed yet again into pigeons. Though the meaning of these birds cannot be translated into precise, rational terms it is clear, at least, that they are symbols of life, of sex and flight. The sexual overtones are more insistent in the bird imagery used to describe the sleeping Amabel. "He had lain in the shadow of it under softly beaten wings of her breathing . . ." (p. 176). "She lay on his shoulder in this ugly room, folded up with almost imperceptible breathing like seagulls settled on the water cock over gentle waves. . . . Lying in his arms . . . her hands drifted to rest like white doves drowned on peat water . . ." (p. 226).

The imagery of this novel is, in fact, extraordinarily profuse and diverse. Other recurring motifs are water (e.g. "As pavements swelled out under this dark flood", p. 14; "swarming ponds of humanity", p. 26; "like November sun striking through mist rising off water", p. 28; "She still swayed him like water moves a trailing weed", p. 179): lower forms of life (e.g. "crawling worms", p. 15; "water-beetles", p. 27; "sheep in a market", p. 43; "sheep with golden tenor voices", p. 153; "cattle waiting to be butchered", p. 169; "like rats smelling food when they have been starved in empty milk-churns", p. 178; "as does, in moonlight in cold deep-shadowed other day, push him out of his burrow and kick the old buck to death", p. 180; "like cats over offal", p. 181; "fought everyone and themselves and were like camels, they could go on for days without one sup of encouragement", p. 196; "like a cat that has just had its mouse coming among other cats who had only had the smell", p. 241): flowers (e.g. "like two lilies in a pond", p. 27; "hands with rings still on her fingers were water lilies done in rubies", p. 165). Some of the most elaborate and extraordinary images are the geographical metaphors which present the human face and body in landscape terms, in which Melchiori finds echoes of Donne. "When he opened his eyes close beside her in the flat she had blotted out the light, only where her eye would be he could see dazzle, all the rest of her mountain face had been that dark acreage against him" (p. 176). ". . . she fixed him with her eyes which drew him like the glint a hundred feet beneath and called on him to throw himself over" (p. 215). ". . . looking down on her face which ever since he had first seen it had been his library, his gallery, his palace, and his wooded fields he began at last to feel content and almost that he owned her" (p. 226).

The examples quoted do not by any means exhaust the kinds of imagery present in the novel, but they may be sufficient to suggest something of its complexity and ambiguity of tone. If much of its imagery conjures up an impression of death, desolation and aridity, much also conjures up a counterbalancing impression of vitality and wonder. Beauty and ugliness, poetry and barbed satire, the grotesque and the ornate are all inextricably blended. *Party Going* has sometimes been compared to the novels of Kafka, and it undoubtedly has much of their nightmare strangeness. Several of the minor characters—the nannies dressed in granite, with their infallible instinct for disaster, so solid and real, yet with something supernaturally portentous about them; the queer individual whom Alex mistakes for the hotel detective, who varies his speech from Yorkshire to Brummagen to "educated accents" with such disconcerting facility; the enormously fat people in the hotel reception hall, especially the glass-eyed man, who after much indecision, tries to light his cigar and instead explodes his box of matches—would be quite at home in Kafka's world. The general atmosphere of the strain and nervous tension of protracted waiting is also Kafkaesque. So too is the setting: as in *The Castle* or *The Trial* familiar and ordinary things are seen from a new and startling angle and invested with a weird poetry. Just as one of the most lasting impressions of *Living* is of the din and blackness of the foundry, so one of the most unforgettable things about *Party Going* is the station, so vast, yet so densely crowded, so commonplace and yet so mysterious, with its huge vault of green (or blue) glass, its tunnels and stairways, with the fog slowly filtering in, blending with the smoke of countless cigarettes to blur and smudge everything and everyone.

"Fog burdened with night began to roll into this station striking cold through thin leather up into their feet where in thousands they stood and waited. Coils of it reached down like women's long hair reached down and caught their throats and veiled here and there what they could see, like lovers' glances. A hundred cold suns switched on above found out the coils where, before the night joined in, they had been smudges and looking up at two of them above was like she was looking down at you from under long strands hanging down from her forehead only that light was cold and these curls tore at your lungs" (p. 199).

It is impossible to ascribe to the setting of the novel any single, definite meaning. *Party Going* is not an allegory, but a symbolic novel which can be interpreted on various different levels. But like many symbolic novels (even like *Wuthering Heights* and *Moby Dick*, though it is not, of course, suggested that this *divertissement* is of comparable stature) *Party Going* is, at one level, a social allegory. The railway station, as well as being "death's dream kingdom" is, as Arnold Kettle has remarked, "in a sense the social fabric". For, Kettle elaborates the point, "within it life accumulates and is organized . . . The absurd, dignified station-master, king of the place, yet the puppet of voices at the other end of a telephone wire, moves majestically through the crowd, prepared at a crisis, like a competent R.S.M., to rebuke the junior officer who is letting down his class. And within the station human life is divided. While the people wait for their trains under the great roof, the rich repair as a matter of course to the hotel, and the richest take suites of rooms in which to wait and drink and bath and be in a position to fornicate." [22]

John Lehmann similarly interpreted the novel as "a parable of the predicament in which the British ruling classes found themselves at the worst of the crisis between 1929 and 1931" [23] —the predicament being, presumably, their isolation, disunity and uselessness. There is certainly much to support this view. There is, for example, the description of Angela and Robin. "Like two lilies in a pond, romantically part of it but infinitely remote, surrounded, supported, floating in it if you will, but projected by being different on to another plane . . . stood Miss Crevy and her young man, apparently serene, envied for their obviously easy circumstances and Angela coveted for her looks by all those water beetles if you like, by those people standing round" (p. 27). But the party of which they are members is only "*apparently* serene"; some at least of them are alarmed by the pressure of this vast mass of people, though they are reassured by their confidence in the crowd's docility and passivity (it is in connection with the crowd that the sheep and cattle imagery is used), and by the steel doors which keep it out of the hotel. Julia looking down at the crowd "felt encouraged and felt safe because they could not by any chance get up from below; she had seen those doors bolted, and through being above them by reason of Max having bought their room and by having money, she saw in what lay below her an example of her own way of living because they were underneath and kept there" (p. 152). The most important passage is the long interior monologue of Alex Alexander which orchestrates all the important themes and symbols of the novel—the dead pigeon, the party going where?, the disunity and antagonism, the spiritual emptiness, the animal imagery. "That is what it is to be rich, he thought, if you are held up, if you have to wait then you can do it after a bath in your dressing-gown and if you have to die then not as any bird tumbling dead from its branch down for the foxes. . . . Again, no standing, no being pressed together, no worry since it did not matter if one went or stayed, no fellow feeling, true. . . . And in this room, as always, it seemed to him there was a sort of bond between the sexes and with these people no more than that, only dull antagonism otherwise. . . .

"It was all the fault of these girls . . . he thought, who never banded together but fought everyone and themselves and were like camels, they could go on for days without one sup of encouragement. Under their humps they had tanks of self-confidence so that they could cross any desert area of arid prickly pear without one compliment . . ." (p. 195). The last sentence provides the most direct reference to *The Waste Land* and "the prickly pear "of *The Hollow Men*; but Alex's reflections also remind one of some of the comments of Thomas Quayne and St. Quentin Miller in Elizabeth Bowen's *Death of the Heart*, which had been published in the previous year. ("As a matter of fact I don't think we get together. We none of us seem to feel very well, and I don't think we want each other to know it. I suppose there is nothing so disintegrating as competitiveness and funk and that's what we all feel. The ironical thing is that everyone else gets their knives into us bourgeoisie on the assumption we're having a good time . . . They seem to have no idea that we don't care much for ourselves. . . ." [23])

But there is much in the novel which defies any attempt to force it into a political or social allegory. Perhaps it could be maintained that Miss Fellowes' physical illness is a representation of the spiritual condition of her class, or that this whole class is a "dead pigeon". But this would certainly be arbitrary indeed. Any attempt to define the theme of the novel in a single phrase is doomed to failure.

The novel is, as Mark Schorer has remarked, about "the disruption of manner in the upper classes",[24] but it is about much more than that. It is about the spiritual emptiness of humanity in the modern world; it is about the plight of the ruling caste; it is about the latent hostility between social classes; it is about the false and uneasy relationships between men and women of the upper class who, having no spontaneous wish for each other, can only scheme to use one another to their own advantage. But it is also about the enchantment of beauty, the desire to love and be loved. And despite the seriousness and penetration of its perceptions, it always remains high comedy—light-handed if not exactly light-hearted.

<h1 style="text-align:center">4</h1>

The themes of *Caught* have already been touched on in other contexts. *Caught* is a novel arising from, but not entirely dependent for its interest on, the special conditions of the War. On the topical level, as a piece of contemporary history, it is concerned with the chaotic disruption of normal existence—the mobilization of men of military age, the enforced contacts between members of different social classes, the dispersal of families—and with the break-down of conventional standards and values under the impact of war-time conditions. On this general level *Caught* is an anti-heroic novel and a very poor piece of war-propaganda. It conveys no idealized impression of an indomitable people preparing with efficiency and speed for the wrath to come, but a far more credible impression of confusion and muddle, nepotism and self-seeking, pettiness, shirking of responsibility and moral laxity. It conveys very well the fevered, unreal atmosphere of a time of constant meetings and partings, when uniforms still had a strange fascination. "In night clubs ... or wherever the young danced, couples passed the last goodbye hours abandoned to each other and ... when these girls were left behind alone as train after train went out loaded with men to fight, the pretty creatures must be hunting for more farewells. As they were driven to create memories to compare, and thus to compensate for the loss each had suffered, he [Richard] saw them hungrily seeking another man, oh they were sorry for men and they pitied themselves, for yet another man with whom they could spend last hours, to whom they could murmur darling, darling, darling it will be you always; the phrase till death do us part being, for them, the short ride next morning to a railway station; the active death, for them, to be left alone on a platform; the I-have-given-all-before-we-die, their dying breath" (p. 63).

But all this is background; even Prudence and Ilse, the two girls who become involved with the life of the sub-station, are not vitally important characters. In the foreground are Pye and Roe, two of the most memorable of Green's gallery of lonely men, and on the more personal (yet at the same time more universal) level the theme is one of harassment and strain, apprehension and loneliness. As previously mentioned the book concerns the disintegration, through a combination of internal and external pressures, of sub-officer Pye. This is the most tragic of Green's novels; indeed it is the only one in which one of the leading characters dies—and Pye, in utter despair, dies by his own hand. (But he is careful to turn off the automatic burners in the boiler before he puts his head in the gas oven.) But it must be stressed, in opposition to critics like Orville Prescott, or even like Giorgio Melchiori (who finds in this, and other novels of Green's, "a feeling of futility common to many sensitive writers in this century" [25]) that the novel also concerns the achievement of identity, the reintegration with life, through his enforced participation in the experience of other people, of Richard Roe. In this, as in Green's novels generally, if there is defeat, there is also victory, and the victory is no less real because it is muted.

Mark Schorer has remarked that besides these two themes (the topical and contemporary; the individual and universal) there is a still larger element, "a larger ambiance if not a larger story, and that is London. It is chiefly London at night". [26] It has previously been shown that the amount of description is very much greater in *Caught* than in either of Green's earlier novels. One thing that quickly strikes a reader is that *Caught* is a vastly more colourful book than either *Living* or *Party Going*. In this novel, for the first time, colour becomes an important means of conveying feeling. Like all romantic writers, Green relies heavily on the appeal to the senses through the creation of images and colour is an important part of this sensuous appeal. A comment made by one of Hawthorne's critics applies equally to Green: "When we speak of Hawthorne's use of colour, we are not merely speaking of description. He uses colour for descriptive purposes, but it is a means and not an end. It is more to him than a mere pigment for painting a description. It is part of a larger device designed, in Conrad's phrase, to 'reach the secret springs of responsive emotion'. It is an emotional element rather than a merely descriptive one; it is used for its emotional and mood value rather than its intellectual and descriptive value." [27]

The obvious preliminary to any attempt at an analysis of Green's use of colour (which cannot hope to be more than tentative and fragmentary, since this branch of literary study is scarcely out of its infancy) is to ascertain which colours he uses in *Caught* and the other novels, and with what frequency. Even this apparently straightforward task is beset with difficulties. One difficulty is that colour-adjectives are not the only means of suggesting colour. Objects are often included by Green, as by other writers, partly at least for their colour effect, though their colour is not explicitly stated. Some of the most obvious examples are blood and snow, grass and fire. Even more puzzling are light and shadow, which frequently have strong suggestions of colour, without precise definition. Another difficult question is whether every single colour mentioned should be listed, or whether various shades should be grouped together in a few general categories—red, blue, etc.

It seems most practicable to concentrate on actual colour-adjectives, though it is recognized that to rely wholly on lists and percentages is dangerous, since this means ignoring subtleties of connotation and suggestion. It also seems best (mainly because the alternative is too unwieldy) to group the different variants of the basic colours together. The results of the analysis are given in the table on the next page.

The first thing one notices about these figures is the very wide range of variation, in the total number of colour-words used in the different novels, and also in the blending of colours in the different books.

The next observation to be made is that the total number of colour-adjectives in each book corresponds fairly closely (as one would expect—or, at least, hope) with the percentage of description as given previously (p. 75). Since the novels vary considerably in length, the average number of colour-words in

	Living	Party Going	Caught	Loving	Back	Concluding	Nothing	Doting	Total
White	7	12	39	40	18	61	20	6	203
Red	5	10	33	31	36	31	6	5	157
Black	17	3	31	22	14	37	7	3	134
Blue	6	8	41	29	10	22	6	6	128
Yellow	7	7	23	35	6	30	5	3	116
Pink	3	7	24	12	13	15	8	5	87
Green	6	5	9	19	11	14	1	2	67
Purple	5	—	12	14	3	5	1	6	46
Grey	6	2	11	10	1	7	3	—	40
Brown	1	3	10	1	11	6	—	—	32
Orange	1	—	4	1	—	—	—	—	6
Silver	2	—	—	2	—	1	—	—	5
Total	66	57	237	216	123	229	57	36	1,021

The following shades (most of them occurring only a few times) were included under the various main heads.

Red: blood-coloured, blood-dark, blood-red, carmine, crimson, copper, coppered, flame, fox-dyed, reddish, ruby, rust, russet, scarlet, sunset, vermilion, wine-coloured. (A total of 32 occurrences.)

Blue: azure, Eton blue, gentian, ice-blue, indigo, sapphire (11 occurrences).

Yellow: gilt, golden (49); apricot, brass, cream, ginger, honey, khaki, mustard, primrose, saffron, sand-coloured, tow (17).

Pink: rose, rose-coloured, rosy (25); coral, flesh-coloured (4).

Purple: violet (15); grape, mauve, plum-coloured (7).

Grey: granite, pewter (2).

every seven pages is here given, and compared with the actual percentage of description (not taken to the nearest complete percentile as before).

	Percentage of Description	Colour-words in seven pages
Caught	8·4	8·5
Concluding	7·6	6·3
Loving	4·9	6·6
Party Going	3·9	1·5
Back	2·9	4·1
Living	2·6	1·7
Nothing	2·5	1·6
Doting	2·2	1·0

There are, it will be noticed, two discrepancies. One of these is too small to be significant—the slightly higher concentration of colour-words in *Loving* than in *Concluding*, despite the higher percentage of description in the latter. The other is much more glaring—the very low concentration of colour in *Party Going* as compared with *Back*, which has a good deal less description. Actually this is quite readily explicable, for in this fog-bound novel there can be no natural colour. Almost the whole action takes place indoors in the late afternoon; even in such sequences as the descriptions of Julia and Amabel walking to the station through the Park the fog has blotted out the sky and reduced visibility almost to zero, and the only colour that is seen is of "the leaves brilliantly green veined like marble with wet dirt" (p. 17), picked out for a moment by the headlights of passing cars. But this is not the whole reason; even where one might expect colour, for example in the women's dresses, there is none. Julia, Evelyn and Amabel are described in general terms as being beautifully dressed, but the only clothing colours that are actually specified are those of the anonymous women of the crowd—"in low green and mustard colours" (p. 28)—and of the two nannies—"dressed in granite, with black straw hats" (p. 8). The dominant "colour" of the novel (if a colour occurring only a dozen times can be called dominant) is white; it is the white of old age, of useless beauty ("her hands were ridiculously white", p. 26), of illness ("very white she lay still as death", p. 125). There are a few splashes of colour in Julia's childhood memories of her umbrella "quartered in red and yellow silk", but most of the little colour in the novel is concentrated round Amabel, with her blue eyes and her vermilion finger-nails, her hands "like white doves". Indeed almost one-sixth of all the colour-words in the novel are concentrated in the three-page description of Amabel having a bath—an elegantly voluptuous study in pink and white.

The near-colourlessness of the novel may be in part due to fidelity of observation and accuracy of description, but it is also in part due to conscious restraint. This "albino" quality un-doubtedly contributes greatly to the total effect of the book; any more colour, or any more vivid colour, would have con-flicted with the "death's dream kingdom" atmosphere. In this novel Green's skill as a descriptive writer is most frequently seen in patterns and contrasts of light and darkness; and of pale and dark. (A good example is the description of the crowd "with some kind of design made out of bookstalls and kiosks seen from above and through one part of that crowd having turned to-wards those who were singing, thus lightening the dark mass with their pale lozenged faces" (p. 150).

Living has little more colour than *Party Going*, but what little there is is effectively used to create an impression of drabness and dinginess. Here the dominant colour is black—the black of the burnt sand of the foundry floor, of the smoke which besmirches everything. "Everything but the grass is black with smoke, only thin blue waves of smoke coming up from the dark crowds already waiting gives any colour, and the pink brick" (p. 266). This sentence epitomizes the colour scheme of the book. The occasional splashes of colour—Lily's hair "like short golden rivers"; "the orange roses with a few curly green leaves" on the paper doylies in the pub; the "fierce red eye" of the pigeon; Mrs. Eames' plum-coloured coat—only accentuate the prevailing black and grey. Lily, half-walking, half-dreaming, on a hill above the city with Jones, sees everything "black with smoke, here even, by her, cows went soot-covered and the sheep grey. She saw milk taken out from them, grey the surface of it. . . . Yes and in every house was mother with her child and that was grey . . ." (p. 108).

The effect of *Caught* is vastly different and vastly more com-plex. There is twice as much black in *Caught* as in *Living*, three times as much white as in *Party Going*. But neither of these is dominant, for there is as much blue as white, more red than black. Indeed there is more yellow and more pink in *Caught* than there is black in *Living*, as much purple (and violet) in

Caught as there is white in *Party Going*. This is the only novel of Green's in which the number of colour-words exceeds the number of pages (though both *Loving* and *Concluding* also have averages close to one per page).

It is in *Caught*, then, and the three novels that succeed it (for *Back*, too, has more than twice as much colour as the two early and the two late novels) that colour becomes a means of great importance of reinforcing meaning and evoking feeling, as a passage from the novel itself suggests. "For both it was the deep colour spilled over these objects that, by evoking memories they would not name, and which they could not place, held them and led them both to a loch-deep unconsciousness of all else" (p. 12). But as the passage also suggests, the problem of interpreting Green's use of colour in these books is not easy. In each single instance one is faced with the question whether he used this particular colour because descriptive accuracy demanded it, or simply because of a personal liking for it, or because of some symbolic value it has for him. Undoubtedly much of the colour of *Caught* (and in all the other novels) can be ascribed to the first cause. Obvious examples are the blue of the firemen's uniforms, the red of fire-engines, the black of their boots, leggings and helmets. But in many of his uses of colour Green transcends the limits of descriptive realism. In examining these more subtle, atmospheric, emotive and thematic uses of colour, however, one must heed the warning of a leading authority on colour in literature, Sigmund Skard: "The symbolic content of a colour rarely is tangible like the meaning of a riddle or an allegory . . . but rather may be compared to a vague resonance, an undertone which gives the description a note of mysterious depth, but defies definition." [28]

I shall attempt only to suggest how Green, in a few crucial scenes, releases associations that have gathered round various colours, so that the meaning is greatly enriched. In one such instance, in which white is the dominant colour, colour and metaphor are inextricably fused. Actually there is in *Caught* a good deal more whiteness than the colour-count indicates. It has previously been claimed that the winter snow and ice of the opening chapters (in which the word "white" is not used) are an important means of obliquely suggesting Roe's state of frozen death-in-life. We are subtly reminded of the winter landscape which symbolizes his emotional state in the love scene with Hilly, which marks an important stage in Roe's "rebirth". (This passage with its echoes of Donne and Carew, continues a type of imagery already noticed in *Party Going*.) "The relief he experienced when their bodies met was like the crack, on a snow silent day, of a branch that breaks to fall under a weight of snow, as his hands went like two owls in daylight over the hills, moors, and wooded valleys, over the fat white winter of her body" (p. 117). Here, then, two traditional connotations of white are pitted against one another—the white of cold, fixity, desolation and death, and the white of beauty, happiness and life.

There is another example of this poetic use of colour a few pages later, but here the colour is pink (or rose). *Caught* is rich in all shades of red, which carry all the age-old connotations of this most powerful, most attractive and most repulsive of colours —fire, war, tragedy, danger. But rose and pink are for Green, as they were for Keats and for Meredith, the colours of love. There are hints of this in *Party Going*, but the identification is much clearer in *Caught*, as in the passage just referred to.

"They lay on a sofa, naked, a pleasant brutal picture by the light of his coal fire from which rose petals showered on them as the flames played, deepening the flush spread over contented bodies" (p. 120).

Pink is a dominant colour even in the mad love of Pye's sister, deprived forever of motherhood by her incestuous defloration, for the young Christopher. "At the angle she now held herself she lost those rose diamonds in her eyes, these were shaded, and so had gone an even deeper blue" (p. 14). "She did not turn on the light, so that he could see her eyes only by their glitter, a sparkle by the fire, which as it was disturbed to flame, sent her shadow reeling, gyrating round sprawling rosy walls" (p. 15).

Blue is actually the most frequently recurring colour in *Caught*. Like pink it first becomes prominent in the abduction episode in the toyshop, which is at once one of the most gorgeous and one of the weirdest passages in all of Green's work. The description of the toyshop, in which everything is flooded with blue light from the sea in the stained-glass windows, a blue which both blends with and contrasts with the pink from the ceiling neon lights, must surely have been in Philip Toynbee's mind when he claimed that Green's "almost unique gift is for hallucination", which he defined as "a bewildering ability to see far and wide over the landscape, and to see everything through strange-coloured glass".[29] The "hallucinatory" quality of this episode certainly does not undermine its reality; in fact if it had been presented in any less bizarre setting it would have lost much of its effect of tension and abnormality.

There is certainly nothing accidental about this association of blue, as well as pink, with Pye's sister. This eerie, transfiguring blue light is later implicitly linked with "that winding lane between high banks, in moonlight, in colour blue" (p. 40), that figures so prominently in Pye's memories of his first sexual experience thirty years before. It would be absurd to say anything as simple as that, in this novel, blue (traditionally the colour of fidelity, serenity, constancy, truth and divine love) becomes the colour of incest and psychological aberration. But it would be blindness not to notice how much the unexpected recurrence of blue enhances the emotional effect of these two incidents, and, even more strikingly, that of Pye's last appearance in the novel, which reflects back both on the scene of his incest, and on the scene of his sister's final lapse into insanity. In these few pages (pp. 162–8), in which Pye plays truant in the vast moonlit night, driven by a fury of lust, which "had recently been the effect of his worrying about his sister", driven also by the urge "to find how much he could recognize by this light in the bright river of the street", in a despairing effort to convince himself that he could not have been so horribly mistaken so long ago, blue is evoked again and again. "In the radiance, against which . . . were triangular dark *sapphire* shadows . . ." Pye hopes "to get a girl for the evening, out of the *blue*". "The milk moon stripped deep *gentian* cracker paper shadows off his uniform." A tart accosts him, and, "when she snapped down the light, was again, and at once, *indigo*". He speaks aloud, and is startled when a voice answers him from "a depth of *indigo* shadow". Resuming his walk, "he imagined women where none were. He spoke suggestively to *gentian* hooded doorways". But, instead of the flaxen-haired girl he hopes for, he encounters "a small rough boy with snot pulsating at his nostrils. . . . Immediately the mucus reappeared, almost *Eton blue* in this brilliant light." And it is this boy, whom Pye out of kindness takes back to his room at the sub-station for the night (paralleling his sister's abduction of Christopher Roe), who proves his final undoing.

Green's use of colour in *Caught* cannot be schematized without simplifying and distorting his extremely subtle artistry. His colours are part of an intricate web of insinuation through which a frightening vision of the world is conveyed. But it can at least be said that the strange and complex emotional states of the novel are not merely enhanced by, but partly conveyed by, its abundant and variegated colour. And one can sense, even if one cannot satisfactorily define, correspondences between various colours and various psychological and emotional conditions.

5

It is even more difficult to define the themes of *Loving* than those of its predecessors. This is due partly to the different method of presentation which Green adopts. *Loving* consists almost entirely of dialogue, stage directions and description; here there are neither the author's interpretative comments nor the dips into the minds of his characters which provide some clues to his intentions in *Living*, *Party Going* and *Caught*.

But, different as *Loving* is from the earlier novels, at least some of its themes are the same. For one thing, though the focus of interest is altered, so that now the servants instead of the masters are the central figures, the novel carries on into a time of war the study of the disintegration of the class system, of the hostility—or, even worse, the complete incomprehension—between social groups, adumbrated in *Living* and developed in *Party Going*. The vast Irish castle, English owned and inadequately staffed, is no less a symbol of the social system than the railway terminus of *Party Going*. Like the earlier novel, *Loving* presents the contrast between the effete, functionless, selfish upper class and their servants, who, for all their rivalries and antagonisms and treacheries, are alive and have some traces of solidarity and "fellow feeling". The servants have lost all respect for their masters; the masters regard the servants as mad, and at the same time almost fear them, because they recognize how completely dependent on them they have become. As Mark Schorer puts it, one theme of the book concerns "the illusion of permanence that the settled structure of an earlier time still held for some, and the actual fact of its corrosion".[30] The idea of the impermanence and instability of this world is implicitly emphasized throughout, through the gradual whittling away of its indispensable supports; the butler dies, the head housemaid and the nanny are old and ill, the cook is drunken and unreliable, the pantry-boy absconds, and finally the acting butler and one of the under-housemaids elope. That this world is doomed is hinted early in the novel in the casual comment "For this house that had yet to be burned down . . . was a shadowless castle of treasures" (p. 62).

But *Loving* is about more than the twilight of feudalism and the disappearance of the servant class. Again like *Party Going*, it has a level deeper than the merely social and contemporary. On this level, Kinalty is a place of enchantment and illusion and evasion of responsibility, a kind of lotus land, seductively beautiful but morally unhealthy. Raunce and Edith can only begin to live when they break its spell and escape back to the real world.

In this novel, too, the theme of love versus loneliness becomes more pronounced than ever before, as the title indicates. Practically all of the characters are in a state of loving, but few of them are loved. The loneliness of the other characters—of Agatha Burch, who had loved the dead butler, Mr. Eldon; of the pantry-boy, Albert, who loves Edith; of Kate, who loves Raunce, but turns to the uncouth lamp-man, Paddy; of Mrs. Jack, with her adulterous passion for Captain Davenport which she must overcome; of Nanny Swift, who loves Mrs. Jack, but whose usefulness to her former charge is over—is accentuated by the spectacle of Raunce and Edith, strangely assorted pair though they are, falling in love before their eyes, and caring little for their pain and desperation.

As Robert Phelps has remarked: "This obliviousness is the crucial point about love in Henry Green's world. It amounts to a second innocence, a re-entry into Eden. . . . The most self-absorbed, and inadvertently the cruellest people in Henry Green's novels are the lovers. . . ."[31] And so, just as Lily Gates had eloped with Bert Jones in *Living*, abandoning the old and sick Mr. Craigan to his fate, at the end of *Loving* Raunce and Edith slip quietly away, without a word of farewell and, presumably, without a thought for those whom they leave behind. But it is doubtful whether Phelps' comment that love in Green's world "is non-Christian in the sense that instead of shouldering more awareness, more responsibility, more knowledge, it sheds them" really applies to Raunce and Edith. Raunce's motives for returning to England are intricate and confused; it could as plausibly be maintained that his defection is a shouldering of responsibility (at least of his responsibility as a son, if not as a citizen), not an evasion of it.

In *Loving*, more than in any previous novel—more even than in *Party Going*, which does use something approaching interior monologue quite freely—Green relies on symbols, poetic scenes and patterns of colour, on (to use his own phrase) "a conspiracy of insinuations" to suggest meaning. Probably more readers have been left by this novel than by any of his other books, except perhaps *Concluding*, saying with Virginia Woolf's Lily Briscoe "What does it mean then, what does it all mean?" For as we read, we constantly feel that more is here than meets the eye, that we are missing some clue that would enable us to understand the whole.

The difficulty is, however, that in *Loving*, as in most of Green's novels, there is no single, central, all-important "clue"; there is no "key symbol". Moreover there is not, as there was in *Living*, any assistance in interpretation from the author; the symbols remain much more free and unassigned. William York Tindall, a leading authority on symbolism, especially in modern literature, has distinguished three varieties of symbolic novel. "Sometimes they are centred in narrative or character, sometimes in an image surrounded by assistants, and sometimes in a concert of reflexive concretions."[32] His examples are, of the first variety, *A Portrait of the Artist as a Young Man*; of the second, "Heart of Darkness" and *Passage to India*; of the third, *Party Going* and *Loving*. Speaking of Green's novels, he remarks, "Not central image as in 'Heart of Darkness' or attendant image as in *A Portrait of the Artist* but a multitude of glancing reflections assures the unity and effect of this form, a third among symbolic kinds."[33]

In *Party Going*, as I have indicated, we have the station, the fog, the dead pigeon, the mysterious illness of the elderly spinster, the unidentified birds under the arch, the unidentified stranger, the clump of artichokes, with their "buried treasure", all enigmatically inter-relating and reflecting mysteriously on one another. Similarly in *Loving*, we have the castle, the rococo trappings, the dovecote, the doves, the peacocks (living and dead), the peacock eggs, the artificial ruined temple, again the "buried treasure" in the bog, the weathervane that points in the wrong direction because there is a live mouse caught in its cogs. And once more it is quite impossible to reduce the intricate interplay, the perpetual cross-flickering of the symbols to any simple statement of meaning. The most one can hope to do is to extract a few of them and hazard guesses about what they imply and insinuate.

Perhaps the nearest approach to a "key symbol" is the ring, lost by Mrs. Tennant, found, lost and recovered by Edith, and eventually restored to its owner. Mrs. Tennant is a constant mislayer of valuables but this loss has more serious repercussions than usual. James Hall is right, I think, in his comment that "Mrs. Tennant's loss of the ring implies loss of direction and loss of capacity for loving, while its passing to Edith, who has both in plenty, is the passing of a symbol of power".[34] As far as the servants are concerned it is an "engagement ring", both literally and metaphorically. For Edith and Raunce become engaged almost simultaneously with the finding of the ring, and Edith wants to keep it as a sort of dowry. It is partly as a result of the anxiety caused by the ring's second disappearance and the visit of the farcically menacing insurance investigator that Raunce and Edith eventually elope, thus declaring their engagement not only to each other, but also in the general danger of their country.

Birds had almost disappeared in *Caught*, though the few that are mentioned—the remembered rooks caught in the trap, the pigeons caught by the dockyard fires, "flying about burning" or "walking in circles into the flames"—have their place in this novel about people caught in the trap of war and in the fire of lust. But they return in full force in *Loving*. Most spectacular are the hundreds of strutting peacocks, so zealously tended by Paddy, but to Mrs. Tennant merely part of the *décor*. Green gives no explicit indication of their "meaning", but we come to see them as complex symbols of pride, vanity, beauty, sex and greed. No less important are the doves which combine with the peacocks and the beautiful housemaid to make the last picture. "For what with the peacocks bowing at her purple skirts, the white doves nodding on her shoulders round her brilliant cheeks and her great eyes that blinked tears of happiness, it made a picture" (p. 229).

The doves are leading actors in one of the most subtle

symbolic episodes in the novel. In Chapter 7 (pp. 53–8) Nanny Swift, old, deaf and growing simple, takes up her station near the Tower of Pisa dovecote (itself suggestive of social decline and moral obliquity) and entertains her charges (Evelyn and Moira, the daughters of the adulteress, Mrs. Jack, and their Cockney evacuee playmate, the cook's nephew, Albert) with a tedious, feeble and insipid allegory about love among the birds. While she drones on, with eyes closed, the life of the dove cote (fluttering, quarrelling, murdering and making love) goes on uninterrupted, oblivious of the children who watch with rapt eagerness and of the housemaids who watch with surprise and embarrassment. Not only is the passage beautifully written, with a ballet-like quality and a precise rendering of gesture and movement which remind of Sterne and Borrow, but, as Ernest Jones has remarked, "within the novel this episode . . . is laden with significance. It is a token of strife between the old and the young, between the effete genteel and the pushing vulgar; between sexuality and the denial that it exists; between the classes. It is also about beauty which is inseparable from reproductive and excremental functions."[35] The scene is, in fact, almost a microcosm of the whole novel.

Since *Loving* is so much less tense and tragic than *Caught* it is natural that its colour-scheme should be quite different. There are here none of the dark-blue shadows, and none of the lurid reds of *Caught*. Red has much less effect than the number of its occurrences might suggest; more than half the occurrences are completely neutral, carrying no emotional charge. The same is true of black (Mr. Eldon's red and black note-books are mentioned repeatedly; so is the Red Library). The blues are generally pastel shades; the only variant used is azure, whereas in *Caught* Green had used the full range of gentian, indigo and sapphire. The main difference from the colour-scheme of *Caught* lies in the greater prominence of white, yellow (or, more accurately, gold and golden), green and purple.

Jean Howard, writing, in a review of *Concluding*, of "the pattern and integration, the colour and imagery of [Green's] earlier books", comments on the "purples and blues, the doves, the white lilac under green and all the peacock colours of *Loving*".[36] Though this list does not correspond exactly with the actual number of occurrences of the various colours, the colours mentioned are, on the whole, those which impress themselves in the reader's mind. For they are the colours which recur most frequently in those hauntingly poetic scenes which carry deeper undertones of meaning and which have a greater emotional resonance.

There are many such scenes. One of the most deservedly famous passages in Green's work is the description of the two young housemaids, the working-class enchantresses, Kate and Edith, waltzing together in the vast, disused ballroom amongst the sheeted furniture. But there are many other trivial, commonplace incidents which Green somehow invests with beauty. There is the scene of the younger servants' picnic with the children on the beach on a day when the wind "drove the girls' dresses onto them like statues", and they, themselves in a state of unfulfilled yearning, tease and torture the infatuated Albert, while the children watch and, for diversion, stone crabs to death. There is the extraordinary description of the unkempt Irish lamp-man snoring among his peacocks. All these, and many more, are mannered perhaps, but they are the writing of a man with a vision as fresh and original as if the world were newly created.

6

In *Back* we find a compound theme fundamentally similar to that of *Loving*—the escape of two people into an oasis of happiness and contentment in a world of social and moral upheaval. But the cast of players and the setting are quite different; here a small section of the business world is the test-tube in which a sample of the chaos and disintegration caused by the war is studied. Business life is so hedged about with governmental priorities and regulations that it can barely survive. But *Back* is not merely, or mainly, a satirical exposure of the hamstringing effect of bureaucratic control. The maze of government bureaux, ministries and agencies all known by mystifying initials, the pitfalls, the intrigues and the struggles for power, which face Charley Summers in his efforts to maintain his firm's production of parabolam, are chiefly important in the novel as an externalization of the bewilderment, incomprehension and obsession within his own mind, which arise from the death, while he was a prisoner-of-war, of his sweetheart Rose.

Charley is a man almost fatally wounded. His external

wound, the amputated leg, is a visible token of his crippled
psychological condition. His predicament is that if he is to live
he must both remember and forget Rose. To remember her is
anguish and suicidal despair; to forget her is betrayal and
emotional destitution. The whole novel is his quest for Rose—
the woman and the symbol of ideal love—whom he must find,
and eventually does, in the person of her half-sister Nancy.

   Back is unusual among Green's novels in being constructed
around a focal symbol—or rather a complex of symbols, the
woman Rose, the flower rose, and the colours of roses, especially
red and pink. Not only are vivid memories of the red-haired
Rose constantly present in Charley's mind ("dear Rose,
laughing, mad Rose, holding her baby, or, oh Rose, best of all
in bed, her glorious locks abounding") but she is, Giorgio
Melchiori claims, "evoked with obsessive insistence by the rich
and frequent imagery connected with the flower".[37] The colour,
rose, as previously mentioned, is always, in Green's work,
associated with love and emotional crisis. (In *Loving*, as well as
in *Caught*, it is present in almost all the love-scenes. "Lying back
he squinted into the blushing rose of that huge turf fire as it
glowed, his bluer eyes azure on which was a crescent rose
reflection. . . . Her eyes left his face and with what seemed a
quadrupling in depth came following his to rest on those
rectangles of warmth alive like blood. From this peat light her
great eyes became invested with rose incandescence that was
soft and soft and soft." This is the scene of Raunce's proposal—
Loving, p. 142.) But in *Back* the concentration of red and pink
is far greater than in any other novel; they constitute no less
than forty per cent of the colour-words in the novel.

   Imagery derived from roses, or at least from flowers, is
especially noticeable in the early chapters, before the appearance of Nancy, and frequently in quite unexpected contexts.
"The prisoners' camp had flowered with initials" (p. 8). "These
forms and reference numbers bloomed into flesh and blood, a
young woman, with shorthand, who could type" (p. 37).
". . . with fingers terribly white, pointed into painted nails like
the sheaths of flowers which might at any minute . . . mushroom
into tulips" (p. 43). There is even, occasionally, a type of
metaphor far more commonly found in poetry than in prose—
a piece of Sitwellian synaesthesia. "For there was a bicycle bell,
ringing closer and closer by the church, clustering spray upon

spray of sound which wreathed the air much as those roses grew around the headstones" (p. 6).

This love-death imagery, the motif of the roses twining the headstones, is carried on even in the apparently photographically realistic description of Nancy's apartment, before Charley knocks on her door for the first time, to be confronted by, he so believes, Rose herself. "He read her name, Miss Nancy Whitmore, in Gothic lettering as cut on tombstones. . . . He ran his eye over this door which was painted pink. The wall-paper he stared at round the door, was of wreathed roses on a white ground. . . . And her card was held in place by two fresh bits of sticking plaster, pink" (p. 46).

But too much can be (and by some critics has been) made of the novel's imagery. Few of Green's novels have less description than *Back*; a great deal of the novel (more than of any preceding novel except *Loving*) consists of scene—conversations between Charley and his boss, Corker Mead; his secretary, Dot Pitter; his dead mistress's husband, James Phillips; his raffish acquaintance, Arthur Middlewitch; his landlady, Mrs. Frasier; Rose's parents, the Grants; and of course, Nance. Always Charley is haunted by Rose, and by his delusion than Nancy is actually Rose herself, alive and pretending to be someone else. But all of these conversations Green keeps firmly on the prosaic level. There are, in fact, in the whole novel, only three passages of genuinely poetic passion, in which can be traced the major developments of the rose theme.

The first, of course, is the opening chapter in the cemetery, where Charley seeks Rose's grave. This is a scene of death-in-life; not only is Rose dead, but Charley himself is virtually dead. His state of blank, frozen misery is accentuated by the luxuriant mid-summer burgeoning of the roses. Green does not, as one might expect, place this scene of desolation and numb despair in winter. Perhaps one reason is that he had already done this in the opening chapters of *Caught*. But, apart from this, the simpler form of pathetic fallacy would not be sufficient here (though he does secure the co-operation of the weather by making it rain). Green was seeking a more complex effect; Jean Howard must surely have meant this scene, when, speaking of "the passages of greater intensity" in Green's novels, she gives as an instance "the passage in the deserted garden in *Back* . . . flowering with positive force against the strained terrifying

negation of the shell-shocked man's existence".[38] ("Garden"
is presumably a slip—an unfortunate one since it causes some
confusion with a later scene. It is true, however, that Green
does refer to the cemetery as "this sort of sad garden"). He
wanted this abundant natural life to emphasize by contrast
Charley's state, and he wanted to establish the roses as a
dominant motif as symbolic of the power over Charley still
wielded by the dead Rose. It is noticeable, however, and
undoubtedly deliberate, that although the roses are in full
bloom, the colour of only one is specified; it is not red, but
"ivory pink".

The second scene is that in the blitzed rose-garden, several
months later (pp. 176–8) when Nancy kisses Charley for the
first time, and life begins anew. The two scenes are carefully
linked by verbal echoes. The passage ". . . briars that had borne
gay rose, after rose, after wild rose, to sway under summer rain,
to spatter the held drops, to touch a forehead, perhaps to wet
the brown eyes of someone idly searching these cypresses for an
abandoned nest" (p. 177) recalls "rose after rose after rose"
(p. 5), "the rose sprinkled held raindrops on his eyes", "his
glance was held by a nest" and "so the rose softly thumped his
forehead" (p. 8) and the summer rain (p. 9) which drives
Summers to shelter in the church-porch. This is obvious enough.
What is perhaps not quite so obvious is that this scene, in
contrast to the earlier, is one of life-in-death. It is now autumn
instead of summer; the roses are dead ("Petals that had dropped
some months back and rotted, traces of a summer now gone,
were covered by the brown leaves . . .", p. 176). But Charley
who had been dead is alive again. (One of the meanings
suggested by the title is "Back from the dead".) It is one of
Green's most subtle artistic feats that this whole scene, in which
no roses bloom, is suffused with their colour, from the light of
the setting sun. In barely two pages there are no less than a
dozen occurrences of the word "red" and its equivalents. "Both
instinctively looked back to find whether they are being followed,
but all they saw was the red mound of light rubble, with the
staircase and chimney lit a rosier red, and, as they turned again
to themselves in the garden, the briars wreathed from one
black cypress to another were aflame, as alive as live filaments
in an electric light bulb, against this night's quick agony of
sun."

"The night, on its way fast, was chill, and now he had again that undreamed of sharp warmth moving and living on his own, her breath an attar of roses on his deep sun-red cheek, her hair an animal over his eyes and alive, for he could see each rose glowing separate strand, then her dark body thrusting heavy at him, and her blood dark eel fingers that fumbled at his neck" (p. 177).

Green has here (probably unwittingly) written a scene that Nathaniel Hawthorne had designed more than a century before. A comment from Hawthorne's note-books (1838) shows how similar to Green's was his feeling for red. "The red light which the sunsets at this season diffuse; there being showery afternoons, but the sun setting bright under cloud and diffusing its radiance over those that are scattered in masses all over the sky. It gives a red tinge to all objects, even to those of sombre hue, yet without changing the hues. The complexions of people are exceedingly enriched by it; they look warm, and kindled with a wild fire. The whole scenery and personages acquire, methinks, a passionate character. A love-scene should be laid on such an evening." [39]

The third passage is the briefest. It is the second last paragraph of the novel. It is Christmas, and there is snow on the ground when Charley has "under his eyes the great, the overwhelming sight of the woman he loved, for the first time without her clothes". Here, at last, Nancy, now loved for herself, again becomes Rose; the real and the ideal merge, and what had seemed lost for ever is regained. This passage, one of the most lyrically lovely that Green has ever written, brings the rose theme to its perfect and triumphant finale. "And because the lamp was lit, the pink shade seemed to spill a light of roses over her in all their summer colour, her hands that lay along her legs were red, her stomach gold, her breasts the colour of cream roses, and her neck white roses for the bride."

7

Back, like *Loving*, ends with a promise of happiness and fulfilment. Not so *Concluding*, which ends with no decisive resolution —neither equilibrium nor catastrophe. With the mystery of the missing girl unsolved, with nothing certain in the future except the intensified malignity of his antagonist Miss Edge, Mr. Rock at last falls asleep. But he is—though why he should be is, like everything else, unexplained—"on the whole well satisfied with his day".

What is *Concluding* about—this strangest and most perplexing of all Henry Green's novels? One can say, in general terms, that it continues into a near imagined future Green's treatment of the theme of dissolution, and gives a glimpse of what may replace the disintegrating society of the present. But *Concluding* is more than a conventional anti-Utopia; there is nothing bare, arid or doctrinaire about it. It is too rich in contradictory, wayward, capricious life to be confined within an allegorical strait-jacket. Its strength, like that of all Green's work, derives at least as much from its sympathy as from its satire, from its understanding of, and its refusal to over-simplify, the complexity of the human predicament. No one has brought out the multiple nature of *Concluding* better than Jean Howard in a review written before the novel was published. "*Concluding* . . . is not only the story of the sadness and dignity of an old man, not only an allegory of mankind on the edge of darkness, but also about the desires and fears behind an old man's fear of the dark in a forest, about the trepidations and uncertainties beneath the summer airs and azaleas of adolescence, desires and hostilities that are the same for all ages. . . . Individual man is still the centre of [Henry Green's] world. Without sacrificing the framework of the novel or his preoccupation with human problems he contrives . . . to draw up from the deeper levels of the unconscious evidence of emotions that are inexpressible except through certain media such as that of poetic imagery. Simultaneously and through this same poetic process he suggests the shadow of an allegory behind the individual, and places mankind in relation to the vast ill-comprehended landscape of his own time."[40]

In *Concluding*, then, Green has developed even further the poetic methods which enable him to present, at the same time, several different aspects or levels of reality—the contemporary and the timeless, the specific and the universal. As individuals Mr. Rock and Miss Edge are completely real, but it is clear that they are figures larger than life, that they stand more for themselves. Mr. Rock may be regarded as the representative of liberal humanism and the last apostle of the individual's right to shape his own destiny, Miss Edge as standing for the rigid, bureaucratic regimentation of the human spirit into state-ordained moulds. But the novel is based on something much more complicated than a simple, clear-cut conflict between these two forces. There are other conflicts as well. One that is even more fundamental is suggested by the whole setting of the novel. On the one hand is the former great house, now a training school for girl civil-servants, and now even more out of touch with human and natural realities than it had been (like the similar great house in *Loving*) in its obsolescence as the fortress of aristocracy. But on the other hand is the forest surrounding the school, which, as suggested in an earlier chapter, stands for the elemental, instinctive life which mankind tries to deny but which will not be denied. Nigel Dennis has remarked that the school is "such an official outrage that Nature herself attacks it with every malicious trick in her bag strewing sordid bluebottle flies over the formal azalea flowers, ... loosing owls and bats, making every human cry echo three times, tormenting the spinster matrons with a gross old man. To these barren ladies-of-the-state their academy is a Garden of Eden which it is their duty to keep free from vulgarity and serpents—and the total reply of Green's symbols is that such an attitude to life is, in effect, a baleful attempt to choke the very source of life."[41]

In this conflict it is clear enough where Miss Baker and Miss Edge stand. They continually insist that they "love this Great Place". But their love is completely selfish. They regard *their* beautiful Park in much the same way as Mrs. Tennant regarded her peacocks—as a collection of beautiful objects, to be plundered for the adornment of the Founder's Day Dance, but not to be respected for its own independent life. Mr. Rock's position, however, is somewhat equivocal and ambiguous. He seems, reduced as he is almost to peasant status, to be closer to "the source of life" than they. He has a strong appreciation of natural beauty—by daylight. To him the singing of the starlings, as they settle at dusk, is "the greatest sound on earth". He has a goose and a sow which he tends with affectionate solicitude, while Miss Edge abominates and even fears (or pretends to fear) them. But Daisy and Ted are dependent and domesticated creatures, tokens of the victory of man's intelligence over nature. They are as much the captives of Mr. Rock as the myriad M-initialled girls are captives of the state. Altogether, if

Mr. Rock is to be made a figure of allegory, he is essentially a figure representing the massive, scientific, rational intelligence of the nineteenth century. His fear of "the forests of the night" is symptomatic of his rejection and distrust of the unconscious and irrational elements in himself and in humanity generally —an uneasiness which comes out explicitly in his relationship with his grand-daughter Liz, and even more clearly in the scene of his initiation into the secret society of the girls in their underground meeting place (of which, no doubt, much could be made). It seems, then, that Mr. Rock, infinitely preferable to his antagonists though he is, is not a complete man; he too is stunted and limited—a relic of the past rather than a hope for the future.

Where then does hope lie, or is there none? It does not lie in Liz, who represents what these children are to become— neurotic, broken, despairing in her sensuality. Perhaps there is a hint that, if anywhere, hope lies in the character whom we never see—in the schoolgirl Mary who has escaped. But again, for all we know, Mary may be dead (as Mr. Rock believes). And perhaps, after all, that is the message of the book—that the best hope of the world lies in the end of humanity. Philip Toynbee has said of the novel that it is not "cruel in any obvious way, but by the curious purity of its negation it inspires a sort of chilly despair".[42]

It is paradoxical—but with this writer one expects the un-expected—that *Concluding* is both Green's most pessimistic and his most poetic novel. It is poetic (though one probably uses this term only because poetry is usually thought of as having closer affinities than prose has with music and painting) in the highly charged, lyrical natural description, in the extraordinary profusion of its imagery (unequalled by any other novel, except perhaps *Party Going*), in its whole structure and organization. In this novel the normal temporal-causal sequence has been abolished; the book has the quality of a nightmare, not only in the way it constantly suggests the presence of evil forces, just outside our range of vision, always about to materialize, but never quite doing so, but also in its formless coherence. Mark Schorer has remarked that "we go in and out of this novel in the way that the mind goes in and out of a dream".[43]

It is thoroughly appropriate, therefore, that the novel should begin in a fog, through which Mr. Rock and Adams, the woodman, laboriously make their way up to the academy. The description of the fog in the woods is the first taste of the novel's weird beauty; it is as impressive as the description of London fog in *Party Going*—and indeed some of the conceits are reminiscent of those of the early novel. (E.g. "At this instant, like a woman letting down her mass of hair from a white towel in which she had bound it, the sun came through for a moment, and lit the azaleas on either side before fog, redescending, blanketed these off again; as it might be white curtains, drawn by someone out of sight, over a palace bedroom window, to shut behind them a blonde princess undressing", p. 7; ". . . the sun coming through once more, made it for a second so that he might have been inside a pearl strung next the skin of his beloved", p. 8.)

Equally remarkable are the descriptions of the summer sunlight, sunlight which is so strong that Green frequently uses auditory images to render its quality ("a great shaft of early sunlight which . . . shone so loud", "the megaphone of light", p. 21; "with the great sun beating stretched earth as a brass hand on a tomtom", p. 75); of dusk; and of the moonlight in which Mr. Rock and Liz Wade reach the house and through which they wade homeward, as in the morning he had waded through fog. It is, of course, equally appropriate that the novel should end in this eerie, deceptive light, in which the most familiar things are transformed. "For their moon was still enormous up above on a couch of velvet, blatant, a huge female disc of chalk on deep blue with holes around that, winking, squandered in the void a small light as of latrines. The moon was now all powerful, it covered everything with salt, and bewigged distant trees; it coldly flicked the dark to an instantaneous view of what this held, it stunned the eye by stone, was all-powerful, and made each of these three related people into someone alien, glistening, frozen eyed, alone" (p. 189).

As for the novel's imagery, one immediately notices that the birds, almost banished from *Back*, return, literally in flocks, in *Concluding*. Perhaps the most extraordinary passage in the whole novel is the description of the starlings settling for the night. "Then as they came to where the trees ended, and blackbirds, before roosting, began to give the alarm in earnest, some first starlings flew out of the sky. Over against the old man and his granddaughter the vast mansion reflected a vast red, sky above

M

paled while to the left it outshone the house, and more starlings crossed. After which these birds came in hundreds, then
suddenly by legion, black and blunt against faint rose. They
swarmed above the lonely elm, they circled a hundred feet
above, until the leader, followed by ever greater numbers, in
one broad spiral led the way down and so, as they descended
through falling dusk in a soft roar, they made, as they had at
dawn, a huge sea shell that stood proud to a moon which, flat
sovereign red gold, was already poised full faced to a dying
world.

Once the starlings had settled in that tree they one and all
burst out singing.

Then there were more, even higher, dots against paler pink,
and these, in their turn, began to circle up above, scything the
air, and to swoop down through a thickening curve, in the
enormous echo of blood, or of the sea, until all was black about
that black elm, as the first mass of starlings left while these
others settled, and there was a huge volume of singing" (pp.
176-7).

It would be foolish to attempt to reduce such a passage to a
bald "prose" meaning; it has the quality of a lyric of making
a moment permanent and of suggesting feelings that cannot be
defined. But it should at least be noticed that this is not a
completely isolated passage, with no connection with anything
else in the book. The starlings are to be in some way connected
with the girls. This connection is first hinted at dawn, when Miss
Edge, watching a cloud of starlings rise from the nearby wood,
"was about to exclaim in delight when, throughout the
dormitories upstairs, with a sound of bees in this distant
Sanctum, buzzers called her girls to rise so that two hundred
and eighty nine turned over to that sound, stretched and
yawned, opened blue eyes on their white sheets to this new
day . . ." (p. 19). Later, Ma Marchbanks, interviewing Moira
about the disappearance of Mary and Merode, tells the girl
" 'Besides we rely on you senior girls, you realise, before the
bird is flown, so to speak, you know' " (p. 50). A group of girls
observe Sebastian Birt bringing Merode, whom he has found in
the woods, to Mr. Rock's cottage. "This set them off in whispers,
as a cloud passes the moon, like birds at long awaited dusk in
trees down by the beach" (p. 59). At lunch the noise of the
students' talking "was a twitter of a thousand starlings" (p. 98).

As the staff file in "that clatter of conversation stilled as, with a rustle of a thousand birds rising from willows about a warm lagoon the girls stood in silence to mark the entrance. Then, after Miss Edge had been last to sit down, the three hundred budding State Servants, with another outburst of talk as of starlings moving between clumps of reeds to roost, in their turn, left to collect plates of cold meat and vegetables . . . (p. 99). As well as this frequent likening of the conversation of the girls to the chattering and whistling of the starling flocks as they jostle for roosting places, there is clearly a link between the quoted description of the black mass of birds circling and swooping, accompanied by the music of its singing, and that of the white mass of girls whirling and swaying to waltz music. Perhaps it all "means" no more than that the girls still have a grace, a freedom and an irresponsibility that their elders have lost; it may suggest that they are closer to "the source of life", not yet deformed and denatured by the iron regulation, the restrictions and taboos of the society in which they are growing up. But possibly there is a deeper implication. Starlings are migratory birds, and the vast congregations of these birds at dusk, which Green has described so memorably, are a prelude to migration. Is there perhaps a hint in these two passages (as there is more openly in Mary's disappearance) that the only hope for these girls is in flight? But again one asks—flight whither?

Starlings are not the only creatures invoked in the novel's imagery. Natural imagery is more plentiful in *Concluding* than in any novel since *Party Going*. Mr. Rock and Adams, making their laborious progress towards the house are described as moving "like slow, suiciding moles in the half-light" (p. 8). Mr. Rock, gossiping in the kitchen with Mrs. Blain, while the orderlies listen, "felt a tide of female curiosity flow up over him, so strong it was like the smell of a fox that has just slunk by" (p. 24). For Miss Marchbanks the worry of the two girls' disappearance is "like an ulcer high under the ribs, where it fluttered, a blood stained dove with tearing claws" (p. 47). Liz, kissing Sebastian Birt, fastens "her mouth on his as though she were an octopus that had lost its arms to the propellers of a tug, and had only its mouth now with which, in a world of the hunted, to hang onto wrecked spars" (p. 55). The eyes of the girls are "like jewels enclosed by flesh coloured anemones beneath green clear water when these yawn after shrimps . . ."

(p. 109). Miss Baker, startled in the woods by the derisive laughter of the unseen Liz, "looked back the way she had come, like a hen, at night, watching behind for a fox" (p. 154). Sebastian and Liz, dancing as though glued together, are watched with palsied indignation by Misses Baker and Edge who glare "like a couple of old black herons" (p. 219). Green, in fact, shows an even more remarkable fertility than usual in the coining of new, or the enlivening of old, animal metaphors for the definition of many kinds of human feeling—anxiety, desire, indignation, apprehension, inquisitiveness.

Another strain of imagery, into which, highly conventional as it is, Green manages to infuse new life, is that of jewels (again reminiscent of *Party Going*). This is partly responsible for the aura of glamour surrounding the horde of adolescent girls, particularly at the dance. The complex simile already quoted ("eyes . . . like jewels enclosed by flesh coloured anemones . . .") is several times repeated in various forms ("those . . . eyes, much greater than jewels"; "children . . . with more fabulous gems for eyes"; "the rajah's hoard of her eyes"). But another reason is the haze of literary reminiscence in which these girls move; behind them we sense the shadowy presence of such famous ladies as Cleopatra, Imogen, Dido, Lamia, Belinda and Eliot's nameless society-lady. Giorgio Melchiori has convincingly demonstrated a parallel between the rich and sensuous description of the girls awakening from their afternoon sleep (p. 109) and the famous "The chair she sat in" passage of "A Game of Chess".[44]

The passages quoted have given some indication of the profusion of colour in the novel. There is the red of girls' hair and lips and nails (and pyjamas), of leaves and rhododendrons and sunsets; the gold of girls' hair and legs, of leaves and azalea and moonlight; the blue of eyes and sky and shadow; the green of trees and water. And yet none of these is the dominant colour of the novel. Actually the colour-adjective most frequently used is, as in *Party Going* and *Loving* (and, later, in *Nothing*), white. But the proportion of white in the spectrum of *Concluding* is far higher than in either of the two earlier novels. Numerically, the second most important "colour" is, as in no other novel, black. (In *Living* black and white are also the two most prominent colours, but in reverse order.) At first blush it may seem extraordinary that in this novel, which seems full of vivid and variegated colour, the two no-colours are almost as prominent as all the genuine colours. But a little examination reveals that this opposition between black and white on the one hand and the vivid reds and greens, blues and yellows on the other emanates from, and in turn reinforces, some of the basic conflicts of the novel.

It is, as has already been suggested, dangerously misleading to ascribe to colours independent and self-sufficient meanings, or to seek absolute correlations of colour and emotion. There is no doubt that in *Concluding* many of the uses of white and black may be attributed mainly to descriptive accuracy. There are white sheets, white faces, white legs, white flowers, white dust, white teeth, white arms, white heads, white dresses; there are black hats, black dresses, black trees. But one cannot but feel that the insistence on these two "colours", particularly in combination, carries deeper implications. The phrase "black and white" occurs at least a dozen times in the novel; any doubt we may have that this is accidental is dispelled when, at the dance, Miss Edge daintily fans herself with "a lace bordered black and white handkerchief" (p. 215). Indeed this whole ball sequence is a study in black and white—the girls are all in short white frocks; Liz, Miss Baker and Miss Edge in long black gowns; Mr. Rock and Sebastian Birt in black suits. (What the other teachers are wearing is not specified.)

Black is, of course, traditionally a colour of negation and death; white has, among many others, connotations of purity and abstraction. The two together, in common usage, carry such meanings as restriction and regulation, precise definition, the strict letter of the law, the reduction of everything to formulas. There is no doubt that this is the force of "black and white" in *Concluding*. Early in the novel, when Edge and Baker are discussing the "Rock imbroglio", Baker reminds Edge of the "original directive" in which it is laid down "in black and white" that Mr. Rock is to keep his house for life. "Black and white" is the symbol of bureaucracy, of legalism divorced from all human feeling.

The other colours of the book—the reds and greens, blues and golds—are the colours of nature, of life, passion and vitality. The opposition of colours in this novel is, in fact, virtually the same as that in the later apocalyptic poems of Edith Sitwell. There are at least a couple of occasions when this

opposition comes to the surface, though, of course, its significance is never defined. One of these is the description of the walls
of the headmistresses' Sanctum. ". . . this receding vista of white
and black lozenges set from the rugs to four feet up the walls,
in precise and radiating perspective, seemed altogether out of
place next British dragons in green and yellow . . ." (p. 12).
(It is typical of Green's refusal of any simple allegory, however,
that it was Miss Edge herself who was responsible for having
part of the tiled floor covered with the "state imitation Kidder-
minster rugs".) It is this black and white, geometrically-precise
dado which mesmerizes the red-haired Merode (who had been
found amid the green and gold of the fallen beech), when she
is interviewed by Miss Marchbanks. "No longer blinded in
sunlight, her eyes had caught on one of the black squares, as
that pyjama leg had earlier been hooked on a briar. And while
her horror at this interview increased, so the dado began to
swell and then recede, only to grow at once even larger, the
square in particular to get bigger and bigger till she felt she had
it in her mouth, a stifling, furry rectangle" (p. 69).

The other occasion is the conversation at lunch, when the
lovesick Winstanley, hopelessly infatuated with the indifferent
Sebastian, offers a topic to bridge the awkwardness caused by
Miss Edge's forgetful mention of Mary.

" 'Ma'am,' she said. 'Have you ever thought of Chinese
pheasants for our grounds?'

" 'Chinese?' Miss Edge enquired.

" 'The plumage,' Winstanley explained. 'A perfect red and
gold. . . .' "

Miss Edge seizes an opportunity for a few thrusts at Mr. Rock
and Sebastian Birt, when Miss Baker breaks in. " 'Where I was
brought up there used to be a black and white farm,' Baker
announced. 'A half timbered place, piebald horses, black and
white poultry and so on' " (p. 100).

At the end of the meal, Winstanley returns to the subject.

" 'The great thing is, ma'am, they're to all intents and
purposes practically self-supporting,' Winstanley began once
more.

"Because Miss Edge had just asked herself if the horror Rock
could have sheltered Mary she was startled.

" 'How do you mean?' she fiercely enquired.

" 'The Chinese pheasants.'

" 'Yes I had gathered that,' she lied. 'But the point occurred to me, how would they do in winter, in snow?'

" 'Oh ma'am, I'm sure they must be hardy. Why think of the giant panda,' Marchbanks said.

" 'Yes, there's another black and white animal,' Miss Baker agreed" (p. 105).

All of this appears perfectly natural and unobtrusive, but it has no obvious point on the "story" level. One can only assume that it has been carefully planted to work on the fringes of the reader's consciousness, underlining a basic conflict of the novel between age, negation, regulation, inhumanity on the one hand and youth, nature, vitality, feeling on the other.

8

In Green's two latest novels, *Nothing* and *Doting*, colour has ceased to be important. With the almost exclusive concentration on dialogue, description has faded almost to nothing. *Nothing* has considerably less description, but exactly the same number of colour-words as *Party Going*; the predominance of white (hands, table-cloths, ties) together with the smaller infusions of rose (fire-light), red (nails and mouths) and blue (eyes) reflects the similarity between the two novels, especially the prominence in one of an Amabel, in the other of a Jane Weatherby. In *Doting* the proportion of description is lower than in any other book, and the number of colour-adjectives falls to only one in every seven pages. Actually of the thirty-six colour-words in the novel, twenty-two occur in the first thirteen pages (the scene in the night club). After this first section there is an average of only one colour-word in every seventeen pages. "Purification" could hardly be carried further than this.

From these novels the birds have also been banished; there are no flocks of starlings, no screaming peacocks, no disorderly doves in these bare, abstract novels. Perhaps it is mere perversity on the reader's part, but the sections of these novels that seem to have the strongest hold on the reader's imagination (and it is none too strong) are the very passages which, according to Green's new theory of the novel, are illegitimate and redundant—the description of the private room in the great hotel, where the twenty-first birthday party is to be held in one novel; in the other the opening and closing scenes in the

night clubs, with their snake-dancers and jugglers and changing
lights. The juggler who performs his miracles of skill, ignored
by the Middletons and Annabel, in the opening chapter,
reappears in the different night club of the last chapter, to be
greeted by an "Oh God!" from Peter Middleton, Nigel Dennis
has commented that when the juggler reappears "the reader
dimly suspects that he has missed something".[45] It is a sufficient
indication of the difference of these novels from their predecessors that this is the only occasion in either novel when the
reader *has* such a suspicion; their "meaning" is not superficial,
but it is seldom conveyed by oblique, "poetic" methods. Nigel
Dennis explains the juggler as the representative of "a world in
which optical illusion, smiling care and enviable sleight-of-
hand matter most . . . [His] first appearance is for the purpose
of luring the reader into a dream of romantic deception; his
second appearance when the characters have played out their
parts is to indicate the dream is over, that 'the wheel has turned
full circle'."[46] He does not go on to suggest, however, as might
very well be suggested, that the juggler, who balances ivory
billiard balls and pint beer mugs with such dexterous aplomb,
is really Green himself, who in this novel juggles his men and
women with equal adroitness. It is scarcely fanciful to see the
women of this novel as ivory balls—smooth, hard and im-
penetrable—and the men, particularly the bibulous Charles, as
beer mugs!

Little needs to be added to what has already been said, in
other contexts, about the themes of these two novels. In them
Green seems to have deliberately limited the range of his
sympathies and judgment, but there is more to them than some
reviewers thought—Marghanita Laski, for example, described
Nothing as "a novel of society with (O blesséd relief!) no wider
social implications whatsoever, and possibly no implications of
any sort at all".[47] Actually *Nothing* is an extremely acute study
of the almost disintegrated society of the well-to-do; for all its
frivolity, its apparent triviality, its steady stream of dialogue
which carefully avoids discussion of serious issues, it exposes (if
"exposes" is the right word for a book which so scrupulously
refrains from comment or judgment) the moral and emotional
impoverishment of the smart set, shows parental duty reduced
to a cold-hearted parental cannibalism—more subtle and
civilized, no doubt, and cloaked by "charm", but essentially

no better than that of Dickens' Mr. Turveydrop. There are still, for the older generation, the elaborate and impeccably cooked and served luncheons and dinners, but it is clear that these are the last vestiges of a way of life that is fast disappearing. Jane Weatherby and John Pomfret are the last representatives of a moribund class, the leisured, parasitic class which is on the verge of being taxed out of existence; the twenty-first birthday party for Jane's son, Philip, which is really Jane's own show, is like the ritual dance of an effete and dying culture.

Interwoven with this theme is another—the reversal of the traditional roles of parents and children. It is the parents who are the rebels—their attitude to life has still the irresponsible, adolescent hedonism of their youth in the twenties—while their children, as typified by Philip, are the conservatives, the traditionalists, the responsible, though arrogantly priggish, members of society. Their parents have no concept of society; for them "society" simply means themselves and their friends. This theme of the incomprehension and failure of sympathy between the generations is yet another version of what is perhaps the most constant of all Green's themes—the impossibility of any human being really knowing and understanding any other.

Doting presents this same shattered world, but more fully illuminates another aspect of it—the predicament of the young woman of the upper middle-class, who in former times would have been launched on the world to acquire a suitable husband in a series of dinners, balls, house-parties (like Hannah Glossop in *Living*, and the girls in *Party Going*), but who, now, finds nowhere to begin. This situation is explicitly discussed by two of the members of the older generation, one of whom has capitalized on it, while the other would very much like to.

" 'Then you blame me, old man?'
'I? Not the least bit in the world' Middleton said, with
evident sincerity. 'No, if you want me to put my
finger on the spot, I'd say it was taxation.'
'By making everything more expensive?'
'Precisely, Charles. They don't get asked out any more.'
'Except for the old, old reason?'
Mr. Middleton laughed. 'How then are they to meet any-
one nowadays?' he demanded" (p. 224).

So this novel also, underneath its shimmering lightness, its polished inanity, is actually a serious anthropological study of the break-down of the elaborate mating procedures of the past, and the resultant moral confusion.

These two novels do have important themes, but they are not, one feels, themes important enough to engage the exclusive attention of the author of *Caught, Back* and *Concluding.* The themes are too much confined to the topical, the transitory; the dimension of universality present in the earlier novels is lacking. There seems to be nothing more to say on these themes, or on this segment of society. It is now six years since *Doting* appeared —the longest gap in Green's work since the ten-year hiatus between *Living* and *Party Going.* One cannot help wondering whether these two most recent books were signs of the withering of the creative impulse in Green, and whether he now prefers silence to repetition and self-imitation.

Styles and Manners

> Prose is not to be read aloud but to oneself alone at night, and it is
> not quick as poetry but rather a gathering web of insinuations
> which go farther than names however shared could ever go. Prose
> should be a long intimacy between strangers with no direct appeal
> to what both may have known. It should slowly appeal to feelings
> unexpressed, it should in the end draw tears out of the stone.
>
> (*Pack My Bag*, p. 88)

I

IN this chapter I propose to discuss Henry Green's style—or
rather styles, for his novels vary as much in their handling
of language as they do in technique. Since Green's use of
metaphor, especially recurrent metaphor, in several novels has
already been commented on, I shall here be concerned chiefly
with vocabulary, syntax and sentence structure—with the words
that Green uses and the patterns into which he combines them.
One purpose will be to discover and record Green's deviations
from normal usage. But, as René Wellek has pointed out, "this
method of stylistic analysis—of concentrating on the peculiarities
of style . . . —has obvious dangers. We are likely to accumulate
isolated observations, specimens of the marked traits, and to
forget that a work of art is a whole. We are likely to overstress
'originality', individuality, the merely idiosyncratic."[1] A second
purpose, therefore, will be to discover at least a few of the
more important general features of Green's style (or styles)—i.e.
features which, although within the bounds of accepted usage,
are characteristic of the novelist, or of the particular novel. The
most important (and the most difficult) purpose will be to
interpret any discoveries that may be made as indications of the
novelist's intentions or, more precisely, of the deeper significance
of what he writes.

2

Before attempting this analysis, however, some consideration of
the general question of the importance of style in the novel, and

particularly in the novels of Henry Green, seems desirable. Is a
minute scrutiny of the actual words that any novelist uses really
necessary? In a challenging and stimulating article, published
recently, Philip Rahv maintains that, generally, it is not. This
critic protests vehemently against "three biases" in contemporary criticism of fiction which, he claims, "can be traced directly
or indirectly to the recent infection of the prose sense by poetics".
The second of these biases is "the one identifying style as the
'essential activity' of imaginative prose"; this identification,
Rahv claims, "confuses the intensive speech proper to poetry
with the more openly communicative, functional and extensive
language proper to prose".[2]

Developing his argument against this bias, Rahv maintains
that the novel secures its effects "not locally, in the short run,
but in the long run, by accumulation and progression", and
that more important criteria in estimating a novel's value than
style are "character—creation . . . the depth of life out of
which a novelist's moral feeling springs . . . the capacity in
constructing a plot".[3] He quotes with approval the view of the
Russian critic Zhirmunsky who, in opposition to the more
extreme formalists, maintained that "a novel and a lyric poem
are not to be equated as works of verbal art because the relationship in them between theme and composition is quite different.
Words in a novel . . . are closer to everyday speech and openly
communicative in function, whereas in a poem the verbaliza-
tion is wholly determined by the aesthetic design and is, in
that sense, an end in itself."[4] Rahv also quotes with approval
the distinction made by Christopher Caudwell (in his book
Illusion and Reality) between poetic and prosaic language. "The
poetic word is the logos, the word-made-flesh, the active will
ideally ordering, whereas the novel's word is the sign, the
reference, the conversationally pointing gesture."[5] And again,
"The poem and the story both use sounds which awake images
of outer reality and affective reverberations; but in poetry the
affective associations are organized by the structure of the
language, while in the novel they are organized by the structure
of the outer reality portrayed. . . ." Hence, says Rahv, "the
emotional associations of the novel are attached not to its words
but to the mock-reality which they bring into being". He
endorses also Caudwell's view that "rhythm, preciousness and
style are alien to the novel [for] novels are not composed of

words. They are composed of scenes, actions, *stuff*, and people, just as plays are. A 'jewelled' style is a disadvantage to a novel because it distracts the eye from the things and people to the words—not as words, as black outlines, but as symbols to which a variety of feeling-tone is directly attached."[6]

Rahv's conclusion is that "All that we can legitimately ask of a novelist in the matter of language is that it be appropriate to the matter in hand. What is said must not stand in a contradictory relation to the way it is said, for that would dispel the illusion of life and with it the credibility of the fiction."[7] In the course of the essay he does, however, admit some qualifications. "There are, of course, poetic passages in novels (as in Melville and Lawrence) as there are novelistic passages in poetry, but that in no way changes the characteristics of the two genres."[8] "There is such a thing, to be sure, as a purely formal prose, in which the elements of style and composition dominate . . . but it is precisely the 'ornamentalism' of such prose that basically differentiates it from the narrative language of novelists like Stendhal, Tolstoy or Dostoievsky, who achieve expressiveness chiefly through extensive rather than intensive verbal means." He suggests that "in English the work of Virginia Woolf would to some extent correspond to what the Russians mean by 'ornamental' prose fiction [which, he explains, is not the same thing as 'ornate prose' but is 'mainly distinguished by the fact that it keeps the reader's attention fixed on the small detail: the words, their sounds, their rhythm'] as would a novel like *Nightwood*; and among the younger American novelists there are not a few 'ornamental' writers of prose to whom the test of local exemplification would apply, for the effects they seek depend almost entirely on stylization, on the perceptibility . . . of the mode of expression".[9]

Following the suggestions of Philip Rahv and the various critics whom he quotes (without necessarily accepting their valuations, explicit or implicit, of the novelists they mention) it seems possible to group novelists roughly into five categories, according to their differing attitudes towards the language they use, and according to the relative importance in their work of what is said and how it is said—or to use the phrase that Rahv borrows from the formalists, according to the degree of perceptibility of the mode of expression. I must emphasize, however, that I am not suggesting that the novelists in each of the various groups are of even approximately equal stature.

1. At one extreme there are those novelists who gain their effects almost entirely by accumulation and progression, whose imaginations are so stirred by a large-scale vision of human life that they take comparatively little interest in, and little trouble with, the actual details of expression. This group includes such novelists as Dostoievsky and Tolstoy, Balzac and Stendhal, Dickens and Hardy—novelists, who are undeniably among the greatest, but prose-writers whose styles, if examined in detail, are often disappointingly careless. R. A. Sayce's comment on Balzac applies fairly well to all: "An exceptional imagination, expressing itself in transforming imagery, seizes trivial reality and remodels it in a manner which may be called, in a technical sense, sublime. The faults are not thereby annihilated but their relative size is reduced to insignificant proportions. Instead of occupying the centre, they are pushed out to the surface and appear as mere accidental excrescences."[10]

2. Next are those novelists who are primarily concerned with what they have to say, but who are, nevertheless, distinctive and careful prose stylists. Here I am thinking particularly of those novelists who (unlike the writers of the first group) have little or nothing of the poet in their make-up—novelists like Fielding, Jane Austen, Thackeray (at his best), George Eliot, Butler, Bennett and such contemporaries as Isherwood, Waugh and Graham Greene.

3. A third group is made up of those novelists who, generally concerned with the total, over-all effect rather than the local effect, are in the main content (in Sartre's phrase) to "utilize language", but who sometimes use language poetically. Philip Rahv's examples, as already mentioned, are Melville and Lawrence.

4. Next are those novelists in whom subject-matter and theme are still extremely important, but who are also unremittingly concerned with style, with the rhythms of the paragraphs, the vividness and expressiveness of their prose; those who share Flaubert's ideal, as defined by Ernst Robert Curtius, "to transmute reality into imperishable verbal substance",[11] and who frequently borrow the devices of poetry—the evocative power of words, figurative language, alliteration, repetition, grammatical and syntactical distortion. Conrad

is of this company; so is Faulkner; so is Joyce; so is Virginia Woolf.

5. Finally there are those novelists who, in Bacon's phrase, "study words and not matter", the highly mannered writers of jewelled, precious prose who are so preoccupied with style as an end in itself that they have little concern with anything else. E. M. Forster would probably relegate Meredith and even James to this category[12] (as Philip Rahv would similarly relegate Flaubert and Virginia Woolf), along with Walter Pater and Oscar Wilde, and all the Firbanks and Douglases, the Cabells and Hergesheimers and Van Vechtens.

To which of these categories does Henry Green belong? It is clear, at least, that he does not belong to the first; indeed it is doubtful whether any important contemporary novelist does. (Perhaps that uneven, neglected, but sometimes extremely impressive novelist, James Hanley, does.) In the days before Flaubert and Turgenev and Henry James it was possible for novelists to be blithely indifferent to the novel as a form of art; it has hardly been possible since. It is equally clear that Green does not belong with the "non-poetic" second group. It is very easy to under-estimate the importance of the colloquial, vernacular element in Green's work, but obviously Green's conception of prose, as defined in the passage quoted at the beginning of this chapter, is different from that of most novelists of his generation. In practice the essential difference is that whereas writers like Christopher Isherwood attempt to make of language a kind of transparent medium through which we view the action, Green has experimented with language in an endeavour to make prose the embodiment of sense-impression and emotional experience.

To which of the three remaining categories does Green belong? His hostile critics, like C. P. Snow and Orville Prescott, would, no doubt, summarily dismiss him to the last category. But the views of two other critics, who are much more favourably disposed towards Green, Robert Phelps and Philip Toynbee, deserve attention. Phelps in his study of Green describes him as a "writer in whose work the marriage between vision and medium is so exceptional that in reckoning with him we have to acknowledge a difference in kind". Comparing Green's prose with that of his near-namesake, Graham Greene, Phelps remarks that Greene's novels have "virility of vision and [are] masterfully made", but claims "yet Graham Greene's prose, for all its aptness of simile, is more housekeeper than wife to what he is saying. It speaks up distinctly and it never lies. But it is never bedded down with or instinctively begotten upon, as the most casual passage in Henry Green may be." And, quoting the long sentence describing the juggler in *Doting* (p. 8), he asks: "With the exception of Faulkner, is there anyone else writing English today who could, or would, write as sure, resourceful and original a sentence as this one?"[13] To Phelps, then, Green is a novelist of the fourth group.

Philip Toynbee has also discussed this question of style in the contemporary novel. He detects four attitudes towards language among English writers. Two groups, whom he calls the "dandies" and the "archaists" (who seem to correspond approximately to the fifth category I have mentioned) are small and negligible. Toynbee sees "the real linguistic war" as between the upholders of the predominant view, the writers of vernacular prose, who use the language of contemporary speech with little transmutation (the best of whom would be included in my second category) and "a small but formidable band of terrorists" (those "who confront their language as a wrestler confronts his adversary, knowing that they must twist it and turn it, squeeze it into strange shapes and make it cry aloud, before they can bring it to the boards"). The terrorists, led by Joyce, include such diverse writers as Thomas Wolfe, Virginia Woolf, Henry Miller and Henry Green [and surely Faulkner?]; as Toynbee remarks, they have nothing in common except "a conscious assault on the "linguistic medium". Sometimes, he says, they are defeated by it, and their failures "can be justly accused of affectation, of pretentiousness and of exhibitionism".[14]

With this view (which, in the terms I have suggested, would make Green essentially a writer of the fourth category who occasionally lapses into the fifth group) I substantially agree. But I am doubtful whether, in some of his novels, Green can properly be termed a "terrorist of language". The question of Green's handling of language is closely related to the other question of his variations of method. In the novels which consist largely of direct scene, of the meticulously accurate rendering of "pedestrian conversations" (to use Green's own phrase), Green, it seems to me, is a novelist of the third category. In these novels he is generally content to "utilize" language; only

occasionally does he use language poetically. Robert Phelps is
a little disingenuous when he uses the phrase "the most casual
passage in Henry Green" and a little later quotes a sentence
which is, in fact, unique in *Doting*. There are only three sentences
in the whole of this novel which are even half as long and as
syntactically elaborate as the one he quotes. Two of them, also
in the opening pages, describe the snake-dancer who precedes
the juggler in the floor-show at the first night-club; the other,
near the end of the book, describes the second night-club which
is the setting for the final scene. They are anything but casual
passages; stylistically they are exceptional.

I should say, then, that in four of the eight novels since
Blindness—in *Nothing* and *Doting*, the two most recent, in
Loving, which most closely resembles them in method, and even
in *Back* (in which, I have previously claimed, there are only
three passages of genuinely poetic passion)—Green is a novelist
of the third group. In the other four—*Living, Party Going,
Caught* and *Concluding*—he is a novelist of the fourth category.
In each of the novels of this second group there is an occasional
passage which may, with some justification, be regarded as
precious, affected and pretentious, but to no novel, as a whole
(not even to *Party Going*), do these adjectives apply. And Green's
novels, it must be stressed, *are* wholes. While he clearly regards
prose as an art as arduous and exacting as poetry, his quoted
comment shows that he is keenly aware of the difference between
them. His comment clearly implies the wholeness and unity of
a novel; it certainly does not seem to approve any "declaration
of independence by the smaller unit" or to suggest that Henry
Green would view with favour the test of "local exemplification" which Philip Rahv deplores.

3

I have previously claimed that all of Green's novels are unmistakably his own, and that, although he has made many
different experiments with language, some features of his style
have remained constant. Before discussing the variations of
style from novel to novel, I propose to examine some of these
continuing characteristics—first a few minor idiosyncrasies,
quirks and mannerisms, then some more important features.

Almost as certain an indication of Green's authorship as the

N

presence of birds (and chandeliers) in his novels is his unusual trick of introducing a relative clause with a redundant conjunction. This is by no means habitual, but every novel has at least a few examples.

"Craigan and Joe Gates and Dale stood by their box ready weighted for pouring *and* in which was mould of one of those cylinders" (*Living*, p. 33).

"There it lay and Miss Fellowes looked up to where that pall of fog was twenty foot above *and* out of which it had fallen . . ." (*Party Going*, p. 7).

"Immediately the mucus reappeared, almost Eton blue in this brilliant light, *and* which trembled, weaving with each breath he took . . ." (*Caught*, p. 168).

"Over a corn bin on which he had packed last autumn's ferns lay Paddy snoring between these windows, a web strung from one lock of hair back onto the sill above *and* which rose and fell as he breathed" (*Loving*, p. 51).

". . . the girl began, raising limpid, spaniel's eyes to Miss Edge, *and* that were filling with easy tears . . ." (*Concluding*, p. 90).

The examples quoted will also serve to illustrate the most frequently recurring of all Henry Green's verbal habits—the replacement of the article (either indefinite or definite) or the possessive pronoun (his, her, etc.) by demonstratives (this, that, these, those). Demonstratives are normally used either to point out something obvious in the situation or to draw special attention to something previously mentioned, but in Green's novels they often do not have either of these functions. For example the sixth sentence of *Back* reads: "As he looked up he noted well those slits, built for defence, in the blood coloured brick." The slits have not been mentioned before and are not to be mentioned again; there seems to be no reason for the use of "those" beyond the desire to avoid using, whenever possible, the completely neutral definite article. The frequency of occurrence varies a good deal from novel to novel, but none of the novels has less than a dozen quite perceptible examples. And each of them has at least a few which must strike one as distinctly odd. ". . . and *that* promise of the birds which had flown under the rock she stood on would be fulfilled . . ." (*Party Going*, p. 151). "He raised a vinegar-coloured palm to his chin, which was covered by *that* four-day growth of bristle" (*Caught*, p. 50).

". . . then with a toss of *that* drooling, over-weighted head . . .
she trotted off" (*Concluding*, p. 159). Almost as frequently Green
replaces the third person pronouns "it" and "them" by "this"
and "these" (e.g. "When she had drained her cup, she reached
up to put this away on the trolley . . ."). And again Green is
fond of referring to his characters not by name, or as "he", or
"she" or "they", but as "this man" (or "the man"), "that one",
"these two", etc.

These are minutiae and perhaps trivia, but they do contribute to an identifiable distinctiveness of expression in Green's
prose. (One might also mention Green's liking for the word
"regard", where most people would use either "watch" or
"look at", and for "looked to" where most would use "seemed
to" or "appeared to"). These minor deviations from the expected
show that Green is constantly concerned with how a thing is to
be said, that he is not prepared to use mechanically even those
most inconspicuous of all monosyllables—the articles. On the
other hand he may sometimes be justly accused of using
mechanically his own pet deviations from normal usage.

Turning now to more general considerations, it would
probably be agreed that the study of the sentence is one of the
basic methods of getting at the essential qualities of any writer's
style. If this is so, then the first important thing to be stressed
about Henry Green's style is that its basis is the short, syntactically simple sentence. Since this is hardly the impression given
by most critics who have commented on Green's prose,
statistical confirmation of the claim is probably necessary. This
is given in the table on page 192, but a few comments on
how the statistics were obtained are also necessary.

The table gives the results of a study of ten samples of one hundred sentences of "non-dialogue" from each of Henry Green's
novels. Henry Green has an extremely accurate ear for dialogue;
his characters always speak in their own character, not in his.
There is generally in his novels, therefore, a sharp distinction
between conversational and non-conversational elements
(though in some novels the former does colour the latter). Since
the purpose of this chapter is to examine Green's style, not the
styles of his characters, all dialogue has been excluded from these
samples, but everything else (including "stage directions" in
"scenes") has been included. This means, of course, that the
sampled fraction of any book depends on its technique. So, for

example, only eighty of the 190 pages of *Caught* are included in the ten samples. This is the smallest portion—forty-two per cent —but it is too large to be seriously misleading. On the other hand about 150 of the 225 pages of *Back* are included, and all of the "non-dialogue" in *Nothing* and *Doting*. In fact in neither of these novels are there a thousand sentences of non-dialogue, and in both cases the figures given are estimates based on 700 sentences.

Number of sentences of various lengths, per thousand

Sentences of – words	Living	Party Going	Caught	Loving	Back	Con-cluding	Nothing	Doting
1–10	414	183	406	522	495	444	536	550
11–20	301	262	316	293	317	298	274	306
21–30	156	246	154	117	112	121	107	82
31–40	74	139	48	42	34	68	29	30
41–50	31	86	36	13	19	30	24	18
51–60	14	56	16	7	8	11	14	6
61–70	4	18	6	5	7	11	—	2
71–80	3	7	3	1	2	6	1	1
81–90	1	1	7	—	2	5	6	3
91–100	1	1	1	—	1	2	3	1
101 & over	1	1	7	—	3	4	6	1

This table reveals several things. It shows, firstly, that in each of the novels, except one, over forty per cent of all sentences are no longer than ten words, and that in each novel, with the same solitary exception, more than seventy per cent of all sentences are twenty words long or less. In the absence of similar studies of other novelists one cannot categorically assert that these percentages are remarkably high. But comparison with the figures, given opposite, for half-a-dozen other fairly representative twentieth-century novels shows that they are, at least, higher than in many novels.

Secondly it does bring out fairly clearly the different handling of language in the novels in which the element of scene is highest (*Loving*, *Back*, *Nothing*, and *Doting*) and the remaining four novels. In the first group half or more of all sentences have ten words or less, and over four-fifths have twenty words or less.

Thirdly it points up unmistakably the fact, previously hinted at, that *Party Going*, stylistically, is quite exceptional among

Green's novels. But since we are at present concerned with general features, not with variations, further comment on this novel will be deferred.

What all this amounts to, in general terms, is that, if *Party Going* is excluded, almost half the sentences in Green's novels (forty-eight per cent) are of ten words or less and almost four-fifths (seventy-eight per cent) are of twenty words or less. Green's most characteristic sentences are not those describing the juggler in *Doting*, or those describing the roses in *Back*, or those describing the starlings in *Concluding*. They are sentences like "They stood by, two by two, holding ladles, or waiting" or "There was no room for Richard, who had to draw up a beer crate to get next Ilse" or "The passage carpet was so thick you never could hear anyone coming" or "Charley re-entered the

	Sentences of 1–10 words (per cent)	Sentences of 11–20 words (per cent)	Sentences of 1–20 words (per cent)
Elizabeth Bowen: *To the North*	20	40	60
E. M. Forster: *A Passage to India*	29	31	60
Graham Greene: *The Power and the Glory*	29	36	65
V. S. Pritchett: *Mr. Beluncle*	35	30	65
William Faulkner: *Light in August*	38	31	69
L. P. Hartley: *The Shrimp and the Anemone*	34	36	70

living-room, sat down, put his hands on his face" or "Miss Edge watched her colleague out of the room" or "He rattled the cocktail shaker". There are literally hundreds of such sentences in Green's novels, yet, so far as I know, only one critic has remarked on Green's "frequently exhibited control of possibly the most difficult of artistic media, the declarative sentence".[15] The very foundation of Green's style, then, is a terse, un-adorned, precise and economical prose as colloquially unobtrusive as that of his most distinguished contemporaries.

It may, of course, be objected that the important thing in giving a writer's style its distinctive character is not the ratio of short *sentences* to long, but the ratio of *words* that occur in short sentences to those that occur in long. This is a substantial objection. It is a matter of simple arithmetic that a single sentence of over one hundred words is approximately equivalent in bulk to a score of sentences of from one to ten words (average 5·5 words); indeed a long sentence of this kind attracts much more of the reader's notice than its verbal equivalent in short sentences, especially when these are not combined in paragraphs, but interspersed among the spoken words of the characters, as they so often are in Green. Green is obviously keenly aware of the staccato monotony of the Macaulayesque pistol shot style; except in *Back*, there are few longer *sequences* of very short sentences in his novels than this one, from *Caught* (p. 172): "He slept in the hired car. He went straight to bed when he arrived. He slept another sixteen hours. Then he got up. The ground was under snow." (The function of this curt broken-rhythmed paragraph of suggesting and reflecting Roe's blitz-shattered condition is obvious enough.) I do not maintain, therefore, that the long elaborate sentence is unimportant in Green's prose. What I do maintain is that such sentences are never the foundation of Green's prose, but are used carefully and deliberately for special purposes. Giorgio Melchiori, quoting one such sentence from *Concluding* (p. 109), aptly describes it as "one of the richest passages in Green's prose; one of those passages approaching the florid diction, the syntactic freedom and the sensuous imagery of poetry, which stud all his novels up to *Concluding* [and after]—unexpected flourishes of feeling, fanciful word-pictures departing from his more restrained style in the same way as a complicated stucco scroll will suddenly break out of the quiet and balanced form of an arch or balustrade in a seventeenth century building".[16]

Statistical confirmation of this picturesque architectural simile is given in the table below, which is based on the same samples as before, but is arranged in ascending order from the novel with the fewest words per thousand in short sentences to the one with the most. The table does indicate the importance of the long sentence—the "complicated scroll-work" in most of the novels, but it also establishes beyond doubt that the "restrained style" is the staple of Green's prose. In only one novel, *Nothing*, do we find as many as ten per cent of the total words of non-dialogue in sentences of over eighty words, and in this case, it must be remembered, non-dialogue is, at most, ten per cent of the whole novel. On the other hand, in all the novels, except one, the greatest number of words (never less than a quarter of the total) is contained in sentences of eleven to twenty words. The table also shows more clearly the division previously noticed. For whereas in the four most scenic novels the second highest number of words is contained in sentences of one to ten words, in *Living*, *Caught*, and *Concluding* the second greatest number of words is contained in sentences of twenty-one to thirty words. Finally the uniqueness of *Party Going* is even more clearly evident.

Number of words per thousand in sentences of various lengths

Sentences of – words	Party Going	Caught	Living	Con-cluding	Back	Nothing	Loving	Doting
1–10	46	137	148	157	204	216	232	250
11–20	160	275	280	264	331	287	332	360
21–30	243	219	237	184	198	186	223	160
31–40	193	95	163	143	83	70	111	83
41–50	156	91	84	81	59	77	44	60
51–60	126	49	41	36	38	55	28	26
61–70	45	23	15	41	32	—	24	7
71–80	21	13	14	26	11	8	6	8
81–90	3	44	5	25	12	34	—	19
91–100	3	5	6	11	7	19	—	10
101 & over	4	49	7	32	25	48	—	17

Sentence-length is, of course, not the only important consideration in a study of style. Other matters that must be investigated are the extent to which modification is introduced, the order in which the various elements—the phrases and clauses—of a sentence are introduced, and the relationship between these elements. These matters will be considered in the discussion of the individual novels. But sentence-length, after all, is basic, for the obvious reason that no sentence of half-a-dozen or even a dozen words can be highly complex. My main aim here has been to demonstrate that a very high proportion of Henry Green's sentences are of this kind.

4

My discussion of the individual novels will not be strictly chronological. It is better, I think, to consider the eight novels in the two groups of four that I have indicated—those in which dialogue is of supreme importance, and in which there is, in the non-dialogue, an especially heavy reliance on the short sentence; and those in which other elements are as important as dialogue, and in which the style in the non-dialogue is more elaborate or more constantly "perceptible". It is convenient, however, to begin with the two early novels which represent two different extremes of Green's stylistic experimentation.

The styles of *Living* and of *Party Going* provide as sharp a contrast as do their subjects and their themes. The style of *Living* is more startlingly distinctive than that of any later novel, and its peculiarities are easier to catalogue, if not to explain, or justify.

The feature that no one fails, or could fail, to notice is the almost total warfare declared on the definite article. Actually it is not only definite articles that are eliminated literally by the hundred. ("Thousands came back from dinner along streets." "Noise of lathes working began again. . . ." "Hundreds went along road." "Some had stayed in iron foundry shop. . . ." All these are in the first half-page.) The indefinite article frequently has the same fate. ("They sat round brazier. . . ." "This man scooped gently at great shape cast down in black sand in great iron box." "He was very clever man at his work." These also occur in the first four pages.) So do possessive pronouns. ("Then blowing ash from cigarette." "She wiped red, wet hands on dishcloth." "Baby howled till mother lifted him from bed to breast. . . .") In one sample of four thousand words there were 144 such omissions; from these figures one can reach the rather startling conclusion that if all the missing articles were restored the novel would be some five pages longer!

Green does not completely extirpate the articles, but it seems to be impossible to discover any principle by which their fate is decided; the few survivors seem to owe their existence to accidental oversight rather than judicial leniency. "Thousands came up the road to work. . . . Then road was empty. . . ." One could perhaps develop a subtle argument that a thronged road requires an article, a deserted road does not—but what about this passage? "The foreman stood near by. They waited. Gates was tired. Foreman stood near by." Why an article in the first sentence, but not in the otherwise identical fourth?

Another linguistic peculiarity is the frequent omission of

"there". There are scores of sentences like "When party went he stayed on over—was nothing for him to do in London"; "Anyway was no hanky-panky about her"; "And again, this was to be lucky night, was no one to receive them"; "Is nothing wonderful in migrating birds". Yet another is the number of fragmentary, verbless "sentences". (In four one hundred sentence samples there were eight.) The novel opens with the words or sentences or paragraphs:

> "Bridesley, Birmingham.
> Two o'clock."

and there are many others—"Sun", "Evening", "On the ceiling", etc.

Again there are frequent inversions and distortions of normal word order—sentences like "Mr. Bridges went down through works in Birmingham till Tupe he found"; or "So came they home at evening"; or "Lily Gates shook hands, holding limply out hand"; or "Plump she was". Sometimes all these features are combined, as in one of the most frequently quoted passages in the novel:

"Evening. Was spring. Heavy blue clouds stayed over above. In small back garden of villa small tree was with yellow buds. On table in backroom daffodils, faded, were between ferns in vase" (p. 11).

Green also makes fairly frequent use of repetition: "And now time is passing now"; "Was low wailing low in her ears"; "He had on bowler hat, high, high crown"; "These took no notice of the crowd, no notice"; "She was blank, blank"; "She clung to man and said she had dreamed, had dreamed, had dreamed"; "Just then Mr. Dupret in sleep, died, in sleep."

Elsewhere I have mentioned Green's use, in this novel, of the extended comparison, introduced by "as ... so". Frequently in developing these comparisons Green slips in a redundant "so":—

"But as sometimes, coming across the sea from a cold country to the tropics ... *so* as you are coming tropical birds ... settle to rest on the deck ... so things she remembered of him came one by one back to her mind" (p. 156).

"*So*, as pigeon when she had watched out of kitchen window ... so she drew back ..." (p. 206).

"Then as after rain *so* the sky shines . . . so her sorrow folded wings . . ." (p. 239).

Yet another peculiarity is the occasional use of "like" instead of "as if" or "as though": "Some years of his life had been staked on her, like impaled". (The word-play is no doubt deliberate too.) "She began to run after him, still not realizing and like obediently . . ." Another small matter that should be mentioned, because it does make a difference, however indefinable, to the "flavour" of the book, is that numbers are hardly ever spelt out, but are given as Arabic numerals. There are examples on almost every page: . . . "Joe Gates laughing with Mr. Tupe when $\frac{5}{8}$ spanner fell from above . . .", ". . . no word was said between them not while their 8 ton of metal was carried them in a ladle . . .", ". . . her eyelids fold up and her 2 eyes . . . blink", "Party in front, 4 girls, 4 young men, the girls on one pavement men on the other side, 2 parties but 1 at same time . . ." (Again 1 wonders why the inconsistency.)

Critical opinion on the reasons for the adoption of this highly individual manner and on its degree of success has been divided. Walter Allen, in the earliest published essay on Green's work, characterized the style accurately as "bare, repetitive, harsh, angular, sometimes deliberately clumsy" and asserted that it was "an admirable medium for the expression of the blackness and din of the foundry".[17] This is undoubtedly true; one of the passages most memorable in its concrete vividness and in the way the very arrangement of the words mirrors the action described is this one.

"In the foundry was now sharp smell of burnt sand. Steam rose from the boxes round about. On these, in the running gates and risers, metal shone out red where it set. On Mr. Craigan's huge box in which was his casting Mr. Craigan and Jim Dale stood. They raised and lowered long rods into metal in the risers so as to keep the metal molten. Steam rose up round them so their legs were wet and heat from the molten metal under them made balls of sweat roll down them. Arc lamps above threw their shadows out sprawling along over the floor and as they worked rhythmically their rods up and down so their shadows worked" (p. 34).

This style, however, is not used only for the parts of the novel concerned with the foundry; it is used also to present the domestic life of the Craigan-Gates and Eames households, the love affair between Lily and Bert, their elopement, Lily's return and so on. It is notable, however, that in depicting the life of the wealthy Duprets, Dick's infatuation with Hannah Glossop and Hannah's with Tom Tyler, and the disappointed hopes of both, this style is considerably modified. In the early chapters there is no clear demarcation (e.g. "She pushed button of bell; this was in onyx. She laid hand by it on table and diamonds on her rings glittered together with white metal round onyx button under the electric light. Electric light was like stone. He was cut short by her. He was hurt at it. He kept silence then", p. 37), but in many later passages there are few traces, or none, of the special features listed. (E.g. "Some time passed before young Mr. Dupret could recover from his surprise at this visit. To his friends in London he talked with horror about the cynical attitude of older women towards sex. There was so much horror in the tone of his voice that his friends asked themselves what could have happened to him and talked of it to each other. But while he soon recovered his old assurance it was some time before he could go into his father's room" (pp. 92–3).

The bald, clipped, staccato, almost telegraphic style with all its naïveties and distortions of word-order is, then, essentially the industrial workers' style. But it is fitting that there should be traces of it, for example, in the episode when Richard Dupret, disappointed in the hope of catching Hannah on the rebound, rows on the Thames and determines that work is what he needs.

"River was brown and flowed rapidly down to the sea. On either side the violet land under this grey sky. Trees on either side graciously inclined this way and that, leaning on his oars he watched these and rooks that out of the sky came peaceably down on fields" (p. 170).

Philip Toynbee regards the style of *Living* as a failure. "We feel at once that an effect is being striven for. . . . The assault has been too sudden. . . . And in this case the eccentricities seem somehow trivial. The omission of the definite article irritates by its self-consciousness and seems to contribute nothing to the perfectly ordinary statements which are being made." He also criticizes as pointless the emphatic inversions and "quotes" one sentence ("Again was first day outside, another fine evening") which he claims to be typical and which he finds "frankly incomprehensible". It may be "incomprehensible", but it is hardly typical. In fact after reading the novel some half-dozen times and making a thrice-repeated sentence-by-sentence check I am convinced that the sentence is *not* in the novel! Nor can I find any other "incomprehensible" sentence.

Toynbee considers that the "motive for Green's oddities of diction" was an "aversion to the *looseness* of modern English prose". But he maintains that Green's "method of confronting the contemporary linguistic problem" was "wholly mistaken". "It is true that a great fault of current speech lies in the pro-liferation of superfluous and meaningless sounds. . . . Some severity is needed. But 'the' is both an innocent and a useful word and to concentrate so heavy a gun against it seems a curious misdirection of this writer's fire-power." [18]

Giorgio Melchiori agrees that the "arresting mannerism" of omitting the definite article is "tiresome, and at times it seems to be done by mere mechanical revision, with resulting artificiality". But he sees it as an early example of "the poetic stimulus at the root of Green's prose". He claims that "it is significant that the same device is largely used by Auden in the poems written at the same time as Green's *Living* . . . and there is little doubt that Green got it from him". [19] This may be so, but *Living*, after all, did appear in the year before Auden's *Poems*, and it may be that the device was taken independently from the same models—perhaps Hopkins and Anglo-Saxon. Green did remark in *Pack My Bag*: "I had taken English as my school and that meant learning Anglo-Saxon. This I found I could not do." But this much at least he may have learnt.

Whatever the origins of this device, and of the highly un-orthodox way of arranging words, Melchiori's further comment is valid: "He realized the potentialities of the device as a means of reaching in description the same effect that Impressionist painters had achieved in their landscapes; the simplification of natural forms, heightening the emotional quality of the picture by concentrating on the really significant features." [20] Most of the passages in which Green achieves a combination of lyrical beauty and bare strength have already been quoted in this or previous chapters—notably the descriptions of the pigeons, and of the foundry, especially the scene in which the Welshman, Arthur Jones, sings at his work because "That night son had been born to him". In such passages as these, at least, all the peculiarities of style are triumphantly justified.

Party Going is much less obviously eccentric in style than *Living*. It does begin with a sentence which appears to be a hangover from the abrupt article-less style of the earlier novel ("Fog was so dense, bird that had been disturbed went flat into a balustrade and slowly fell, dead, at her feet"—one notices how carefully that word "dead" is isolated and emphasized) but thereafter with very rare exceptions (perhaps half a dozen in the whole book) articles are to be found in the expected places. More accurately, there is always *something* where we expect an article, but it is not always an article. Indeed the most distinctive verbal feature of this novel is the frequency with which "this / that / these / those" replaces the article. This device is comparatively rare in *Living*. There are only a dozen or so clear-cut examples in the earlier novel, but in *Party Going* there are at least six times as many (considerably more than in any other novel). Again there are a few "likes" for "as". ("So like when you were small. . . ." "She was made better at once, for like delicate plants must be watered"), and once or twice there is something not, I think, to be found in *Living*—an adjective instead of an adverb ("One rough-looking customer in particular eyed her rather close." At this point, incidentally, we are seeing things through the eyes of the two nannies.). Also on a couple of occasions there is another new mannerism —"and this" instead of "which". ("She entered a tunnel . . . and this had DEPARTURES lit up over it . . ."; "But it had its ticket and this had Marriage written on it.") But these are all inconspicuous trifles.

I have previously claimed, however, that *Party Going*, in style, is unique among Henry Green's novels. The statistical tables already given show that it is the only novel in which the 1–10 word sentence does not predominate. Indeed it has only eighteen per cent of such sentences, compared with forty-one per cent in *Living* and *Caught* which have next fewest. Again it is the only one in which the largest fraction of the total number of words is to be found not in sentences of 11–20 words, but in sentences of 21–30 words. Averages are far less important than range in a study of sentence-length, but for what it is worth, the average sentence-length in *Party Going* is 25·5 words, compared with 17·3 in *Caught*, the next highest, and 12·6 in *Doting*, the lowest.

Actually average length of sentences means a little more in

Party Going than in any other novel. One important feature of *Party Going* is its uniformity. The ten samples (of a hundred sentences each) vary in total length only from about 2,400 to about 2,900 words; the ten samples from *Living* vary from 1,300 to 2,300 words, as do those from *Caught*. There are similar variations in the samples from *Back* (1,000–2,200 words) and *Concluding* (1,200–2,450 words). *Loving* is the only novel which approaches *Party Going* in this respect; its samples range from 1,100 to 1,600 words.

All this does not mean, however, that *Party Going* has a large number of very long sentences. On the contrary it has fewer sentences of over 80 words (seven in the whole novel) than any other novel except *Living* (five), *Loving* (nil) and *Doting* (four), and a lower percentage of words contained in sentences of over 80 words (one) than any other novel except *Loving* (nil). What *Party Going* does have is a great number of sentences that are not short, and not (by Green's standards at least) really long; it has more sentences per thousand in the twenties (246—nearest rival *Living* with 156), thirties (139—again *Living* nearest with 74), forties (86—*Caught* is nearest with 36), fifties (56—almost four times as many as *Caught* with 16) and sixties (18, to 11 in *Concluding*) than any other novel.

What I am trying, laboriously, to demonstrate is the remarkable stylistic evenness of the novel, so far as this is reflected in sentence-length. For whatever purposes the sentences are used —indirect scene, interior monologue, commentary—they seldom deviate either into the curt, terse and laconic or into the highly elaborate, complex and involuted.

Giorgio Melchiori has remarked on Green's "growing taste (in *Party Going*) for elaborate imagery and mixed metaphor" and has claimed that his "preoccupation with style is so strong that the content is overpowered. It is easy to isolate and examine that style, already fully mature which Green used later in *Caught*, *Loving* and *Back*. It is extremely artificial and ornate. Green is not afraid of using the most flamboyant rhetorical devices."[21] Here, it seems to me, Melchiori is generalizing, as critics of style generally are prone to do, from a few carefully selected examples. While admitting "the growing taste for elaborate imagery" (which I have discussed in the previous chapter) I would maintain that the style of most of the novel is the reverse of flamboyant and ornate. I would also contend that, so far from exhibiting "the involutions of a Jamesian style", the majority of sentences in the novel are loose, compound, multiple sentences, based on co-ordination much more than subordination. Often it is merely the substitution of "ands" for full-stops which converts three or four short sentences into one substantial one. ("She turned and she went back to where it had fallen and again looked up to where it must have died for it was still warm and, everything unexplained, she turned once more into the tunnel back to the station.") But one has only to make the alteration to realize how much difference it makes to tone and tempo. ("She turned. She went back to where it had fallen. Again she looked up to where it must have died for it was still warm. Everything unexplained, she turned once more into the tunnel back to the station.") As a matter of fact a number of the shorter sentences would, if normally punctuated, be parts of longer compound sentences, for many sentences, and even a few paragraphs, begin with "and". ("He said it was good for everyone after a hard day and you drank it, went to have your bath and then sat down to begin tea. And now how extraordinary she should be here, drinking in tea rooms with all these extraordinary looking people. And there was that poor bird.")

The general sentence-structure of *Party Going* is most skilfully adapted to the subject and theme of the novel. In this novel, which preserves unity of time and place, and which concentrates attention on a homogeneous group of the people of the same age, social class and attitudes, it is right that the sentences should be fairly uniform in length and structure. And in this novel, in which instead of anything happening the characters wait—not in despair, hope or tense expectation, but just wait—for the fog to lift, it is right that the sentences should be the kind they are. It is a fundamental stylistic axiom that a series of short sentences generally conveys an impression of speed, activity, decisiveness. These were the last things that Green wanted to convey. Monotony, lassitude and boredom were what he wanted to convey and these loose rambling sentences were the ideal means. Moreover these sentences, so vague and indefinite in structure, not only directly present the fog of uncertainty and incomprehension, subterfuge and evasion in which the characters have their being ("Max, when he saw Hignam, thought it best to find out what he could about Amabel rather than pretend he had always known she would be coming, for there was no knowing what she might have said while she was alone with them, so he asked him, 'What's this about Amabel?' ") but are a sort of syntactic equivalent of the fog which is the dominating force in the novel.

But *Party Going*, of course, is more than a satirical and comic exposure of triviality and futility. In his broadcast talk on the novel in 1950 Green asked: "How can the novelist communicate obliquely with his readers and yet retain their interest, let alone do for them what I regard as indispensable, namely to quicken their unconscious imagination into life while reading? . . . How is the reader's imagination to be fired?" He answered: "For a long time I thought this was best lit by very carefully arranged passages of description."[22] Like all of Green's novels *Party Going* has a dimension of poetry and wonder; there are at least a dozen scenes, episodes and passages in which Green endeavours to fire the reader's unconscious imagination into life. In these passages the style becomes more colourful, imaginative and metaphorical in language, more developed in rhythm, and more complex in syntax. In these passages (generally, but not invariably, descriptive passages) we for a time escape from the banal consciousness of the characters; or, more accurately, we have superimposed on the characters' consciousnesses the poetic vision of Green himself. They include descriptions of the fog, the station, the crowds thronging into the station and seen from above, of the muffled noise of the crowd heard by the people inside the hotel, of Miss Fellowes' delirium, of Amabel—especially of Amabel having her bath.

It is worth noticing that all the half-dozen longest sentences in the book are of great thematic and symbolic importance. (In this the book differs from *Living*—but there is good reason. In the earlier book the important themes are centred round Lily and Mr. Craigan; syntactic elaborateness would have been inappropriate. Almost all the long sentences are ironical commentaries on the Duprets. The longest sentence *is* concerned with Lily, but it is a highly repetitive and syntactically primitive piece of indirect scene in which Lily talks with Mrs. Eames about Jim Dale (pp. 41–2).) The long sentences in *Party Going* include the passage comparing Angela and Robin to "two lilies in a pond, romantically part of it but *infinitely remote*", surrounded by a crowd of "water-beetles" (p. 27); the passage in which Alex, thinking of Amabel, compares her to "ground so high, so *remote* it had never been broken" (p. 144); the passage in which Max and Julia look down on the crowd below, and cannot "but feel *infinitely remote*" (p. 150). Another is the description of the faint whisper of the crowd's hubbub reaching Alex, Amabel and Angela through "curtains so thick and heavy they seemed made of plaster on stage sets" (p. 149—again the idea of remoteness is emphasized). The last two are the description of the crowd, seen as ruins of a forgotten civilization (pp. 201–2), and Julia's memory of the birds which had flown under the arch (p. 151). In the previous chapter I have tried to show the importance of these passages; it is clearly no accident that they are also the passages of greatest stylistic elaboration and complexity. The longest, and one of the most elaborate, of all is this one:

"Looking down then on thousands of Smiths, thousands of Alberts, hundreds of Marys, woven tight as any office carpet or, more elegantly made, the holy Kaaba soon to set out for Mecca, with some kind of design made out of bookstalls and kiosks seen from above and through one part of that crowd having turned towards those who were singing, thus lightening the dark mass with their pale lozenged faces; observing how this design moved and was alive where in a few lanes or areas people swayed forward or back like a pattern writhing; coughing as fog caught their two throats or perhaps it was smoke from those below who had put on cigarettes or pipes, because tobacco smoke was coming up in drifts; leaning out then, so secure, from their window up above and left by their argument on terms of companionship unalloyed, Julia and Max could not but feel infinitely remote, although at the same time Julia could not fail to be remotely excited at themselves" (p. 150).

This sentence is somewhat obscure both in meaning and syntax in the dozen words of parenthesis between ". . . carpet or" and "with some kind . . .". But otherwise its structure is quite clear, even though we have to wait for nearly 150 words before the subject, "Julia and Max", is reached. Although there is a good deal of subordination in the various parts of the sentence, especially the first, its basis is co-ordination. It is rather like a clothes-line with the sequence of participles ("looking", "observing", "coughing", "leaning" and "left") the pegs, from which hang clauses of various sizes and shapes. So far as meaning is concerned it could have been written:

o

"Julia and Max looked down . . . faces (and) observed . . . writing (and) coughed . . . drifts (and) as they leaned . . . above, left . . . unalloyed, they could not . . . themselves." Equally, of course, it could have been written as four sentences. But it does not violate any of the rules of syntax; it merely takes a common construction and multiplies and elaborates it to the utmost.

Another, and perhaps an even better, example of the characteristic sentence-structure in this novel is this one:

"Where ruins lie, masses of stone grown over with ivy unidentifiable with the mortar fallen away so that stone lies on stone loose and propped up or crumbling down in mass then as a wind starts up at dusk and stirs the ivy leaves and rain follows slanting down, so deserted no living thing seeks what little shelter there may be, it is all brought so low, then movements of impatience began to flow across all these people and as ivy leaves turn one way in the wind they themselves surged a little here and there in their blind search behind bowler hats and hats for trains" (p. 202).

The basic meaning of this sentence—the comparison of the crowd to a ruined city, and of the movements of impatience that sweep through the crowd to the stirring of the ivy leaves covering the ruins in the wind at dusk—is perfectly clear. But the syntax is deliberately deranged to create the same effect of uncertainty and confusion noticed in the less elaborate sentences. The first seven lines of the sentence are heavily dependent on apposition and co-ordination—"ruins", "masses of stone"; "grown over", "unidentifiable", "with the mortar fallen away . . ."; "loose", "propped up", "crumbling"; "starts", "stirs", "follows". But the most unusual feature is that one of the phrases qualifying "ruins" ("so deserted . . . it is all brought so low") is deliberately misplaced; logically this should come after "crumbling down in mass", or even after "where ruins lie". The other peculiarity is that Green does not use the conventional words for introducing an elaborate comparison of this kind ("as . . . so"); instead he uses "then as" and "then". In fact he encourages the reader to take the wrong path by following "then as a wind . . ." with "so deserted". It would be easy enough to reconstruct the sentence so that, despite its length, everything is crystal clear. But something would be lost—the element of ambiguity and obscurity is, in this novel, essential.

5

Caught and *Concluding* are perhaps the most interesting of all Green's novels from a stylistic point of view. Despite their differences in subject-matter (fire-station and girls' school), time-scheme (months in one, hours in the other) and technique, they have certain similarities in style.

They are alike, in the first place, in that they have no startling peculiarities of language. Each book has its occasional adjective for adverb ("He saw plain", "He looked helpless about"), its occasional demonstrative for article (they are more frequent in *Caught*), its occasional redundant "and" in relative clauses. But these features are less prominent than in most of Green's novels.

More positively, they are alike in distribution of sentence-lengths. About forty-one per cent of the words of non-dialogue in *Caught* are in sentences of 1–20 words, and about forty-two per cent of those of *Concluding*. *Living* is very similar in this regard with forty-three per cent, but *Living* differs from the two later books in that sentences over eighty words long form only two per cent of all its non-dialogue, compared with ten per cent in *Caught* and seven per cent in *Concluding*. The basis of the non-dialogue of *Caught* and *Concluding* is, as in all of Green's novels except *Party Going*, the short sentence, but this base is varied with really long and really elaborate sentences to a far greater degree than it is in *Living*, or any other novel except *Nothing*, in which non-dialogue is an insignificant fraction of the whole book.

It is unnecessary to comment at length on the "basic" style of the two novels. One point that should be made, however, is that because of the different subject-matter and technique a reader is likely to be more conscious of the shorter sentences, the more abrupt style, in *Caught* than in *Concluding*, despite the fact that, according to the statistics, there is a higher percentage of such sentences in *Concluding*. This is because more happens in *Caught*, and because in *Concluding* the short sentences tend to occur singly or in pairs, intermingled with dialogue, whereas in *Caught*, where there is much more scene without dialogue, scene in indirect speech and summary, they often come in fairly large clumps. The difference is illustrated in the following typical paragraphs.

"It seemed a long time before they drove out through the

slush, but they were quite fast. In those early days taxis drew the pumps. Richard was upset that Chopper, who was in charge of the appliance, should ride standing on the step and not use the seat made for him next the driver. They careered along. They stopped. Pye's appliance had drawn up in front. Pye and Chopper plunged through a peacefully open door. 'It can't be,' Richard thought. But it was. He looked up. From a window came a blind of smoke, as though rolls of black-out material, caught in the wind, had been unwound and been kept blowing about. Just like the smoke from one of their bonfires at home. He said to himself, 'So it is, at last' " (*Caught*, p. 79).

"Soon after, he got up and left Miss Edge. The lady was so obviously lost in happy contemplation of her charges. And he felt he had done enough. Honour was satisfied, he thought" (*Concluding*, p. 215).

Another difference to be noticed is that in *Caught*, which is concerned with people of diverse classes and backgrounds, Green occasionally does something that he was to do constantly in *Loving*; he allows the idiom of the working-class characters to carry over into the narrative.

"As she fussed a way for them through the crowd, regardless, knocking knees right and left with the case she carried, she said to herself it was awkward as much as to be seen with him, the useless good for nothink" (p. 113).

"She sat on, found another woman from London, and was well away by closing time" (p. 115).

"Nothing had been right after it came, it was such a worry, a girl didn't know what, not for the best she didn't. It was so difficult and she was no hand at it" (p. 120).

"Yet he had known subs in those times, real officers mark you, who didn't look no different" (p. 133).

Much of the language of both books, and especially of *Caught*, is plain, incisive and economical. But these adjectives clearly do not apply to everything in the two novels. In both, and again especially in *Caught*, there are very pronounced variations of style from the simple to the elaborate, from the prosaic to the poetic (and sometimes pseudo-poetic). Since, in *Caught*, at least, luxuriance of diction and complexity of syntax usually go hand-in-hand, I propose to isolate the sentences of eighty words and over, to see for what purposes they are used, and to try to determine whether they contribute anything of value to the novels as wholes, or whether they are merely exercises in fine writing.

There are twenty-six such sentences in *Caught*, far more than in any other novel. Twelve of them are concerned with the inner lives of the characters—their memories, reveries, emotional states and momentary impressions. Sometimes they record the characters' thoughts and feelings immediately, without interpretation; sometimes they translate and interpret them. Of these the most unquestionably necessary are the two long sentences which form part of Pye's reverie, as, on the night of the mobilization, he remembers his youth and his first girl.

"In the grass lane, and Pye groaned as he lay on the floor, his head by a telephone, that winding lane between high banks, in moonlight, in colour blue, leaning back against the pale wild flowers whose names he had forgotten her face, wildly cool to his touch, turned away from him and the underside of her jaw which went soft into her throat that was a colour of junket, oh my God he said to himself as he remembered how she panted through her nose and the feel of her true, roughened hands as they came to repel him and then, at the warmth of his skin, had stayed irresolute at the surface while, all lost, she murmured, 'Will it hurt?' " (pp. 40-1).

This sentence and its companion, beginning "And as he came along in shadow . . ." (p. 41), most of which has been quoted elsewhere (p. 59), are not an exact reproduction of Pye's thought-processes; they skilfully blend his thoughts with sensuously vivid description which, one feels, emanates from the author, not from the character. But we stay close enough to Pye's mind for the passage to be convincing. The sentences have no definite structure; the syntax is confused and broken. This, of course, is justified, since it perfectly conveys Pye's emotional condition and the way that experiences long past recur in one's mind with startling clarity and immediacy as one waits for sleep. The importance of this passage in the book has been emphasized already; this, in itself, is sufficient justification for a certain elaborateness.

At the other extreme, however, is this passage, describing the emotional condition of Mary Howells, after her daughter has left her husband and come "home".

"For she mourned the fruit of her own body, what had, so to

say, been grafted on her by Howells, but which in the fullness
of time, when ripe, had dropped away alive, with a live life of
its own she did not comprehend, to be grafted by a stranger
with this helpless bundle that in spite of the process was
part of Mary's flesh and blood, this baby that bore a strange
name; this it was she mourned, not for the marriage, the
flowering, the development or for that its mother had borne,
all these being in the course of nature, but she mourned the
mother, her own daughter, that she had come back" (pp.
81–2).

It is very difficult to see the need for this passage; it merely
tells us verbosely and magniloquently what we already know.
If it is an attempt to dignify Mrs. Howells it fails; to me, at least,
the inflated language seems to have the reverse effect of mocking
her very real grief.

Most of the other passages of this kind concern Richard Roe
—his memories of his boyhood, of his first experience of heights
in Tewkesbury Abbey, of his wife among the roses at his country
home, of his early training at the fire-station, of Christopher's
abduction from the toy shop, as he imagines it. These passages
again are not pure interior monologue. Green says of Roe,
"His feelings were usually uppermost", and these passages are
rather attempts to convey the quality and the origins of his
feelings than attempts to reproduce trains of thought exactly.
One of the most vivid and immediate is the description of his
wife as he remembered her, before their marriage, in the rose-
garden. One sentence of this passage (p. 64) may well have
been the origin of *Back*; it is, at the least, a first draft of the
opening page of the later novel. More typical in feeling,
language and syntax, however, is this sentence, describing Roe's
reactions to the house and gardens where he grew up, which
remain unchanged after twenty years.

"It was he who had changed, who dreaded now, with a
hemlock loss of will, to evoke how once he shared these scenes
with no one, for he had played alone, who had then no inkling
of the insecurity the war would put him in, and who found,
when confronted by each turning of a path he knew by heart
but which he could never call to mind when he closed his eyes,
that the presence, the disclosure again of so much that had not
changed and shewed no immediate signs of changing, bore him
down back to the state he wished to forget, when he was his

son's age and had no more than a son's responsibility to a father" (p. 32).

Apart from the adjective "hemlock" there is nothing unusual in the language of this sentence, but its syntax is extremely complex. The most notable features are the separation of relative clauses from their antecedents by interpolated phrases and clauses (". . . *he* had played alone, *who* had then . . .") and the extraordinary number of clauses. There are no less than seventeen finite verbs, of which, strictly speaking, only the first ("was") belongs to the top syntactic level, and only three others ("had changed", "dreaded", "found") belong to the next level. The sentence, not only through this tangle of subordinate clauses, but even more perhaps through the unemphatic, muffled rhythms, which, if analysed, would be found to contain a large number of paeons ("who dréaded now", "with a hémlock", "for he had pláyed") and anapaests ("It was hé who had chánged" and "and who foúnd") communicates perfectly Roe's emotional state—a sort of grey, brooding, lethargic regret. The passage presenting (partly through Roe's memory and imagination, mainly through omniscient narrative) Christopher's abduction from the toyshop I have described as one of the most gorgeous and one of the weirdest passages in this novel (or any other of Green's), and I have tried to show its place in the symbolic colour pattern of the work. But though most of its ornate bizarrerie does compel the reader's imagination, there are times when it seems overdone and meretricious. In the following sentence, for example, one feels that Green, in his quest for "poetry" has worked desperately hard for very little result; the result, if my reaction is typical, is exasperation and bewilderment. "What is all this about?" one asks, and if one takes the trouble to unravel the meaning one does not feel adequately rewarded.

"He imagined that, his pink cheeks grape dark in the glow, Christopher had leant his face forward, held to ransom by the cupidity of boys, and had been lost in feelings that this colour, reflected in such a way on so much that he wanted, could not have failed to bring him who could have visited no flower-locked sea on the Aegean, and yet, with every other child, or boy at school, with any man in the mood, who knew and always would that stretch of water, those sails from the past, those boats fishing in the senses" (p. 13).

If this whole sequence seems even more febrile and hectic than the woman's derangement and the child's terror justify, it is, one suspects, because Green is trying to divert the reader's attention from the coincidence, crucial to the plot of the novel, that it is Pye's sister who abducts Roe's son.

The other main purpose for which the long sentence is employed is description, sometimes mingled with scene. Here again there are occasions when one feels that Green, forgetting the larger design of the novel, is merely giving a display of fanciful virtuosity. Is there any need, for example, for the elaborate description (p. 53) of the smells which accost Piper as he goes in quest of a cup of tea, or of the even more elaborate description, complete with a carefully worked out synaesthetic conceit, which celebrates the sole appearance of Fat George and his coffee-stall?

I have less doubts and reservations about another ostentatiously flamboyant section of the novel—the night-club scene. In this section we find, as Melchiori has observed, "the furthest point Green has reached in contriving elaborate adjectival expressions . . . a transference into prose of a way of constructing images characteristic of poetry".[23] In a passage of five pages, half of it dialogue, there are four very long sentences, studded with phrases like "each girl's bare, sapphire, gleaming head", "this soft evening aching room", "bottles on tables held stifling moonlight", "fat, soft and soft-eyed, with sea flower fingered hands", "this murmuring, night haunted, softness shared", "whose clouded heads", "this hyacinthine, grape dark fellowship of longing". This is very different in tone from Auden's description of a similar scene:

> Join there the insufficient units
> Dangerous, easy, in furs, in uniform
> And constellated at reserved tables
> Supplied with feelings by an efficient band . . .[24]

But it is not impossible that Green had the last-quoted line in mind when he wrote the description of Hilly's "feelings":

"She had been wafted off, was enchanted not entirely by all she had had to drink and which was released inside her in a glow of earth chilled above a river at the noisy night harvest of vines, not altogether by this music, which, literally, was her honey, her feeling's tongue, but as much by sweet comfort, and the compulsion she felt here to gentleness that was put on her by these couples, by the blues, by wine, and now by this murmuring, night haunted, softness shared" (p. 108).

The difference between Auden and Green is the reverse of the usual distinction between the poet and the prose-writer; the poet here is the detached analytical observer, the prose-writer is the participant. There is great complexity of feeling in this passage; superimposed on the already complex feelings of the fictitious characters (which, they realize themselves, are partly genuine, partly self-willed, partly the bogus product of bottled "stifling moonlight") is Green's own characteristically ambiguous blend of irony, compassion and romantic delight. The scene reaches at least its stylistic climax in the sentence describing the performance of the singer, "the famous coloured lady". But "describing" is not the right word; Green somehow seems to become at once the singer and her rapt audience.

"As she stood there, gently telling them in music, reflecting aloud, wondering in her low, rich voice, the spot light spread a story over her body and dazzled her cheeks to bend and blend to a fabulous matching of the mood in which she told them, as she pretended to remember the south, the man who had gone, as she held all theirs with her magnificent eyes guardedly flashing, slowly turning from one couple to another, then again dropping her voice, almost sighing, motionless, while beads of sweat began to come like the base of a tiara on her forehead as she told the audience that he could see only as the less dark below her and whose clouded heads, each one, drew nearer to a companion's in this forced communion, this hyacinthine, grape dark fellowship of longing" (pp. 111–12).

The prose of *Caught*, then, is at times even more adventurous and experimental than that of its predecessors. It has a greater variety and intensity of experience to convey. The surprising thing is not that it sometimes breaks down, sometimes seems forced and rhetorically magniloquent, or too opulently lush or too self-consciously bizarre, but that it so generally succeeds— especially when one considers the conditions under which the novel was written. The great difficulty of writing at all seems to have made Green determined to avoid the temptation of mere documentary reportage to which so many writers succumbed; it is not to be wondered at that in avoiding this danger he sometimes went to the opposite extreme.

I have grouped *Concluding* with *Living, Party Going* and *Caught*, not because all four books are alike in style, but because in them the mode of expression, in the non-dialogue sections, is more frequently "perceptible" than in the other novels. But it is more perceptible partly, of course, because there is more of it to be perceived, and I realize that other groupings are possible. Another possible criterion would be stylistic harmony, as opposed to stylistic diversity. Using this criterion I would be inclined to group together *Party Going, Loving, Concluding* and *Doting* as novels in which there is something approaching stylistic uniformity. In all four this is connected with unity of setting, for even in *Doting* the settings, except for the night clubs, are so much taken for granted that they merge into one. In all it is connected with unity of time, or at least (in *Loving* and *Doting*) with unity of season. In all it is connected with the homogeneity of the cast. In the other novels there is a much greater mixture of styles. In *Living, Caught* and *Back* this is partly because of the more extended time-scheme and the greater variety of settings. In *Living* and *Caught* it is also partly because of the diversity of characters. In *Nothing* it is because Green had not completely adopted a method to which he was committed in theory. In *Back*, which more than any other novel concentrates attention on one character, there were special reasons for stylistic diversity which will be considered later.

There is, then, a further distinction to be made between the styles of *Caught* and *Concluding*. Because we are more aware of the short sentences in *Caught*, we are also more aware of the long and elaborate ones. We are more aware in *Caught* of the alternation of sharp observation and colloquial realism with opulent rhetoric (sometimes with the modern implication of insincerity and exaggeration) and poetic imagery. In *Concluding*, on the other hand, realism is confined almost entirely to the dialogue; in the non-dialogue there is a constant heightening of language, a constant spontaneous welling-up of imagery.

Some of the images have been quoted previously, but they confront us on almost every page:

". . . the azaleas, which, without scent, pale in the fresh of early morning, had not yet begun, as they would later, to sway their sweetness forwards, back, in silent church bells to the morning" (p. 6).

"The anonymous letter she had torn into little pieces the

night before, now lay like flakes of frost on her white head"
(p. 12).

"The girl and the old man came together over this, in the
megaphone of light" (p. 21).

"Sun, through the bright leaves, lit all this in violent dots,
spotting the cotton with drips as of wet paint, and making
small candle lamps of flesh" (p. 57).

". . . the heavy hair a colour of rust over a tide-washed
stovepipe on a shore" (p. 58).

The long sentence is not as distinct from its surroundings,
then, as it usually is in *Caught*; nevertheless only *Caught* has more
such sentences (of eighty words and over) than *Concluding*. In
Concluding they are used for the same purposes—chiefly for
interior monologue (or something approaching it) and description. Frequently, these two are blended in the one sentence.
This one, for example, is a good illustration of the way that
Green, in common with other modern novelists, makes use of
"Flaubert's great discovery that in fiction no object exists until
it has acted upon or been acted upon by some other object",
how he, like other moderns, makes "*active* those elements which
had hitherto remained *inert*, that is, description and expository
summary".[25]

"But it was not entirely in search of malice that Edge scanned
the now high, almost unbroken ramparts of flowering rhododendron which whisked past in vast, red and white splodges, it was
not, say, for a sight of decapitated frogs the artificial cherries,
which matched the car's paintwork, bobbed and scraped to
either side of her black London hat, nor could it even have been
for the perfume of those eunuch scentless flowers that her thin
nostrils opened and shut like a rabbit's, and little blue eyes,
continually darting sideways to catch up with the car's speed,
found no repose or a girl's face anywhere on which they could
read the answer to the question she dared not put,—where was
Mary, where Merode?" (p. 75).

It is indeed an index of the difference between *Caught* and
Concluding that in the later novel there are only two lengthy
sentences which contain no element of description. One is the
unspoken soliloquy of Mr. Rock (pp. 33-4) about the "Byzan-
tine malice" of the "Babylonian harlots"; the other (p. 110)
takes us into the mind of Miss Edge as she determines that
despite the disappearance of Mary the "little Fiesta" must go on.

At least a dozen of the most elaborate sentences in the novel are purely (or almost purely) descriptive. They include the descriptions of the starlings at dawn (p. 19), the fallen beech (p. 55), the girls with their swags of azaleas (p. 58), the girls waking (p. 109), the kitchen in the late afternoon (p. 113), the hall panelling (p. 125), the approach of evening (p. 168), the starlings at dusk (p. 177).

Almost all of these passages are memorable, and most of them are important in the symbolism of the novel. Perhaps the most spectacular of all is the description of the girls waking:

"Panelling around the walls was enamelled in white paint, as also the bedsteads with pink covers, the parquet floor was waxed and gold, two naked Cupids in cold white marble, and life size, held up a slab of green above a basket grate, while white and brown arms were stretched into the tide of late afternoon pouring by; a redhead caught fire with sun like a flare and, out of the sun, eyes, opening to reflected light, like jewels enclosed by flesh coloured anemones beneath green clear water when these yawn after shrimps, disclosed great innocence in a scene on which no innocence had ever shone, where life and pursuit was fierce, as these girls came back to consciousness from the truce of a summer after luncheon before the business of the dance" (p. 109).

Giorgio Melchiori, commenting on this sentence, which he describes as "one of the richest passages in Green's prose", remarks that "the impression it conveys is obviously of warmth and stillness as well as of richness; but the whole is suffused with a kind of dreamy haziness and unreality, which mellows figures and contours, and this in turn gives a sense of uneasy expectation which suddenly strikes a sinister note in the images of the sea anemones".[26] Melchiori makes a close comparison between this sentence and the opening passage of "A Game of Chess" in Eliot's *Waste Land*, and demonstrates fairly conclusively that "from the choice of words, colours and images it is obvious that the younger writer, during his formative years in the late 'twenties must have deeply felt the pervasive influence of the Eliot of *The Waste Land*".[27]

It is perhaps pure coincidence that the syntactic structure of this sentence is basically similar to that describing the approach of night as the Rocks make their way towards the "vast mansion" for the dance. But this is a type of sentence that

Green writes with superb mastery—the kind of sentence beginning with a succession of co-ordinate elements, the last of which is developed and elaborated in an intricate series of subordinate clauses. The emotional effect of such sentences depends as much on the cadences as on the specific details they present.

"The first blackbird, up on a branch, gave heed that night rode near, the light grew ever softer, rhododendrons stared, air was still, the boots they wore gleamed wet so soon; it was cool, and gnats had departed to the last bars of sun which, high above, slanted from one beech to another that dwarfed the azalea bushes where bluebottles no longer waited, whence butterflies were gone, and whose scent had faded, whose honey was now too late for bees in the hush of sunset preparing in the west that would lie red over the sky like a vast bank of roses, just time enough for lovers" (p. 168).

There is some tendency, in *Concluding*, to dwell on detail, to over-elaborate the poetic fancies (as, for example, the description of Merode's knee), but generally the colourful imagery and the lyrical eloquence are controlled by the needs of the novel as a whole. At least in its natural description the book reached the highest level that Green has attained.

6

In discussing the styles of the remaining novels I shall abandon chronological order and consider first the two latest novels, *Nothing* and *Doting*. There is less to be said about the styles of these two novels, because from them almost everything but dialogue has been banished, and, with very rare exceptions, the brief passages (generally single sentences) of non-dialogue serve merely to introduce the conversations ("That same week, on a summer evening, Mr. Middleton walked a friend home from his club") or to indicate the character's appearance and movements during their conversations ("He came over to sit on the arm of her chair", "His face, which she was watching, took on a look of great sadness"). Frequently the conversations go on for a page or more, uninterrupted even by a "he said". Comments are fewer even than in *Loving*; when they do appear they are usually the kind of non-committal, tentative comments noticed elsewhere in the earlier novel. In conformity with his view that the novelist should not assume greater certainty about his characters' motives than he has of other people's motives in real life, Green seldom makes any definite assertion of what his people are thinking and feeling. The words and phrases mentioned as characteristic of *Loving*—"as if" and "as though", "it seemed", "obviously", "evidently" and "probably" —are present in abundance, varied sometimes by "it can only have been", "with signs of" and "by the looks of it".

The prose generally, then, is muted and colourless, functional and neutral—a vehicle of information or conjecture. It is never careless, however; the second sentence of *Doting*, for example, has "evidently" been very deliberately arranged, even contrived. ("His son only grunted back at him, face vacant, mouth half open, in London, in 1949.") A reader unfamiliar with Green's other works might not notice anything distinctive in the prose, but to the devotee the stigmata are plainly visible. J. D. Scott remarked of *Doting* that the style, "for all its subtlety, its sinuous flexibility, its poetry and wit, is marred by turns of phrase which have become mechanical".[28] The praise may not be justified but the criticism is. For example, some sentences from the farcical seduction-scene in *Doting* (e.g. "Also *this* trolley, between the two of them and *that* fire was hard by his knees", or ". . . he put his free hand round her chin to turn *this* in his direction" (italics mine)) sound like self-parody; it may well be deliberate, but self-parody is a dangerous game.

In the later book, *Doting*, as previously noticed, it is only in the night-club scenes at the beginning and end, especially in the descriptions of the "snake-dancer" and the juggler, whose performances are ignored by the Middleton-Paynton party, that Green attempts anything more elaborate. In the juggler passage Green rivals the juggler himself in his studied, but apparently casual and effortless, artistry. He juggles phrases and clauses with the same dexterous aplomb and assurance as the juggler does his billiard balls and beer mugs. Robert Phelps comments that in this passage "a mirror has been made of the syntax itself" and notices particularly "the apposition at the end balancing there as quietly, as breathtakingly, as the jug on the juggler's toe".[29] (". . . the ball supporting a pint pot, then the pint pot a second ball until, unnoticed by our party, the man removed his chin and these separate objects fell, balls of ivory each to a hand, and the jug to the toe of his patent leather shoe where he let it hang and shine to a faint look of surprise, the artist", p. 8).

In *Nothing*, as the statistical tables show, there are more excursions into elaborateness than in *Doting*. At least some of them, in my view, are failures, which may be justly accused of pretentiousness and affectation. One of these is the opening couple of pages—a passage of indirect scene in which, in a sequence of three long sentences (86, 80 and 91 words), John Pomfret recounts to his mistress, Liz Jennings, his experience of the previous Sunday.

"It was wet then, did she remember he was saying, so unlike this he said, and turned his face to the dazzle of window, it had been dark with sad tears on the panes and streets of blue canals as he sat by her fire for Jane liked dusk, would not turn on the lights until she couldn't see to move, while outside a single street lamp was yellow, reflected over a thousand rain drops on the glass, the fire was rose, and Penelope came in. Jane cried out with loving admiration and there the child has been, no taller than the dark armchair, all eyes, her head one long curl coppered next the fire and on the far side as pale as that street lamp or as small flames within the grate, and she was dressed in pink which the glow blushed to rose then paled then glowed once more to a wild wind in the chimney before their two faces dark across Sunday afternoon.

" 'Then you're to be married' Jane had cried and so it was he realized, as he now told Miss Jennings, that the veil of window muslin twisted in a mist on top of the child's head to fall to dark snow at her heels, with the book pressed between two white palms in supplication, in adorable humility, that all this spelled marriage, heralded a bride without music by firelight, a black mouth trembling mischief and eyes, huge in one so young, which the fire's glow sowed with sparkling points of rose."

This passage is open to the obvious, but perhaps trivial, objection that nowhere else in the book is there any indication that the diabetic snob, Pomfret, is capable of the perceptiveness and eloquence here attributed to him. But pretty and mildly amusing as the passage is, it is open to more series objection. To me it seems a rather painful piece of self-imitation. So many of the familiar Green properties are here—"sad tears", the "rose" fire, the light reflected in a thousand rain drops, "the huge eyes which the fire's glow sowed with sparkling points of rose". The things we have accepted in *Caught*, *Loving* and *Back* as fresh and vivid perceptions here seem stale and shop-soiled.

The second part of the book begins with an even more florid piece of ornamentation. (One almost gets the impression of Green, at the beginning of each part, deliberately demonstrating his strength before donning the strait-jacket of the conversational method; one looks for a similar display at the beginning of the third part, but finds that it has been reserved for the end.) Here, in a sequence of four single sentence paragraphs (of 135, 19, 97 and 88 words) Green presents the luxurious, flower-decked, mirror-lined room in "the great hotel" where Philip Weatherby's twenty-firster is to be held, and Jane Weatherby's entrance. This passage is more successful but it too seems unnecessarily and flagrantly over-elaborate. Here again we have familiar properties—the mirrors and chandeliers, reflecting a "thousand thousand times" that we know from *Loving*, the masses of flowers (daffodils this time) that we know from *Concluding*. It seems as though Green, realizing that he was repeating himself, went to extreme lengths to give a virtuoso performance; in the third paragraph of the sequence he seems to have set out to out-Faulkner Faulkner in fanciful hyperaesthesia (and synaesthesis). "Then with a cry unheard, sung now, unuttered then by hinges and which fled back to creation in those limitless centuries of staring glass, with a shriek only of silent motion the portals came ajar with as it were an unoperated clash of cymbal to usher Mrs. Weatherby in, her fine head made tiny by the intrusion perhaps because she was alone, but upon which, as upon a rising swell of violas untouched by bows strung from none other than the manes of unicorns that quiet wait was ended, the room could gather itself up at last." One is reminded of sentences of Faulkner's like: "It was not completely dark but just enough so that the room's last long instant of illimitable unforgetting seemed to draw in quietly in a long immobility of fleeing, with a quality poised and imminent but which could not be called waiting and which contained nothing in particular of farewell." From neither verbal murk does anything significantly meaningful, or necessary to the total design, emerge.

Two other isolated elaborate sentences seem more successful, possibly because the ironic or mock-heroic note in them is heard more distinctly, not muffled by romantic poeticisms. One is the sentence (p. 109) describing Jane's gracious behaviour after her son's unexpected announcement of his engagement to Mary Pomfret. Here the inflated language, the pompous oratorical rhythms are exactly right; they at the same time perfectly define the reactions of the slightly tipsy crowd of refugees from the twenties, and ironically puncture their pretentiousness (". . . it must have seemed to most the finest thing they had ever seen, the epitome of how such moments should be, perfection in other words, the acme of manners, and memorable as being the flower, the blossoming of grace and their generation's ultimate instinct of how one should ideally behave").

The other is the sentence (p. 243) describing the unfortunate moment when that fool, Dick Abbott, chokes in the middle of kissing Liz. He fights a Homeric battle for breath while Liz thumps his back, fetches a glass of water and utters "ohs" of alarm. The sentence, firmly and clearly structured on a sequence of "soon", "then", "as", "so", "when", is brought adroitly to its blandly malicious close—". . . what was plainly a glow of ease started to pale him, to suffuse his patient, gentle orbs".

One last sentence must be mentioned, if only because it is the longest Green has ever written—243 words. It preludes the very last scene (p. 244) and presents Jane Weatherby and John Pomfret, now engaged instead of their children, sitting on a sofa, in a state of drowsy sensual contentment, before the fire which (of course) "glowed a powerful rose". The sentence is too long to quote, but again one feels that, charming as it is, one has seen it all before, that this is almost automatic writing, that Green could, and perhaps did, write it in his sleep.

Stylistically, *Nothing* reminds me of a pawpaw tree—a leafless, spindly-limbed plant out of which sprout, incredibly, and with no apparent relationship to the slender branches which can barely support them, and from which it is inconceivable that they can draw their sustenance, a few monstrous, globular fruit. That is what strikes one in reading *Nothing*—the disproportion, the lack of connection and relationship, the effect of lush, artfully designed patches of purple (or rather of white, rose and blue) arbitrarily superimposed on the abstract, colourless background. And as the colours, which in earlier novels had

P

strong emotional resonance, have here become mere pictorial clichés, so the long sentences, which in earlier novels had flowered naturally and had almost invariably been of special thematic significance, have here become mere exercises in elaboration.

Loving does not suffer from this stylistic disharmony. Its style is very different from that of *Party Going* but it resembles that novel in the homogeneity of style which matches its unity of setting and atmosphere. Irving Howe, reviewing the novel, referred to Philip Toynbee's description of Green as a "terrorist of language" and remarked that *Loving* belonged to "the post-terrorist phase", that it is "composed in unstrained and unmannered prose".[30] The prose is certainly "unstrained". Whether it is always unmannered is perhaps debatable; certainly it is always distinctive. Henry Reed has pointed out that the fact that the novel consisted largely of a series of dialogues set Green a particular problem—what to do with the surrounding narrative. "The dialogue is mainly between servants, and the servants' world is always present. Green seems to have chosen to let the idiom of the human figures slip beyond the figures' outlines and mildly to invade the landscape and the furniture." [31] This is quite true; the whole book seems to be permeated by the collective consciousness of the servant-characters. "He reached round her middle and drank her in a kiss like a man home after a journey. . . . She sank into him as her knees gave way yet both of them stayed decent." "A ledge of more purple leather on the fender supported Raunce's heels next his you-and-me in a gold Worcester cup and saucer." "When they were established there after she had conducted him as though he was an old man and he had sat himself down heavily. . . ." "For those most greedy of all birds had collected in twos about and behind the lilac trees, on the scrounge for tit-bits." "For what with the peacocks bowing at her purple skirts, the white doves nodding on her shoulders round her brilliant cheeks and her great eyes that blinked tears of happiness, it made a picture."

There are actually, I think, only two recurrent and easily definable idiosyncrasies of expression. One is the very frequent use of "this" or "that" instead of the article. ("That door hung wide once more", "He whipped out the decanter while Bert provided those tumblers that had not yet been dried".) The other peculiarity is that the substitution of the adjective for the adverb, noticed occasionally in *Party Going* and *Caught*, now becomes habitual. ("Bert followed sheepish", "He picked it up off the floor quick", "He said friendly . . .", "Raunce eyed her very sharp", "At last she said quite calm . . .", "He went so soft he might have been a ghost . . .". All these, and a few others, occur in the first ten pages.) The concentration is highest in the early sections of the book, but even in the last few pages Raunce is still gazing "awkward" in Edith's face, and appealing to her "soft". This is probably the most noticeable mannerism in any of Green's novels, apart from the elimination of articles in *Living*; some critics found it irritating, but one quickly gets accustomed to it. It is a simple, but quite effective, device for giving the flavour of unsophistication that Green wanted.

The adaptation of style to the servant-characters is seen also in Green's handling of the sentence. *Loving* is the only novel in which there are no really long sentences. Whereas every other novel has at least a sprinkling of sentences of eighty, ninety or a hundred words, the longest sentence in *Loving* is only seventy-three words long—and it is a merely informative sentence about Raunce's investigations in Mr. Eldon's note-books. Almost eighty per cent of the words of non-dialogue in *Loving* are in sentences of less than thirty words; the figure is higher than that for any other novel, even *Doting*. The average sentence length is only 13·3 words; only *Doting* has fewer. Sequences like the following are not uncommon: "He went slow. He could hear feet slither. Then he turned in a flash. He had Edith. He stood awkward one hand on her stomach the other on the small of her back." But these sentences, one notices, are part of a paragraph (p. 114) made up of sentences of 6, 42, 21, 17, 66, 3, 5, 6, 3, 16 words and their function in describing sudden swift action in the game of blind man's buff is obvious.

Despite the prevailing brevity of the sentences *Loving*, unlike *Doting*, is not a bare and austere novel. One indication of this is that it has a higher percentage of adjectives than any of the novels from *Living* to *Concluding*. (This claim is based on a study of four one-thousand-word samples from each novel. The percentages obtained were as follows: *Loving* 5·9; *Concluding* 5·3; *Caught* 4·8; *Back* 4·1; *Party Going* 2·9; *Living* 2·6.) The unusually high density of adjectives in *Loving* is seen in such sentences as these (as well as in some of those already quoted). "And there it was *close*, on a *low* hill, surrounded by cypresses amongst which grew a palm tree, the *marble* pillars lying beside *jagged cement topped* walls against a *blue* sky with *blue* clouds." (Green's omission of hyphens in compound adjectives and nouns is habitual.)

"Edith laid her *lovely* head on Raunce's *nearest* shoulder and above them, above the *great* shadows laid by trees those *white* birds wheeled in a sky of *eggshell blue* and *pink* with a *remote* sound of applause as, circling, they clapped their *stretched, starched* wings in flight."

"The shape they made was crowned with his head, on top of a *white sharp curved* neck, *dominating* and *cruel* over the blur that was her mass of hair through which her lips sucked at him *warm* and *heady*."

There is at least one Hopkinsian pair of adjectives: "And Edith looked out on the morning, the soft bright morning that struck her *dazzled, dazzling* eyes."

These sentences also illustrate quite well the shapeliness, the perfect poise and grace of sentence-structure that Green attains in this novel. There are no passages of bravura like those in *Nothing*, which seem to have been deliberately manufactured to fill pre-decided positions. Instead Green's vision is constantly freshly alert, illuminating characters, landscapes, interiors, revealing beauty, often in unexpected places—nowhere more unexpectedly than in the wonderful picture of the uncouth, matted-haired lamp-man snoring on a corn bin.

"It was a place from which light was almost excluded now by cobwebs across its two windows and into which, with the door ajar, the shafted sun lay in a lengthened arch of blazing sovereigns. Over a corn bin on which he had packed last autumn's ferns lay Paddy snoring between these windows, a web strung from one lock of hair back onto the sill above and which rose and fell as he breathed. Caught in the reflection of spring sunlight this cobweb looked to be made of gold as did those others which by working long minutes spiders had drawn from spar to spar of the fern bedding, on which his head rested. It might have been almost that O'Conor's dreams were held by hairs of gold binding his head beneath a vaulted roof on which the floor of cobbles reflected an old king's molten treasure from the bog" (pp. 51–2).

It would be difficult to find a passage more clearly illustrat-

STYLES AND MANNERS

ing Green's descriptive prose at its best, yet it occurs quite unostentatiously between two passages of dialogue (and Edith's reaction is " 'Oh, Kate, isn't he a sight and all!' "). Several of the little idiosyncrasies are there—*"these* windows", "a web strung . . . *and* which", "this cobweb *looked* to be". The diction is simple, prevailingly monosyllabic ("sovereign", "reflection" and "reflected" are the only trisyllabic words); there is only one word that is at all unusual—the striking adjective "shafted". But the passage is composed as carefully as a poem; the evenness of sentence length (35, 39, 40, 36 words—45, 47, 49, 46 syllables) makes the passage like a lyric in four stanzas. The passage, indeed, has a strong iambic rhythm. Parts of it can be written as almost regular lines of blank verse:

Into whích, / with the dóor / ajár / the sháf / ted sún
Láy in / a léngth / ened árch / of bláz / ing sóvereigns . . .

and

O'Cón / or's dréams / were héld / by haírs / of góld
Bínding / his héad / beneáth / a vául / ted róof
On whích / the flóor / of cób / bles refléc / ted . . .

No doubt some theorists would object, but these lines have to be torn out of context and isolated before their approximation to regular metre becomes evident. (In any case, as René Wellek remarks: "The artistic value of rhythmical prose is still debated and debatable. In accordance with the modern preference for purity in the arts and genres, most modern readers prefer their poetry poetic and their prose prosaic. Rhythmical prose seems to be felt as a mixed form, as neither prose nor verse. But this is probably a critical prejudice of our time."[32])

Another indication that *Loving* is anything but a bare book is that it has a lower percentage of finite verbs than any of the books up to *Concluding*. This assertion is based on a study of the four one-thousand-word samples already referred to. The results are given in the table on page 226.

The percentages of finite verbs are not in themselves of much significance, as they do not reveal a wide range of variation. More important is the distribution of different verb forms. In any novel, except the very rare ones that use the historic present, one expects the basic tense to be the preterit ("said", "did", "went", etc.). It certainly is in all of Green's books. The revealing and significant thing, however, is the extent to which other tenses are used. As the table shows, the striking thing about *Loving* is that it has more preterit verbs than any other novel, except *Living*, but far fewer verbs of any other kind than any other novel.

	Living	Party Going	Caught	Loving	Back	Con-cluding
Percentage of preterit verbs	11·1	8·0	8·3	9·7	9·6	9·5
Percentage of other finite verbs and verb phrases	4·3	6·6	4·7	2·4	4·6	4·0
Percentage of all finite verbs and verb phrases	15·4	14·6	13·0	12·1	14·2	13·5
Percentage of all *words* (including auxiliaries) in finite verb phrases	19·2	20·7	17·6	14·5	19·0	17·4

(The last line is necessary because the "other verbs" range from "goes" through "will go", "has gone", "was going" and "had gone" to forms like "might have been going".)

The two extremes are *Party Going* and *Loving*. The best way to compare them is by deriving percentages from the first and last lines. It will then be seen that of all the words in *Party Going* (or at least of all the samples studied) which are either finite verbs or constituents of finite verb phrases, only thirty-nine per cent are verbs in the "basic" tense, the preterit; in *Loving*, on the other hand, the percentage of preterit verbs in all finite-verb-forming words is sixty-two per cent.

The distribution of verb-forms in the samples of four thousand words for each of these novels is shown in table on next page.

From these figures a number of inferences may be made. In the first place, the high incidence, in *Loving*, of preterit verbs is an indication of how closely Green concentrates attention on the couple of months which provide the time-scheme of the novel, and how much, within the "fictive present" of the book, he concentrates on action and on observable behaviour. James Hall has claimed that Green's "comic characters have no history";[33] this is true of *Loving*, but the high incidence of the "had done", "was doing" and "did . . . do" forms in *Party Going* shows that the generalization is not entirely valid. (Hall does qualify the generalization, however: "Their pasts, if any,

		Party Going	Loving
1	Preterit (type "did")	319	388
2	"Had done" type	70	28
3	"Might (etc.) do" type	65	18
4	"Was doing" type	43	21
5	"Did . . . do" type	27	8
6	"Do/does" type	24	3
7	Others	37	17
	Total	585	483

(The third line includes all the active verbs formed with the auxiliaries "may", "might", "must", "would", "could", "should"; most of the verbs in the fifth line are in the negative and interrogative forms.)

. . . are backdrops rather than moral evolutions.") The almost total absence from *Loving* of the present tense is an indication of the scarcity of commentary, and of interior monologue. And finally the third line provides another indication of the greater decisiveness, concreteness and immediacy of *Loving*, compared with *Party Going*; or, to put the distinction more fairly, the large number of verbs compounded of "might" and similar auxiliaries indicates that the interest of *Party Going* lies much more in the relationships between actions and in motives, than in the actions themselves.

All of these features—the scarcity of finite verbs, the large number of adjectives (and also of nouns and participles), the perfect "poise" and sinuous flexibility of rhythm—are to be seen in the sentence which is, deservedly, one of the most-quoted that Green has ever written, the sentence describing Kate and Edith dancing together, in the dust-sheeted ballroom.

"Above from a rather low ceiling five great chandeliers swept one after the other almost to the waxed parquet floor reflecting in their hundred thousand drops the single sparkle of distant day, again and again red velvet panelled walls, and two girls, minute in purple, dancing multiplied to eternity in these trembling pears of glass" (p. 62).

This is a passage that is poetic not only in feeling but in form as well. It is chiefly in the last few words ("these trémbling peárs of gláss") that regularity of stress becomes evident, but there are other features that one usually associates with poetry rather than prose. There is, for example, the compound adjective "red velvet panelled". More important is the alliteration, most obvious in the phrase "the single sparkle of distant day", and much more subtle in the intricate interweaving of "l", "t", "s", "n", and "p" sounds in the last three lines, where it is combined with the assonance of "girls", "purple", "eternity".

There is no doubt that *Loving* represents one of Green's peaks as a prose-stylist. He dares less than in *Caught* or *Concluding*, but everything he does attempt is triumphantly accomplished.

7

In *Back* there are few surface idiosyncrasies. There are, of course, a few demonstratives for articles and adjectives for adverbs, but no more than in *Caught* or *Concluding*.

I have claimed previously that *Back*, in technique, is a bridge between the three highly scenic novels and the others. The percentage of scene (dialogue plus stage directions) is much higher than in *Living*, *Party Going* and *Caught* and distinctly higher than in *Concluding*, but it is much lower than in *Loving*, *Nothing* and *Doting*. *Back* is also distinguished from the three latter novels in having a good deal of informal character revelation, often approximating to interior monologue. Since method and style are very closely associated, one would expect *Back* to stand, stylistically, somewhere between the two main groups. And so it does; though I have claimed earlier that *Back* belongs in style with *Loving*, *Nothing* and *Doting*, I have also admitted that a strong case could be made for grouping it with *Living* and *Caught*. It is mainly because *Back* illustrates so well the extremes in Green's handling of language that I have left discussion of it till last.

The table (p. 195) does show that, in distribution of sentence-lengths, *Back* is much closer to *Loving*, *Nothing* and *Doting* than to the other novels. But statistics are notoriously treacherous; or at least they must be kept in their place as useful servants, not allowed to become tyrannical masters. And there is here an important distinction to be made, which the statistical tables do not reveal.

The distinction is similar to that previously made between *Caught* and *Concluding*. The vast majority of the short sentences in *Nothing* and *Doting*, and a very large proportion of those in

Loving, appear singly or in pairs as stage directions in scenes. One typical four-page chapter of *Doting* (pp. 82–5) yields only seven scattered sentences of non-dialogue. In *Back* also the short sentence is frequently used in this way. "Mr. Summers quacked a laugh." "Charley grunted." "Charley was not to be drawn. He sat there, smiling." "Charley leant forward, but kept his eyes on the glass." "There was no response from Summers" (pp. 23–9). But far more often than in the other novels (even *Caught*) we find extended sequences of short sentences, which are not mere stage directions, but which record the actions and reactions of Charley Summers.

"The door was open.

"He went in. He climbed the stairs. He began to regret it.

"Then he was outside an inner door, on which was written her name. Her name was there on a card.

"He read her name, Miss Nancy Whitmore, in Gothic lettering as cut on tombstones. He noticed the brass knocker, a dolphin hanging by the tail. He ran his eye over this door which was painted pink. The wall paper he stared at round the door, was of wreathed roses on a white ground. He looked again" (p. 46).

"He began not to understand. He looked. He saw the cat was there no longer. A kettle was boiling. He tilted again. Her dear face did not even seem to belong, he thought. But he knew it must be all right" (p. 48).

"Then he had another thought. That she'd lost her memory, same as her mother. He knew he must take things slowly. He worked on the chair" (p. 49).

"When he got to the next call box, he rang this man at the C.E.G.S. But he was out. Then Charley walked a great distance unseeing. Until he found himself by a park. He awkwardly sat under a tree. He collapsed at once into deep sleep" (p. 61).

"He hurried. The shop girl had liked his eyes and wrapped the china up. He took this off while he was still on Miss Whitmore's stairs. He knocked, carefully holding the crockery to his chest. Surprisingly enough she was up and in. She opened.

"It was Rose again.

"He forgot the plans he had made" (p. 67).

This, I think, is a fairly accurate description of the style of the quoted passages. "It is for the most part a colloquial and, apparently, a non-literary prose, characterized by a conscientious simplicity of diction and of sentence-structure. The words are chiefly short and common ones, and there is a severe and austere economy in their use. The typical sentence is a simple declarative sentence, or a couple of these joined by a conjunction; there is very little subordination of clauses."[34] This is Philip Young's description of the early style of Ernest Hemingway. I would not say that the passages from *Back* are Hemingway imitation; there are several touches in them that are characteristically Green's, and which one would be very surprised to find in Hemingway. But perhaps these passages might not have been written quite like this, if Hemingway had not established a new tradition in prose-writing. Moreover, if Green's style in *Back* does at times resemble that of Hemingway there is a very good reason for it; Charley Summers, the hero of *Back*, has much in common with the "Hemingway hero". Certainly Charley is no big, tough, outdoor man, but does not this describe him accurately? "He is a sensitive, humourless, honest, rather passive male." "He cannot sleep at night; when he can sleep he has nightmares. He has seen a great deal of unpleasantness . . . in the war; and he has been wounded by these experiences in a physical way, and . . . also in a psychical way."[35] This again is Philip Young's description of the first Hemingway hero, Nick Adams.

In a brilliant commentary on one of the most important stories in which Nick Adams appears, Young also writes: "Clearly, 'Big Two-Hearted River' presents a picture of a sick man, and of a man who is in escape from whatever it is that made him sick. And Nick apparently knows what is the matter and what he must do about it, and must not do. . . . He must not think or he will be unable to sleep, he must not get too excited or he will get sick. . . . It is as though he were on a doctor's prescription, and indeed he is on the strictest sort of emotional diet, but is his own nutritionist."[36] Camped in the woods on his hunting trip Nick finds that "his mind was starting to work. He knew he could choke it because he was tired enough." The next day he spends fishing, and every little thing that he does—a series of mechanical, deliberate, almost ritualistic movements—is presented in a regular and monotonous sequence of curt sentences. As Young puts it, "A terrible panic is just barely under control, and the style is the perfect expression of the content of the story. The tense exasperating effect of this rhythm on the reader is extraordinarily appropriate to the state of Nick's nerves, which is above all what Hemingway is trying to convey."[37]

The similarity of Charley Summers' condition to that of Nick Adams (or of Jake Barnes, the hero of *The Sun Also Rises*, who is also a war-casualty and insomniac) is most obvious in the section near the end of *Back*, when Charley, staying overnight at Redham, because Mr. Grant is dying, is stricken with dread by the roar overhead of, it seems, every bomber in England, and then falls uneasily asleep, only to be wakened by the commotion at Mr. Grant's death.

". . . the culmination of all this was about to remind Summers of something in France which he knew, as he valued his reason, that he must always shut out. He clapped hands down tight over his ears. He concentrated on not ever remembering. On keeping himself dead empty. He made himself study the living room. He forced himself to stay clear. And he saw the cat curled up asleep. It didn't even raise its ears. Then, at the idea that this animal could ignore crude animal cries above, which he had shut out with his wet palms, he nearly let the horror get him, for the feelings he must never have again were summoned once more when he realized the cat, they came back, as though at a signal, from a moment at night in France. But he won free. He mastered it. And when he took his streaming hands away, everything was dead quiet.

"Finally he heard her coming at last. There could be no doubt. Instinct made him switch out the lamp. He waited in darkness" (p. 186).

Any similarity there may be, at times, between the style of *Back* and the famous "Hemingway style" is not due to any merely superficial imitation; it is due to the fact that both writers were presenting characters who are themselves similar, and who have been similarly damaged by the blows—physical, spiritual and emotional—that they have suffered. The curt, laconic understatement of the style reflects in *Back*, as it does in "Big Two-Hearted River" and *The Sun Also Rises*, the barrenness, the "strained, terrifying negation" (to use again Jean Howard's phrase) of the hero's existence, the restraint that Charley Summers, like Nick Adams or Jake Barnes, knows that he must practise if he is to survive, the necessity not to think, not to remember, because that way madness lies.

I have emphasized that, if there is a stylistic resemblance between *Back* and the stories and novels of Hemingway, it is intermittent, not constant. Giorgio Melchiori has very well remarked that, in *Back*, "a frequent recourse to puns and complicated metaphors reveals the author's determination to create a lyrical climate in which the realistic narrative should have acquired a deeper poetical significance".[38] If *Back* occasionally reminds one of Hemingway, it also occasionally reminds one of the even greater American, Faulkner. I suspect that when Green was writing *Back*, he re-read not only Hemingway, but also Faulkner's first novel, *Soldiers' Pay* (1926) in which Faulkner also told the story of the home-coming of a war-shattered soldier. I do not think it is fanciful to detect hints for one of the most lyrical passages in *Back* (pp. 176–8) in the following paragraph from *Soldiers' Pay*.

"The garden was worth seeing. *An avenue of roses* bordered a gravelled path which passed from sunlight beneath two overarching oaks. Beyond the oaks, against a wall of poplars in a restless formal row were columns of a brick temple, yet the poplars themselves in a slim, vague green were posed and vain as girls in a frieze. Against a *privet hedge* would soon be lilies like nuns in a cloister and blue hyacinths swung soundless bells, dreaming of Lesbos upon a lattice wall, wistaria would soon *burn in a slow inverted lilac flame*, and following it they came lastly upon a single rose bush. The branches were heavy and knotted with age, heavy and dark as a bronze pedestal, crowned with pale impermanent gold" (Chapter II, I).

In *Back*, we find (p. 176) "But when they got round the red garage, which was intact, and a *privet hedge*, which in this light, and because it was shaded, *burned a dark glowing violet*, they found what had been *the rose garden* . . .". The privet hedge and the roses are common property, but hardly, one suspects, the metaphorical use of "burn".

Again, however, it is not a question of imitation, but of assimilation. Whatever Green may have taken, consciously or unconsciously, from Faulkner, he made entirely his own. *Back*, I have remarked elsewhere, is unusual among Green's novels in being built round a central complex of symbols—the woman, Rose, the flower and the colour, rose; and I have claimed that in three wonderful passages—the opening scene in the cemetery, the scene in the blitzed rose garden, and the final scene of the "trial-trip"—the major development of the rose theme and symbol can be traced. No one but Green could have written these two extraordinarily elaborate but magnificently controlled companion-sentences (companion, though separated by 170 pages). And though it would be quite wrong to quote these sentences as typical of the style of the novel as a whole, there is no doubt that they (and the passages of almost equal elaboration which surround them) contribute incalculably to the total effect of the book.

"For, climbing around and up these trees of mourning was rose after rose after rose, while, here and there, the spray overburdened by the mass of flower, a live wreath lay fallen on a wreath of stone, or on a box in marble colder than this day, or onto frosted paper blooms which, under glass, marked each bed of earth wherein the dear departed encouraged life above in the green grass, the cypresses and in those roses gay and bright which, as still as this dark afternoon, stared at whosoever looked, or hung their heads to droop, to grow stained, to die when their turn came" (p. 5).

"But when they got round the red garage, which was intact, and a privet hedge, which in this light, and because it was shaded, burned a dark glowing violet, they found what had been the rose garden, enclosed with a low brick wall, and then they had before them, the outlines edged in red, stunted, seemingly withered, rose trees which had survived the blast as though it had never happened, and, for a screen at the back, a single line of dwarf cypresses, five feet high with brown trailing leafless briars looped from one to the other, from one black green foliage to its twin as green and black, briars that had borne gay rose, after rose, after wild rose, to sway under summer rain, to spatter the held drops, to touch a forehead, perhaps to wet the brown eyes of someone idly searching these cypresses for an abandoned nest whence fledglings, for they go before the coming of a rose, had long been gone, long ago now had flown" (pp. 176–7).

If the first part of the second sentence ("But . . . brick wall"), which is only loosely joined to the rest by "and", is disregarded, the similarity of structure in the two sentences becomes more evident. This structure is the reverse of periodic;

so far from the meaning being held in suspense until the end of the sentence is reached, each sentence could end at any of a dozen points. This does not mean that they are compound or co-ordinate sentences; so far from being loose and rambling, each is carefully and minutely planned. It does mean, however, that the essentials of meaning are introduced in the early stages of each sentence. The "top level" of meaning in these sentences is "For, climbing around and up these trees of mourning, was rose after rose after rose, while, here and there, a live wreath lay fallen", and "But when they got round the red garage and a privet hedge they found what had been the rose garden and then they had before them rose trees which had survived the blast and a single line of dwarf cypresses". From this point on, in each sentence, the structure is based on a complicated system of subordination and apposition; as each possible end of the sentence is reached it is elaborated and modified so that the clause which ends each sentence ("when their turn came", "long ago now had flown") is approximately on an eighth level of subordination.

But the pattern of the first sentence is not mechanically repeated in the second. The pattern of the first is quickly established by the "triple" phrase, "rose after rose after rose". This is repeated at almost every level of subordination, first in "a live wreath lay fallen *on a wreath* of stone, or *on a box* in marble . . . or *onto frosted paper blooms*", again in "*the green grass, the cypresses*, and in *those roses*". It is varied slightly in "*stared* at whosoever looked, or *hung* their heads", but reaffirmed in the trio of infinitives, "*to droop, to grow stained, to die*".

The key-phrase of this sentence reappears in elaborated form —"gay rose, after rose, after wild rose"—late in the second sentence. But there is not the same insistent triplicity. Instead, in the middle of the sentence there is a looping appositional effect matching the sense:

> . . . leafless briars looped from one to the other
>   from one black . . . black
>   briars that had borne gay rose

Following a succession of four infinitives ("to sway . . . to spatter . . . to touch . . . to wet") this effect is repeated in the close of the sentence:

had long been gone,
long ago now had flown.

The diction of these two sentences is fairly plain; there are
comparatively few adjectives, particularly in the first (the
second does have "a *dark glowing* violet", and "*brown trailing
leafless* briars"). The language is unmetaphorical (except for
"*burned* a dark glowing violet"). And Green here, more carefully than in some passages previously quoted, avoids poetic
rhythm; there is only one place where the prose threatens to
drop into regular iambics (". . . each bed of earth wherein the
dear departed . . ."). Yet these two sentences, particularly the
first of them, could, one feels, stand alone as elegiac prose-
poems, so perfectly are they controlled and ordered in structure
and sound-pattern.

They do not, however, stand alone. They are parts, and
integral and necessary parts, of a complex organism. Their
function in the novel is as vital as that of the Hemingwayesque
passages quoted earlier. For in *Back* we find ourselves in a
labyrinth of neurotic fantasy and hallucination; it is right that,
on the opening page, we should be led through the labyrinth
of this sentence. And in *Back*, roses are to be the dominant
symbol—the symbol of love-and-death; it is right that in the
opening pages they should be so unforgettably brought to our
notice, in a sentence which grows and burgeons and drops down
to die away as they themselves do.

8

No English novelist who has come into prominence in the last
quarter-century has shown such stylistic versatility, such a
many-faceted mastery over language as Henry Green. His style,
like his presentational technique, has constantly varied, not
only from book to book, but within each book. It has varied
not only to meet the requirements of different subject-matters,
but because it so faithfully reflects his own temperament and
his response to life. Green's is a complex temperament, in which
sensuousness and austerity, wit and melancholy, compassionate
generosity and ironical aloofness, a love of the beautiful and a
fascination with the ugly are strangely blended. He is a realist
and a romantic, an observer and a participant, a satirist and

a poet; it is inevitable therefore that his prose, even within the same novel, should oscillate from spare, curt incisiveness to elegiac lyricism or even flamboyant and opulent rhetoric. No doubt there are times when his style topples into mannerism, times when the habits of language, formed to give exact and vividly memorable expression to distinctive perceptions, become empty and mechanical conventions. But his style, like that of the greatest living master of English prose, the only writer about whom Green has ever been induced to express an opinion, William Faulkner, generally meets triumphantly the test so well defined by J. Middleton Murry. "The test of a true individuality of style is that we should feel it to be necessary and inevitable: in it we should be able to catch an immediate reference back to a whole mode of feeling that is consistent with itself." [39]

Notes

CHAPTER I

1 Quoted by Nigel Dennis, "The Double Life of Henry Green", *Life*, Aug. 4, 1952, p. 85.
2 "The Vision of Henry Green", *Hudson Review*, V, 4, Winter 1953, p. 620.
3 "The Future of Fiction", *New Writing and Daylight*, VII, 1946, p. 77.
4 "Selected Notice" [Review of *Concluding*], *Horizon*, XVIII, 107, Nov. 1948, p. 366.
5 Quoted by Dennis, *Life*, Aug. 4, 1952, p. 84.
6 "Molten Treasure", *Time*, LIV, 15, Oct. 10, 1949, p. 42.
7 *Life*, Aug. 4, 1952, p. 87.
8 Introductory Note, *The Dark Tower and other Radio Scripts* (London, 1947).
9 "An Artist of the Thirties", *Folios of New Writing*, III, Spring 1941, p. 152.
10 Ibid., p. 149.
11 *Life*, Aug. 4, 1952, p. 92.
12 *An Introduction to the English Novel*, Vol. II (London, 1953), p. 191.
13 *Life*, Aug. 4, 1952, p. 92.
14 Preface to "The Lesson of the Master", in *The Art of the Novel* (New York, 1934), p. 230.
15 Ernest Jones, "The Double View", *Nation*, CLXIX, 19, Oct. 22, 1949, p. 402.
16 *Horizon*, Nov. 1948, p. 366.
17 "The Real and Unreal Worlds of Henry Green", *New York Times Book Review*, Dec. 31, 1950, p. 14.
18 *Life*, Aug. 4, 1952, p. 87.
19 "A Novelist to his Readers", *Listener*, XLIV, 1132, Nov. 9, 1950, p. 506.
20 *Horizon*, Nov. 1948, p. 365.
21 *Listener*, Nov. 9, 1950, p. 506.
22 *Life*, Aug. 4, 1952, p. 86.
23 *An Italian Visit* (London, 1953), p. 34.
24 *Listener*, Nov. 9, 1950, p. 506.
25 *Life*, Aug. 4, 1952, p. 85.
26 "Native Boy in Patent Leather Shoes", *New York Times Book Review*, Oct. 7, 1951, p. 1.
27 Ibid., p. 1.

CHAPTER II

1 Quoted by Joan Bennett, *Virginia Woolf* (Cambridge, 1945), p. 23.
2 "The Double Life of Henry Green", *Life*, Aug. 4, 1952, pp. 86, 94.
3 "Back from the War", *New York Times Book Review*, Oct. 1, 1950, p. 28.
4 "The Real and Unreal Worlds of Henry Green", ibid., Dec. 31, 1950, p. 5.
5 *World Within World* (London, 1951), p. 271.
6 "Books in General", *New Statesman and Nation*, XVIII, 150, Oct. 7, 1939, p. 489.
7 George Mayberry, "The Juggling Act", *New Republic*, CXXVI, 19, May 12, 1952, p. 21.
8 "Green on Doting", *New Yorker*, May 17, 1952, p. 125.
9 "Selected Notice" [Review of *Concluding*], *Horizon*, XVIII, 107, Nov. 1948, p. 367.
10 "The Fiction of Henry Green: Paradoxes of Pleasure-and-Pain", *Kenyon Review*, XIX, 1, Winter 1957, p. 85.
11 "Fiction Chronicle", *Partisan Review*, XVI, 10, Oct. 1949, p. 1055.
12 *New York Times Book Review*, Dec. 31, 1950, p. 5.
13 *World Within World*, p. 275.
14 "The Vision of Henry Green", *Hudson Review*, IV, 4, Winter 1953, p. 616.
15 "New Novels", *New Statesman and Nation*, XXIX, 741, May 5, 1945, p. 292.
16 *In My Opinion* (New York, 1952), p. 78.
17 "Henry Green's Technique", *Nation*, CLXXI, 19, Nov. 4, 1950, p. 416.
18 *New York Times Book Review*, Oct. 1, 1950, p. 28.
19 *Kenyon Review*, Winter 1957, p. 77.

CHAPTER III

1 "A Novelist to his Readers", *Listener*, XLIV, 1132, Nov. 9, 1950, pp. 505–6 and XLV, 1150, March 15, 1951.
2 "The Future of the Novel", *Contact*, Aug. 1950.
3 *In My Opinion* (New York, 1952), pp. 104–5.
4 See Leon Edel, *The Psychological Novel 1900–1950* (New York, 1955), p. 85 et seq.
5 *Orion, A Miscellany* (London, 1945), pp. 20–8.
6 *Some Observations on the Art of Narrative* (London, 1946), pp. 2–3.
7 Ibid., p. 15.

8 *Some Principles of Fiction* (London, 1953), p. 68.

9 *Some Observations*, pp. 6–7.

10 *Some Principles*, p. 67.

11 *Some Observations*, p. 7.

12 R. B. Sheridan, *The Critic*.

13 "Green on Doting", *New Yorker*, May 17, 1952, p. 121.

14 "The Double Life of Henry Green", *Life*, Aug. 4, 1952, p. 87.

15 *Listener*, Nov. 9, 1950, pp. 505, 506.

16 "The Vision of Henry Green", *Hudson Review*, IV, 4, Winter 1953, p. 616.

17 "The Novels of Henry Green", *Partisan Review*, XVI, 5, May 1949, p. 491.

18 R. W. Chapman, *Jane Austen, Facts and Problems* (Oxford, 1948), p. 204.

19 *Partisan Review*, May 1949, p. 494.

20 Quoted by N. Dennis, *Life*, Aug. 4, 1952, p. 87.

21 *Hudson Review*, Winter 1953, p. 620.

22 "An Absolute Gift", *Times Literary Supplement*, 2740, Aug. 6, 1954, p. xli.

23 *Life*, Aug. 4, 1952, pp. 87–8.

CHAPTER IV

1 *Aspects of the Novel* (London, 1927), p. 41.

2 *The Art of Fiction* (O.U.P. edn., 1948), p. 16.

3 *Time and the Novel* (London, 1952), pp. 65, 71.

4 Ibid., p. 72.

5 "Books in General", *New Statesman and Nation*, XVIII, 150, Oct. 7, 1939, p. 489.

6 R. Wellek and A. Warren, *Theory of Literature* (London, 1949), p. 226.

7 Quoted by A. K[aun], "Soviet Criticism", in J. T. Shipley (ed.), *Dictionary of World Literature* (New York, 1943), p. 533.

8 *The Tightrope Walkers* (London, 1956), p. 202.

9 *Time and the Novel*, p. 97.

10 "Selected Notice" [Review of *Concluding*], *Horizon*, XVIII, 107, Nov. 1948, p. 366.

11 "An Absolute Gift", *Times Literary Supplement*, 2740, Aug. 6, 1954, p. xli.

12 Ernest Jones, "The Double View", *Nation*, CLXIX, 17, Oct. 22, 1949, p. 402.

13 T. S. Eliot, *Poems 1909–1935* (London, 1936), p. 63.

14 "New Novels", *New Statesman and Nation*, XXIX, 741, May 5, 1945, p. 292.

15 "Fiction Chronicle", *Partisan Review*, XVI, 10, Oct. 1949, p. 1054.

16 See Edith Sitwell's "Aubade", *The Canticle of the Rose* (London, 1949), p. 6.

17 Margaret J. C. Reid, *The Arthurian Legend* (Edinburgh, 1938), p. 201.

18 "Reader's Choice", *Atlantic Monthly*, 186, 4, Oct. 1950, p. 84.

19 "The Novels of Henry Green", *Partisan Review*, XVI, 5, May 1949, p. 493.

20 *The Tightrope Walkers*, p. 203.

21 See *The Dawn of Liberation, War Speeches by the Right Hon. Winston S. Churchill* (London, 1945), Speeches of July 6 and August 2.

22 *New York Herald Tribune Book Review*, Oct. 1, 1950, p. 6.

23 "Back from the War", *New York Times Book Review*, Oct. 1, 1950, p. 4.

24 "The Double Life of Henry Green", *Life*, Aug. 4, 1952, p. 88.

25 *The Tightrope Walkers*, p. 208.

26 Ibid., p. 207.

27 Ibid., pp. 208, 212.

CHAPTER V

1 "The Fiction of Henry Green: Paradoxes of Pleasure-and-Pain", *Kenyon Review*, XIX, 1, Winter 1957, p. 77.

2 "Books in General", *New Statesman and Nation*, XVIII, 150, Oct. 7, 1939, p. 489.

3 "The Novels of George Meredith", *The Common Reader: Second Series* (London, 1935), p. 234.

4 "Introduction to Henry Green's World", *New York Times Book Review*, Oct. 9, 1949, p. 22.

5 "Reader's Choice", *Atlantic Monthly*, 186, 4, Oct. 1950, p. 84.

6 "The Vision of Henry Green", *Hudson Review*, IV, 4, Winter 1953, p. 617.

7 "Back from the War", *New York Times Book Review*, Oct. 1, 1950, p. 28.

8 *Kenyon Review*, Winter 1957, p. 85.

9 "The Novels of Henry Green", *Partisan Review*, XVI, 5, May 1949, p. 490.

10 *The Novel Today* (London, 1936), pp. 37–8, 184.

11 *New York Times Book Review*, Oct. 9, 1949, p. 22.

12 T. S. Eliot, *Poems 1909–1935* (London, 1936), p. 127.

13 "An Absolute Gift", *Times Literary Supplement*, 2740, Aug. 6, 1954, p. xli.

14 James Joyce, *A Portrait of the Artist as a Young Man* (Jonathan Cape, the Travellers' Library, New Edition 1942), p. 256.

15 *The Tightrope Walkers* (London, 1956), p. 214.

16 *Aspects of the Novel* (London, 1927), p. 214.

17 *The Poetic Image* (London, 1947), p. 40.

18 *Rhythm in the Novel* (Toronto, 1950), p. 56.

19 *An Introduction to the English Novel*, Vol. II (London, 1953), p. 192.

20 *The Tightrope Walkers*, p. 194 n.

21 Quoted by Richard Church, *Eight for Immortality* (London, 1941), p. 15.

22 *An Introduction to English Novel*, II, p. 193.

23 *New Writing in Europe* (London, 1940), p. 134.

24 *New York Times Book Review*, Oct. 9, 1949, p. 22.

25 *The Tightrope Walkers*, p. 201.

26 "The Real and Unreal Worlds of Henry Green", *New York Times Book Review*, Dec. 31, 1950, p. 5.

27 Leland Schubert, *Hawthorne the Artist* (Chapel Hill, 1944), p. 97.

28 *The Use of Colour in Literature. A Survey of Research, Proceedings of the American Philosophical Society*, XC, 3, July 26, 1946, p. 178.

29 *Partisan Review*, May 9, 1949, p. 494.

30 *New York Times Book Review*, Oct. 9, 1949, p. 22.

31 *Hudson Review*, Winter 1953, p. 617.

32 *Forces in Modern British Literature 1885–1956* (New York, 1956), p. 287.

33 *Ibid.*, p. 292. For fuller discussion of Green (especially of *Party Going* and *Loving*) see Tindall's *The Literary Symbol* (New York, 1955), pp. 92–7.

34 *Kenyon Review*, XIX, 1, Winter 1957, p. 82.

35 "The Double View", *Nation*, CLXIX, 17, Oct. 22, 1949, p. 402.

36 "Selected Notice", *Horizon*, XVIII, 107, Nov. 1948, p. 366.

37 *The Tightrope Walkers*, p. 203.

38 *Horizon*, Nov. 1948, p. 367.

39 Quoted by Leland Schubert, *Hawthorne the Artist*, p. 96.

40 *Horizon*, Nov. 1948, p. 368.

41 "The Double Life of Henry Green", *Life*, Aug. 4, 1952, p. 88.

42 *Partisan Review*, May 9, 1949, p. 496.

43 *New York Times Book Review*, Oct. 9, 1949, p. 22.

44 *The Tightrope Walkers*, p. 190.

45 *Life*, Aug. 4, 1952, p. 88.

46 *Ibid.*, p. 88.

47 "New Novels", *Spectator*, 6358, May 5, 1950, p. 625.

CHAPTER VI

1 René Wellek and Austin Warren, *Theory of Literature* (London, 1949), p. 185.
2 "Fiction and the Criticism of Fiction," *Kenyon Review*, XVIII, 2, Spring 1956, p. 280.
3 Ibid., p. 290.
4 Ibid., p. 292.
5 Ibid., p. 294.
6 Ibid., p. 295.
7 Ibid., p. 297.
8 Ibid., p. 295.
9 Ibid., p. 292.
10 *Style in French Prose* (Oxford, 1953), p. 135.
11 Quoted by P. Rahv, *Kenyon Review*, Spring 1956, p. 293.
12 See *Aspects of the Novel* (London, 1927), pp. 121, 210.
13 "The Vision of Henry Green", *Hudson Review*, V, 4, Winter 1953, pp. 614–15.
14 "The Novels of Henry Green", *Partisan Review*, XVI, 5, May 1949, p. 489.
15 G. Mayberry, "The Juggling Act", *New Republic*, CXXVI, 19, May 12, 1952, p. 21.
16 *The Tightrope Walkers* (London, 1956), p. 189.
17 "An Artist of the Thirties", *Folios of New Writing*, III, Spring 1941, p. 154.
18 *Partisan Review*, May 1949, pp. 491–2.
19 *The Tightrope Walkers*, pp. 191–2.
20 Ibid., p. 193.
21 Ibid., pp. 196–7.
22 "A Novelist to his Readers", *Listener*, XLIV, 1132, Nov. 9, 1950, p. 506.
23 *The Tightrope Walkers*, p. 200.
24 "Consider", *Collected Shorter Poems* (London, 1950), p. 43.
25 Caroline Gordon and Allen Tate, *The House of Fiction* (New York, 1954), pp. 24, 279.
26 *The Tightrope Walkers*, p. 189.
27 Ibid., p. 190.
28 "New Novels", *New Statesman and Nation*, XLIII, 1105, May 10, 1952, p. 566.
29 *Hudson Review*, Winter 1953, p. 615.
30 "Fiction Chronicle", *Partisan Review*, XVI, 10, Oct. 1949, p. 1052.
31 "New Novels", *New Statesman and Nation*, XXIX, 741, May 5, 1945, p. 292.
32 *Theory of Literature*, p. 167.

33 "The Fiction of Henry Green: Paradoxes of Pleasure-and-Pain",
    Kenyon Review, XIX, 1, Winter 1957, p. 77.
34 Philip Young, *Ernest Hemingway* (New York, 1952), pp. 174–5.
35 Ibid., p. 26.
36 Ibid., p. 19.
37 Ibid., p. 18.
38 *The Tightrope Walkers*, p. 203.
39 *The Problem of Style* (London, 1922), p. 16.

Index

A. HENRY GREEN

B. OTHER REFERENCES AND QUOTATIONS